MARK ROWLANDS

EVERYTHING
I KNOW
I LEARNED
FROM TV

PHILOSOPHY FOR THE UNREPENTANT COUCH POTATO

EBURY
PRESS

For Emma

1 3 5 7 9 10 8 6 4 2

Copyright © 2005 Mark Rowlands

First published 2005 by Ebury Press,
An imprint of Random House,
20 Vauxhall Bridge Road, London SW1V 2SA

Random House Australia (Pty) Limited
20 Alfred Street, Milsons Point, Sydney,
New South Wales 2061, Australia

Random House New Zealand Limited
18 Poland Road, Glenfield, Auckland 10, New Zealand

Random House South Africa (Pty) Limited
Endulini, 5a Jubilee Road, Parktown 2193, South Africa

The Random House Group Limited Reg. No. 954009

www.randomhouse.co.uk

Printed and bound in Great Britain by Mackays of Chatham plc, Chatham, Kent

A CIP catalogue record for this book is available from the British Library.

Cover designed by Two Associates
Interior by seagulls

ISBN 0091898358

CONTENTS

I owe another huge debt of gratitude to the admirable Andrew Goodfellow, my editor at Ebury, who not only suggested that TV might provide a useful medium for my somewhat in-your-face brand of philosophizing, but also, once again, managed to restrain many of my more obvious excesses. Those which remain are due to irredeemable character flaws on my part. Thanks also to Liz Puttick, my estimable agent. Thanks to Emma Harrow, the publicist for this book, and to Caroline Newbury for past and present encouragement. Thanks to Martin Noble who did an excellent job of copy-editing. Thanks to Jennifer, Joe, Jon, Mary, Peter, Rory and Sheila for their encouragement and help. Finally, my greatest thanks to Emma, whose support, lucid intellect, and supreme cocktail-making ability, provided much of the inspiration for this book.

INTRODUCTION

What have the Greeks ever done for us?

Maybe not everything I know I learned from TV – but a lot of it was. And it's not as if my viewing tendencies are particularly high-brow. In fact, they veer steadfastly away from the intellectual; in viewing terms, I'm basically one of the great unwashed. And along with my fellow unwashed, I'm often likely to hear intellectuals telling us just how dumb and stupid we all are. If only – they say – we could be more like the Greeks. Not the modern ones, of course, who are just as unwashed as we are; but the *ancient* ones.

Just look at how much more cultured they were than us. They spent all their time at the market square – the *agora* – discussing all the great questions of life, the universe, and everything. We sit at home scratching ourselves and watching *Big Brother*. But in all this approbation of the ancients and denigration of us moderns, one salient fact seems to be overlooked. Why did the Greeks *have* to go to the market square and talk philosophy all the time? The answer is obvious: *because they didn't have TV*! We don't need to go to the market place to philosophise any more. TV does it for us, in the comfort of our own homes. Philosophy hasn't died in our modern cultureless culture; it has simply relocated.

Lest you think this doesn't affect you – we're all philosophers, whether we know it or not, and whether we've ever picked up a book of philosophy or not. Philosophy is all around us; it's in the culture we inhabit. It trickles out to us from the movies we watch, and the magazines and newspapers we read. More importantly, for the purposes of this book at least, it's in the TV programmes we have been faithfully watching for as long as we can remember. Because of this, philosophy is *in* us. All of us are the authors, co-authors, producers, directors, stars and guest stars in various philosophical questions, issues, disputes, conflations and confusions – even though most of the time we have no idea of this. Being a philosopher is easy, and we don't have much choice in the matter anyway. If you live life and ever think about it you're a philosopher. Being a good philosopher ... now that's a different matter.

The philosophy of the modern age

Yet, while philosophy itself goes on, comfortably adapting to new media and modes of expression, the questions it asks tend to mutate. Philosophy is like that. The questions it asks, and the answers it gives, are often organised around certain, what we might call, *anxieties* – ones peculiar to the age in which we live. The anxieties that afflict us today are quite different from those of earlier times. And so, therefore, is the philosophy we endorse.

We live in the modern world. There is a word people often use in connection with this world: *modernity*. This is one of those annoying words thrown around by pretentious people: the sort of person who also uses words like *paradigm* and *deconstruction* – the sort of person who isn't quite sure what they actually mean. This being so, the fact that I've decided to make modernity the subject of the entire book is, perhaps, a little worrying. In my defence, I don't really have much choice. Most of the good stuff that's offered to us on TV is, at its core, about modernity in one way or another. So, the first question we have got to ask is: *what is modernity?*

Modernity isn't a time. It's an *idea*. Or, rather, it's a whole cluster of them. The sort of person who uses the term *modernity* will also, typically, use the term *ideology*. And what is an ideology? It's a collection of ideas about us, about the world around us, and about our place in that world. Ideology is, basically, a *philosophy*, broadly construed. So modernity, then, is a philosophy. Modernity is the philosophy of the modern age. Of course, this whole definition is somewhat circular, since what counts as the modern age is defined in terms of the ideology of modernity. What makes an age *modern*, chronologically, is the fact that people in it tend to endorse the philosophy known as *modernity*. But you probably get the picture. In eighteenth-century France, certain ideas emerged – ones that later became known as *modern* – and gradually became adopted by large numbers of people. Eventually, these ideas came to form the cornerstone of the political arrangements these people used to govern themselves, and the way in which they understood the world and their place in it.

But now, of course, various further questions have to be asked. First of all, which *people* are we talking about? Secondly, what, exactly, are these ideas that collectively make up the ideology of modernity? The first one is pretty easy, the second really hard.

The people in question are those who populate Western Europe, Japan, Australasia, South Africa, South Korea, large parts of Latin America, probably some parts of China and Indonesia, and, in particular, North America.[1] It's no coincidence that these are the people

---

1. In fact, pretty much anywhere that shows the slightest interest in buying this book.

who make all the really good TV programmes. Other cultures – notably the Islamic cultures – are what we might call *pre-modern*. In saying this, I don't mean in any way to slag them off. We haven't yet worked out if modernity – the ideology not the age – is a good thing. So we certainly don't know that pre-modernity is a bad thing. In fact, what I think we'll find is that modernity is a mixed blessing – there's a good side and a dark side. And, some of the indisputable superstars of modernity's TV offerings – and *Buffy the Vampire Slayer* provides a really good example – are distinctly pre-modern. So I'm not denigrating anybody who doesn't qualify as modern any more than I would say a word against Buffy. And, as you will soon gather, I would never say a word against the *Buffmeister*!

Another qualification is also crucial. I don't think any of us have really got the hang of being modern yet. Not fully or completely. We all give it a go, and some of us are better than others at it, but we all fall short to some or other extent. So, instead of talking about individual people as if they were modern or pre-modern, I think it is better to think of modernity as a kind of *tendency* that is present, to a greater or lesser extent, in each of us. I can't emphasise enough how important this point is. As individual people, we probably embody both modern and pre-modern tendencies. I know I do. That's one reason why the world can often seem so bewildering to us. The modern age, then, is characterised not by the existence of people who are thoroughly modern, but by the marked increase in a certain tendency – a tendency to think a certain way, to adopt a certain philosophy or ideology – that is present, to a greater or lesser extent, in many people.

The second question – what are the ideas that collectively make up the ideology of modernity? – is a lot more difficult. Indeed, once we have got an answer to it, we'll understand one of the reasons why modernity is a mixed blessing. Modernity is a fundamentally confused and inconsistent ideology. The ideology is about as stable as an Italian taxi driver who finds himself trapped behind a convoy of nuns driving up the windy roads to Monte Cassino. That's part of the reason we are all so messed up. We spend most of our lives staring at a TV screen that imparts to us what can only be described, at best, as mixed messages. We are fractured, even splintered, creatures, because we live in an ideology that is at best fractured, at worst splintered. We have a really hard time making sense of ourselves. And a lot of this can be explained by what we watch on TV! Blaming the TV programmes, of course, would be like blaming beer on hangovers. The programmes simply reflect the culture we live in. And that culture, I think, hasn't quite got itself together – not yet, anyway.

Modernity ...

The first big idea underpinning modernity is what's usually known as *individualism*. Individualism is, primarily, a *moral* idea: an idea about what sort of life it is best to live. The best sort of life is one of *self-development*, or *self-realisation*, or *self-fulfilment*. Because this is deemed the best sort of life, you have an overriding moral duty or *obligation*: an obligation to *yourself* to live this life – to be the best you can be and all that sort of stuff. In high culture, people have been carping on about this idea for quite some time. In *Hamlet*, for example, Shakespeare has Polonius, after he gets past all the 'neither a borrower nor a lender be' preliminaries, offering this advice to his departing son: *this above all else, to thine own self be true*. And the nineteenth-century German philosopher Friedrich Nietzsche tells us: 'What does your conscience say? You shall become what you are.' And, here, Nietzsche holds up conscience, your inner voice, against all the voices of other people telling you what you are going to be, or should be. The whole idea of self-realisation is that it is *you* that gets realised or fulfilled, and not other people's version of you.

It would be a mistake to suppose that before modernity came along no one was into self-development, realisation or fulfilment. People have been putting their own development, realisation and fulfilment before everyone else's since time immemorial. What's different about the age of modernity, however, is that people don't feel guilty about this any more. On the contrary – self-fulfilment is now more than merely what many people *actually* do; it is now seen as what all people *should* do. Self-fulfilment is transformed from a *description* about how people actually live their lives, to a *prescription* about how people *should* live their lives. Self-fulfilment is now a *good* thing. It is this moral dimension to the idea of self-fulfilment that is one of the defining features of modernity.

There's another idea that, to many, seems to go hand in hand with individualism. This is *relativism*. According to individualism, your primary obligation in life is to develop, realise or fulfil yourself. You could hardly achieve this primary obligation if everyone else went around interfering with you – preventing you doing what was necessary for your development, realisation or fulfilment. So, the obvious tempting thought is that other people have an obligation not to interfere with you in your quest for development, realisation or fulfilment. Each to his own, or so the idea goes. You should go about fulfilling and realising yourself, and others should go about doing the same for them, and nobody should interfere with anyone else.

This is fine; what we have got so far is a sort of principle of *toleration*. You do what you have to, and let everyone do what they have to. And the only reason to interfere with anyone else is if what they have to do to fulfil themselves prevents you doing what you have to do in order to fulfil yourself. Then, of course, you have a problem. But, short of this problem, the idea is, basically, to *live and let live*.

In the eyes of many, there is but a short step from this principle of toleration to full-blown relativism. To anyone remotely acquainted with principles of logical inference, it is, in fact, a giant leap rather than a short step, but, nonetheless, the idea has caught on. Relativism is the idea that all systems of value are equally worthwhile. Suppose you choose to live your life one way – to fulfil or realise yourself in one way rather than another – then that way is just as good as anyone else's. Conversely, what anyone else chooses to do with their life is just as good as what you choose to do with yours. Different life choices are equally viable, and equally valuable. No one can criticise you for the way you live your life. And, equally, nor can you criticise anyone else for the way they live theirs. All life choices, and so all life orientations, are equally valuable.

Relativism, in this sense, leads to a third component of the ideology of modernity. This component doesn't – yet – have a name; but we might call it *voluntarism*. Voluntarism, in this sense, is a claim about the *origin* of value; a claim about what makes something valuable. Why should it be that everyone's life choices are equally valuable? It seems a bit of a coincidence really unless ... *it is the choice that makes them valuable.* The idea that the value of a choice or decision stems from the fact that it was freely chosen, or *volunteered*, by the individual is what we can call *voluntarism*.

The fourth component of modernity is what we might call *instrumentalism*. The name alludes to what is known as *instrumental* rationality. Instrumental rationality is *means–ends* reasoning. You want something. What's the best way to get it? Instrumental rationality is what tells you how to get what you want. Means are instruments – tools – to achieve ends. The reduction of all of life's decisions to means–ends calculations is also one of the characteristic features of modernity. The other people in your life are evaluated according to how much they bring to your life versus how much you have to put in to them to keep them in your life. They are, when all's said and done, *resources* – whether financial resources, sexual resources, entertainment resources, emotional resources – or simply people with whom you just kill time, as most of us do. Relationships come down to how much you're getting out of them against how much you have to put in – a means–end calculation of a classic sort. And it's not just people. A characteristic of the age of modernity is to make nature itself a resource. The world becomes a collection of *natural resources*, and what we do to the world becomes a matter of what the world can do for us. A mighty river, that in earlier times might have been a source of awe or even reverence, becomes a natural resource – measured in terms of whatever interest we have. Maybe it's the amount of kilowatts per hour it can generate through the hydroelectric dam built on it. Maybe it's the recreational resources it provides us – how much enjoyment and entertainment we can get from canoeing down it, for example. In the age of modernity, everything is calculable. And the formula you use is how much something contributes to you versus how much you have to put into that thing in order to get it to contribute thus.

This is, in fact, all implied in the first, and major, component, of modernity: individualism. According to modernity, your primary goal or directive is to realise or fulfil yourself. To the extent that you have any obligations to other people, these are always secondary to your obligation to live your life in the way you choose, and to realise and fulfil yourself on this basis. So other people become to you as means towards ends. If your primary obligation were to someone else, things might be different. But it is not, it is to yourself. So other people can, in the end, be nothing more than means towards an end – the goal of your self-realisation. That, according to modernity, is the primary value that other people will have to you: they are things to help you get what you want.

So, to sum up, modernity is an ideology that is made up of four principles: individualism, relativism, voluntarism and instrumentalism. The problem is that these principles just won't go together at all. They're incompatible, and modernity is an essentially fractured worldview. And you wonder why you are so messed up!

... and its discontents

So you're an individualist and an instrumentalist? Your highest goal is self-fulfilment and the value of everyone else is a matter of how much they contribute to this goal. Too bad – it's not going to work. The problem is that while you are employing all the means–ends instrumental rationality at your disposal, and ranking everyone on this basis, you can be damn sure everyone else is doing the same as well. And so just as everyone else becomes a resource for you, so you too become a resource for everyone else. If you are weighing everyone else up according to how much they can do for you, everyone else is weighing you up in the same way. The idea behind individualism is that you are a sovereign person, for whom self-fulfilment is the ultimate goal, and with whom no one else has the right to interfere. But the idea behind instrumentalism is, in effect, that you are someone else's – indeed everyone else's – *butt monkey*: merely a means to their self-fulfilment. So, straight away, we have this tension between the individualist and instrumentalist components of modernity.

But this is just to scratch the surface of the farrago of tensions, discrepancies, inconsistencies and contradictions that make up the ideology of modernity. Voluntarism and relativism, for example, are not obvious buddies either. What does voluntarism say? Basically – individual choice is everything. It's your choices that shape you, that make you what you are, and allow you to become what you can be. Your choice is absolutely central to self-realisation and fulfilment. More than this – the life you lead has value precisely because it is one that you have chosen. According to voluntarism it is choice that gives value to what is chosen. But claims about value like this don't sit very comfortably with relativism, because the whole point about relativism is that we can't make true and objective judgments about value. Voluntarism claims that it is *true* that choice bestows value on what is chosen. It claims that it is *true* that a life freely chosen is, thereby, a valuable life. But relativism claims that we can't make true and objective judgments of value. We can be relativists, or we can be voluntarists. But it's not clear that we can be both.

You get a similar problem if you try to be both an individualist and a relativist. Individualism says that self-fulfilment is the highest value. Fulfilling yourself is a good thing, and not doing it is a bad thing. The problem is that relativism won't allow us to say this. If relativism is right, there are no true and objective value statements – all value claims are relative. So, we can't say things like fulfilling yourself is good and not fulfilling yourself is bad because … it's all relative, dude. If we try to combine individualism with relativism we end up wanting something we can't have – an objective standard of good and bad that would allow us to claim that self-fulfilment is a good thing.

And when we turn to the combination of individualism and voluntarism, things get even worse. In fact, here the self-defeating character of modernity is at its most pronounced. What we find is that voluntarism robs the idea of individualism of any purpose. If the idea of self-fulfilment is to have any point, it must surely be necessary that we can make sense of the idea of a *bad* life choice. Or, for that matter, a *good* one. I mean, the whole idea of self-realisation or fulfilment is going to be pretty lame if no matter what you do you end up realising or fulfilling yourself just as well as if you had done the complete opposite. You choose to become a slayer of vampires rather than a cheerleader. You choose to become a *capo di tutte capo* rather than a garbage man. You choose to move to Seattle and host your own radio show rather than stay in Boston married to the unfaithful Lilith. You choose to work your way on to the stand-up comic circuit rather than stay selling umbrellas on the street. You choose to stay working at the nuclear plant instead of becoming a country music manager. All these choices come with alternatives – any choice does. But if the idea of self-fulfilment is going to have any real meaning, there must be some way of ranking the alternatives, some way of ordering them so that some come out as better than others.

You choose to become The Slayer, rather than a cheerleader. There has surely got to be something to the idea that this choice is more important or significant in the process of self-realisation than choosing to go to McDonald's instead of Burger King, or drinking Bud instead of Miller. And if you had decided to become a cheerleader instead of The Slayer, so realising yourself in an entirely different way, it can't automatically be that this choice is just as valuable as the alternative. What's behind all this is a truism – *choices are important only if they are important.* To be more exact, to say that a choice is important is implicitly to suppose that there is gradation or ranking of value in the choices that we might make. For something to be important, other things have to be less important. And if all choices are equally important, then no choice is important. Sad but true.

Individualism needs a way of ranking choices so that some of them come out as more important, and so more valuable in the process of self-realisation, than others. It needs this, otherwise the whole idea of self-realisation or fulfilment basically becomes null and void. But voluntarism can't allow for such a ranking. According to voluntarism, it is the choice itself that makes an action important. Any freely chosen action is equally valuable precisely because it is freely chosen. It is the choice that lies behind it that gives it its value. In short, individualism needs standards that determine or decide whether our choices are good ones – and voluntarism tells us that there can be no such things.

The same is true of relativism. According to relativism, all choices are equally important because there is no objective standard of value that could allow us to rank one as more important than another. So, any way of realising or fulfilling yourself is no more and no less valuable than any other way. And this, for precisely the same reason, robs the idea of individualism of any real content or purpose. Individualism needs standards that allow us to judge whether our life choices are good ones, and relativism tells us there can be no such standards.

The basic contradiction of modernity is now becoming clear. Modernity needs standards that, *by its own principles*, it cannot have. This is why there is a *problem* with modernity.

Yeah, right!

Some people style themselves as post-modernists. I don't know what they mean, and neither, I suspect, do they. But my initial reaction is: *yeah, right*! We haven't even got the hang of being modern yet; post-modern is way beyond our reach. We haven't got the hang of being modern, in part, because it's such a fractured and inconsistent thing to get the hang of. I'm not saying that we absolutely *can't* iron out all the inconsistencies in modernity. But Jesus, it's hard work! And you can't expect us to be ironing out inconsistencies all the time. You come home from a hard day at the office, where all day people have been valuing you only according to how much you contribute to their goal of self-fulfilment, and you're really looking forward to a little identifying and expunging of logical inconsistencies. Yeah, right! Ironing out inconsistencies in the ideology of modernity is not at all the sort of thing you want to have to do when you switch on the TV in the evening. And so you sit there and absorb – all the little discrepancies, ambiguities, incongruities, inconsistencies and conflicts. Even paradoxes. You absorb them all, and as a result, you become a discrepant, ambiguous, incongruous, inconsistent, conflicted, even paradoxical, person.

You doubt me on this? If so, consider some recent work done on the idea of imitation by the Dutch social psychologist Dijksterhuis.[2] If you were ever one of his experimental subjects, this is the sort of thing you could expect. First of all, you might be asked to answer a few questions on something or other. The purpose of these questions is to *prime* you, as psychologists put it, with various stereotypes. For example, answering the questions might require you to use terms stereotypically associated with the elderly – like 'grey', 'bingo', 'slippers' and the like. The result, roughly, is that you are primed to think about elderly people. What Dijksterhuis showed was when you are primed like this, you actually tend to take on the characteristics of elderly people, at least temporarily. For example, right after the priming questions, Dijksterhuis might set you a memory test. And, statistically, you would do worse on this test than people (a 'control' group) who

---

2. A. Dijksterhuis, 'Why we are social animals: the high road to imitation as social glue', in S. Hurley and N. Chater (eds), *Perspectives on Imitation: From Neuroscience to Social Science*, Vol. 2, Cambridge, MA: MIT Press.

had not been primed in the way you had. Chances are you will also tend to walk more slowly and express more conservative attitudes than similar-aged control participants.

Even more striking, and disturbing, is the fact that the same sort of thing applies to intelligence. If you are primed by being asked to answer various questions about stereotypically stupid people – football hooligans, supermodels, or whoever – then you will actually tend to do worse on IQ tests than if you were not thus primed. Or, more precisely, the group of participants primed by thinking about stupid people tended to do worse in Dijksterhuis's experiments than a similar group of non-primed participants. In short, you can become more stupid, at least temporarily, by thinking about stupid people. It's worth remembering if you're on your way to an exam or something. Don't let anyone engage you in conversation about *Pop Idol* – they might as well be beating you around the head with the *stupid stick*.

What does this show? Basically, that we are imitation machines. We are sponges that soak up stereotypical influences around us, even to the extent of taking on the characteristics of those stereotypes. Most of the time, of course, we have no idea we are doing this. But we do it all the same. So, you think you can sit in front of modernity's TV schedule, with its discrepant, ambiguous, incongruous, inconsistent, conflicted, even paradoxical, offerings, without yourself taking on these characteristics? *Yeah, right!*

Modern anxieties

So, modernity has its problems. And we have our problems because modernity has its problems. Lest anyone think that this is part of some anti-TV rant – don't! It's not like TV is the culprit here: it's just the messenger. Modernity is all around us.

Conflicted and paradoxical messages are being served up to us from all directions. They pour out of the crappy magazines and newspapers we read. And just think how many books have been published in the past twenty years on the subject of happiness and how to have it. Besides, while I've been dwelling on the negatives, there is a lot that's good in modernity – we just need to know how to look for it.

Think of what things were like before modernity got its arse in gear. Then we were all part of the so-called *great chain of being*. The universe was a fundamentally ordered place – and in it all things have their place. God, since He made the whole shebang in the first place, was in charge. Below him were the angels, then the seraphim, cherubim, and other assorted *im*s. And below them were humans, who were given dominion over the fish and the fowl and all creatures that walketh, creepeth, slithereth, or in any other way *eth*, upon the earth. God's earthly representatives – the Church and the Monarchy – dealt with the day-to-day running of earthly affairs. And so you knew your place. You lived in a highly structured world, probably doing the same thing as your father, your father's father, and your father's father's father, and his father before him, etc. Your life would have been organised around pivotal social institutions – the church, the meeting hall, the pub – and around the seasons – for sowing, reaping, birthing, sheep-worrying and so on. Your world would have been one resonant with *meanings* and *values*. Things in your ordered world had meaning and value for you because of their place in that world and so their place in your life.

Your fundamental moral obligation was then to play the cards you had been dealt. Modernity changed all that. Now everyone has options. If you don't like the cards you've been dealt – just get a new hand. And options are great. I'm, personally, a big fan of options. They've been very good friends to me, and I like having them around. And certainly very few of us moderns want to go back to the old days of tugging one's forelock to the squire and stuff like that. Nah, most of us will take modernity any day. But the modern way of living does throw up certain what we might call *anxieties*, and these provide recurring themes in the TV programmes we watch. These anxieties all centre on what we might call the *dislocation of the self* that is inherent to the modern worldview.

The pre-modern was characterised by its *order* or *structure* and the *meanings* and *values* that were embodied in it because of that structure. Everything – including you – has its place in the great chain of being, and because it has its place it has meaning and value. The characteristic change that defines the modern age is the dismantling of this sort of picture. The dismantling occurs at both physical and psychological levels. At the gross physical level, mobility is the key. We formerly sheep-worrying, forelock-tugging peasants have been forced to leave the land, first to the cities, then across oceans and continents. Today, we move from city to city – we go where the work is.

This increase in physical mobility is accompanied by an increase in psychological and emotional mobility. The fundamental moral obligation is no longer to play out your allotted role in life, but to be true to yourself. Modern life is all about self-development, self-realisation and self-fulfilment. Be all you can be! And, you know: you can be anything you want to be if you want it badly enough! In the pre-modern age, what you were and what you could be was determined for you by your place in the great chain of being. Now, however, what you are and what you can be is something you have to *choose* for yourself.

This choice breeds a certain cluster of anxieties, ones that we find repeatedly examined, explored and dissected on TV. The anxieties are all variations on a single theme: *what sort of person is it best to be?* The person you are is no longer bequeathed you by your place in the world; it is something you have to choose. The responsibility for this is yours and yours alone. And, when you think about it, that's a lot of responsibility.

The question of what sort of person it is best to be is closely bound up with another, and this provides a similar sort of focus for a cluster of related anxieties: what sorts of values should I choose? That is: *what sorts of values are best to live by?* Cut loose from our structured world of meanings and values, we now have to create them ourselves. And the sort of person you choose to be is, of course, intimately bound up with the sort of values you choose to live by, and vice versa.

These two sorts of anxiety are consistently aired, examined and explored on TV. The best shows – ambitiously – attempt to resolve them, with, I think, varying degrees of success. They do so, of course, in different ways, and the answers they come up with are often quite different. Nor need their approaches be head-on – sometimes it's not obvious that the questions are even being addressed let alone answered. Often, what we tend to find is that a particular anxiety is tentatively approached, aired, let alone for a while, to be returned to later from a different angle. Nevertheless, as I'll try to show in what follows, despite the subtlety of the approaches, we do clearly find, running through the shows we are going to look at, variations on these two related themes: what sort of person is it best to be? What sort of values is it best to choose?

Everything I know I learned from TV

One way of expressing these general anxieties is in terms of the concept of moral value, and, in particular, the question of what *authority* moral values can have over us. In pre-modern times, the standard view was that moral values existed out there in the world. They had an objective existence, independently of our beliefs, opinions, and attitudes about them. The usual story was that they were out there because God put them there. And so doing what is morally right was then a matter of *discovery* – discovering what God wanted us to do. When modernity got its act together, however, moral values became regarded as a matter of *invention* or *creation*. But this change raises a worry about the sort of *authority* moral values can have over us. In a nutshell, the problem is that if we are the creators of moral values, then how can these values in any way *bind* us. How can a creator be bound by what he or she creates? How can the created have any authority over their creator?

When we talk about the *authority* of moral values over us, we usually do so in terms of the notion of *obligation*. We have an obligation – a moral obligation – to do what's right and refrain from doing what's wrong. Or so the idea goes. And in these terms, a characteristically modern anxiety is one about what sort of thing this obligation could possibly be – and, more importantly, how obligations could have any force or authority over us. How can we be in any way constrained by our obligations if we, in effect, created them in the first place? How could we be dictated to by obligations if they are only there at all because of us?

Some of modernity's most sensitive, subtle and sophisticated discussions of the concept of obligation are to be found in the kick-ass TV series *Buffy the Vampire Slayer* and the spin-off series, *Angel*. In these series, we find not only a sophisticated exploration of the concept of obligation, but also an attempt to answer the question of how obligations can be binding. One can, I think, legitimately, dispute whether this attempt is successful. But it's certainly well worth looking at. We'll be looking at *Buffy* in the next chapter.

Modernity, as we have seen, has something of a hard time with the idea of moral value. In particular, its attitudes seem wildly inconsistent. Individualism tells us that self-realisation is valuable – indeed, that it is the ultimate value. Relativism tells us that all values are relative – varying from one person to another. Voluntarism tells us that the basis of value is choice. And, as we have seen, none of these things seems to fit together very well. Perhaps it's for this reason that we find another persistent tendency in modernity. This is the tendency to suppose that if moral values exist at all, then they must really be something else. If you're having trouble explaining or understanding something, then it would be good if that something turns out to be something else – something that you understand a lot better. In recent times, probably the most obvious and influential version of this idea is the view that moral evil reduces to a form of psychological sickness. Being bad is, at the end of the day, simply a matter of being ill.

'You're sick' is, in these times, such a natural response to someone's wrongdoings that it's easy to lose sight of just what is being said. What is being said is that to suffer from a moral deficit is to suffer from a psychological deficit. Moral evil is nothing more than poor psychological health. When people do bad things it is because they are, literally, sick. This idea that we can *medicalise* morality – understand moral right and wrong in terms of psychological health or illness – plays a huge role in modern society. Just think of the billions we plough into psychological counselling every year, and our institutionalised attempts to 'treat' moral transgressors, and so on. But, in fact, the idea that moral right and wrong can be understood in medical terms is not a modern idea at all. It goes all the way back to the ancient Greek philosopher Plato. And, more recently, Sigmund Freud has been banging on about the same general theme.

Can we medicalise morality in this way? Can we understand moral good and evil in terms of psychological health and illness? Of all the recent TV series that deal with this issue, far and away the best is *The Sopranos*. We're going to look at Plato, Freud and Tony Soprano in Chapter 2.

Interpersonal relationships – particularly friendship and love – provide another pervasive anxiety of modernity. The worry, again, stems from modernity's problems in handling the concept of value. It is the instrumentalist strand of modernity that is particularly problematic in this case, because what this strand tends to do is reduce all of life's decisions to means–ends calculations. But, then, a relationship with someone else can only be judged or evaluated in one way: in terms of how much this someone else brings to your life versus how much you have to put in to get them to bring it. That's what other people are: *resources* – financial, emotional, sexual or whatever. Relationships reduce to means–ends calculations, and other people have value only to the extent they can contribute to your overall goal of self-fulfilment, whatever form that should take.

This is one of the real dangers of modernity. You come to see the others in your life *only* in terms of what they can do for you. You find it impossible to think of them in any other way. Try it! If you're with someone at present – a boyfriend, girlfriend, husband, wife or significant other – why are you with them? You might start listing reasons: because they make me happy, because they make me feel good about myself, because they're rich, because they give good head, or whatever. As soon as you start making a list of this sort you're already locked into the instrumental conception of your partner. You're already thinking of them in terms of what they do for you. Indeed, the very asking of the question 'Why are you with them?' invites an instrumental response. The problem is:

it is difficult, genuinely difficult, coming up with any alternative way of looking at the people in your life. Not now, not any more.

And so modernity brings with it a certain sort of anxiety about the possibility of genuine *friendship* and the possibility of genuine *love*. Is it possible to be genuinely friends with someone? Or does friendship always reduce to mutual exploitation? And is it possible genuinely to love someone? Or is 'love' simply a word you use to refer to an especially *satisfying* relationship – that is, a relationship that provides you with a lot of the important things you need?

If friendship and love are simply nothing more than mutual exploitation, then this is, well, somewhat depressing. Some philosophers would describe this sort of situation in terms of what they call *alienation*. Exploitative friendship is alienated friendship; manipulative love is alienated love. Alienation means isolation, separation, distancing, division. It means, above all else, *loneliness*. If all our relationships are alienated ones, then there is a clear sense in which we are truly alone in the world. Each one of us is a point, a focus, of instrumental calculation and exploitation, and everyone else is a resource to be used if circumstances warrant. You are truly alone in the world – alienated from everyone else, as are they from you.

These sorts of themes – the value of other people in your life, the possibility of genuine friendship, or even love – are explored, in somewhat different ways by two highly successful TV series: *Sex and the City* and *Friends*. We'll look at them in Chapters 3 and 4 respectively.

The instrumentalist strand of modernity applies not just in the sphere of personal relationships – love and friendship – but also in the sphere of what we might call, at risk of oxymoron, *impersonal* relationships. And the sphere of impersonal relationships is the sphere of *morality*. Ideally, of course, we'd like to love at least one person, and be friends with some more. And the rest of the schmucks? Well, we'll just have to be moral towards them. But what, exactly, is involved in being moral?

Before modernity got its shit together, there really wasn't much of a problem. Acting morally was acting in accordance with the values that God had put in nature. OK, He may have been a bit of a bastard some of the time. But most of the time He was hard but fair. But with modernity, all this divine guidance is out the window. Now it's all creation of values and stuff like that. So, we want to do the moral thing, let's suppose. How do we do it?

On the one hand, there is a type of moral theory that's just *made* for modernity. It's known as *utilitarianism*. Utilitarianism takes seriously the instrumentalism that is characteristic of modernity. It combines this with the central demand of morality – to be impartial. Instrumentalism claims that everyone else is a means to helping you achieve your goals (self-fulfilment etc). The idea of impartiality requires that everybody is to be treated the same, no matter who they are. We put the two together and what do we get? Obvious – everyone is the same, because everyone is simply a means. But to what end? What is the goal? According to utilitarianism, it's the general welfare: the general happiness of society as a whole.

The counterpoint to utilitarianism in the modern arena is a moral theory associated with an eighteenth-century German philosopher called Immanuel Kant. Without putting too fine a point on things, the difference between utilitarianism and Kant basically comes down to this. Whereas utilitarians incorporated the idea of impartiality into their theory by claiming that everyone is a means, Kant went the other way and claimed that everyone is an end. Because of this, we all have a duty – a moral obligation – to treat everyone as if they were ends. Which they in fact are. At least, that's what Kant reckoned.

There is, in fact, a brilliant examination of the relative merits of utilitarianism and Kantian moral theory. And it's contained in the incomparable *24*. We'll look at *24* in Chapter 5.

A variation on this general theme of how to be moral concerns the role selfishness should be allowed to play in your life. Many people think that the individualism that characterises modernity is simply a form of selfishness. I think they're wrong on this, and I'll explain why later. Nevertheless, I think it is true that individualism is the sort of thing that can easily degenerate into selfishness. Selfishness is a base or corrupt form of individualism, but is something that individualism can easily turn into in certain circumstances. And this raises the question of whether selfishness can ever be a good thing. This idea is explored to great effect by the king of sitcoms, *Seinfeld*. We'll look at *Seinfeld* in Chapter 6.

Another theme that we find running through many TV series concerns the age-old question of the nature of *the good life*. This is really a straightforward approach to one of the characteristic questions of modernity: what sort of life is it best to live? This is, of course, not a peculiarly modern worry – the Greeks were going at this question 2500 years ago. But the advent of modernity, and the resulting dislocation of self from world, sharpens it considerably. The question of how you should live your life is, in effect, an amalgam of our two characteristically modern anxieties: *what sort of person is it best to be?* And, *what sort of values is it best to live by?* The person you end up being depends on the values you choose, and vice versa. Academic philosophers have in recent times – say the last 150 years or so – been almost entirely silent on these sorts of question, preferring to analyse the logical form of action sentences, and wondering whether statements that purport to be about experiences can be analysed in adverbial terms, and fun stuff like that. So, perhaps the most compelling examination of this age-old philosophical question is be found nowhere near anything that looks like any ivory tower, or dreaming spire for that matter. Instead, it's to be found in the activities of a family of little three-fingered yellow people. What sort of a life is it best to live? In *The Simpsons* we find a detailed, comprehensive, and often convincing exploration of many of the more important ancient answers to this question, and also some of the more recent types of answer spawned by modernity. We'll look at *The Simpsons* in Chapter 7.

The final question, I suppose, is: *why does any of this matter?* It's all very well saying things like, 'To thine own self be true.' But does it really matter if you're not? In fact, just what the hell does it mean to say that you have to be true to yourself? If you're going to be true to yourself, then you must have some way of knowing what self it is that you're being true to. But what is this self? And how is it supposed to be? What's the difference between being true to it and being false to it? How do you know any of this? And, in fact, is there any self to be known in the first place?

This issue is dealt with in the sitcom *Frasier*. We'll look at Frasier, Niles and Martin Crane's attempt to answer these questions in Chapter 8.

A modern refrain

I should perhaps lay my cards on the table before we get down to the nitty-gritty of the various TV shows. As you might have already gathered, I'm a big fan of modernity! Generally speaking, I'm all for it! 'Bring it on!' is pretty much what I think. But being a big admirer of something does not necessarily mean being blind to its faults or limitations. Cultural evolution is always, at the same time, cultural *involution* – the withering away of vestigial concepts and ideas. And often what is lost is important and valuable. There is, in fact, a theme that has begun to emerge in this chapter. At the moment, we are just beginning to glimpse its outlines, but it's one that will recur again and again throughout the book. It is, basically, modernity's abiding refrain. The modern world is characterised by a tension – and often an outright contradiction – between *freedom* and *value*.

Individualism is all about freedom. It is about the ability, indeed the right, to choose how to live your life, and to choose the things in which you find fulfilment. This is what I love about modernity, and I wouldn't want things any other way. But the flip side, the *dark* side of modernity, is that this idea has become associated with others that threaten to undermine any credible notion of value. Relativism tells us that all value is relative, and so no life choice is better, or worse, than any other. Voluntarism reinforces this theme with the idea that it is the choice itself that confers value – the value that any life choice has simply results from its being a choice. So any choice is just as good as any other. And instrumentalism tells us that the value of anything outside of ourselves is only instrumental value – the value of other people and other things is a matter of what they can do for us.

So, modernity's laudable emphasis on freedom has left it with a difficult time coming up with any credible conception of value. That is the problem of modernity: the search for value in a world that is oriented around choice. And it's a problem that modernity needs to solve. For, as we have seen, without any credible conception of value, the whole idea of individualism is going to crumble too. In a world where every life choice is just as good as every other, the notion of self-fulfilment – fulfilling yourself through the choices you make – is meaningless. A reconciliation of freedom and value – that would be a postmodernity worth having.

In reality, however, we are nowhere near this. Most of us are, I think, a combination of the modern and the pre-modern. We have our modern tendencies, and these surface most obviously when we are defending our right to live our lives the way we choose. But we also have our pre-modern tendencies, and these come to the fore when we are trying to safeguard the value that we need to find in the world. Each one of us is a curious little hybrid – a funny little muddle, as Bart Simpson once put it. So this book is not about what each one of us is, but about a tendency to be found in all of us, one that is perhaps increasing, but that exists alongside something far older. It is a tendency that is championed in the popular media, and by people who are supposedly experts in telling others how to live their lives. But it is a tendency that has its costs as well as its benefits. These benefits and costs are played out for us each day on the box that sits in the corner of our living rooms.

one
BUFFY THE
VAMPIRE SLAYER

WHAT ARE OBLIGATIONS? AND WHY DO WE HAVE THEM?

Slaying sucks!

It's the old story. A Californian teenager discovers she is the latest incarnation of a long line of Slayers. So she has to give up being a cheerleader, and now spends all her time fighting vampires, demons and other assorted bad things. Her chosen vocation is significantly helped by the fact that her mother has upped sticks and moved to Sunnydale, aka *The Hellmouth*, where the vampires, demons and assorted bad things all hang out. So Buffy has gone where the work is. And she's managed to put together a crew, a collection of sidekicks, known informally as the Scoobies. There's Giles, her Watcher, sent to train her by Watchers' Council. Then there's Willow, the computer nerd who later blossoms into a lesbian and witch. The permanent members of the gang are completed by Xander, class clown and later construction worker. More or less temporary members include Cordelia, class bitch who later buggers off to LA and a larger role in *Angel*. There is Anya, former vengeance demon now trapped in the body of a rather acquisitive teenager. There's Oz, the werewolf and, apparently, the man who turns Willow to lesbianism. And Tara, the witch and lesbian who is the principal beneficiary of this.

I suppose, if there is one thing that we've learned from the seven seasons of Buffy it's this: it isn't easy being The Slayer. From each generation one is born, and if that one happens to be you, then – well, let's face it – you're basically shit out of luck! Just look at the record. Series 1, you die! Series 2, you manage to turn your boyfriend and one true love back into an evil, bloodsucking, creature of the night, just by sleeping with him.[3] That's got to weigh a little heavily on your confidence if not your conscience. And then, just as he turns nice again, you have to kill him in order to save the world. Series 3, your boyfriend returns from whatever hell dimension you sent him to in the previous series only to ditch you and bugger off to LA as soon as he gets a series of his own. Nothing too bad happens in series 4. All you have to deal with is dropping out of college, and your growing realisation that, because you are The Slayer, your life is going to be crap. Series 5, you lose another boyfriend, and die again. Oh, and your mother dies too and your sister turns out to be an instrument designed to destroy the universe. Series 6, you've reached heaven, and just when you think you can take a well-earned rest, you get dragged back to the world by your friend, the same friend who will a few episodes later try to destroy that same world. And by now, your boyfriends, who have become a tad weary of you always putting the world before them, and by your constant disappearances to the hereafter, have all ditched you and/or married someone else, and you've been reduced to working in the fast food industry and shagging a

---

3. This was of course, Angel, the vampire with a soul, who loses it again after shagging Buffy, and who gets it again in series 3. More on Angel later.

vampire who not only has a questionable bleach job, but is refraining from sticking his teeth in you only because he has a chip in his head.[4] And that's more or less it. You die, you get resurrected, and you lose loved ones by the busload. Such is the life of a Slayer.

How did you get into this mess? Well, you're the chosen one, aren't you? You're the *one* of 'from-each-generation-one-is-born' fame. And that makes you unique – apart from, of course, the girl with the dodgy Caribbean accent who came unstuck at the hands of the girl with the dodgy cockney accent. And, of course, Faith, the more than occasionally evil Slayer. But Kendra and Faith were accidents. Kendra appeared because you had temporarily shuffled off your mortal coil at the end of series 1, and Faith appeared because Drusilla clipped Kendra in series 2. So, apart from them, you're unique. And if unique means anything, it means *responsibility*, it means *obligation*. You are, after all, the last bastion of the forces of good against evil. You save the world – a lot!

What's this all about? Some people often claim that *Buffy* is such a great series because Buffy is a post-modern feminist icon. But that's largely wrong. Feminist icon she may be. But there is no way she is post-modern. What Buffy is, in fact, is *pre-modern*. Everyone else is getting all the modernity they want, in fact, all the modernity they can handle. And Buffy? She's missing out on modernity – a lot!

You gave me the world

At the end of series 5, Buffy dies (again). Then, at the beginning of series 6, she gets dragged back to life by Willow and the rest of the Scoobies. After their initial relief that she's not a zombie and that

---

4. Spike, a vampire who, at the time, had a chip in his head rather than a soul, but who gets his soul back at the end of series 6. More on Spike later.

their brains are therefore safe, the Scoobies are all somewhat perturbed by the fact that she doesn't really seem all that happy to be back in the land of the living. In fact, she seems distinctly down in the dumps about the whole thing. A brief chat with Spike, at the end of episode 3, clears things up – for us, if not for them.

After she dived through the interdimensional vortex at the end of series 5, and consequently died, she didn't go to some hell dimension, but to somewhere really rather pleasant. It may have been heaven; at the very least it was a place where she felt at peace. She felt at peace for one very simple reason: she knew that the people she loved were safe. Actually, it's not really clear that she did *know* this at all. After all, the people she loved had apparently spent the whole off-season trying to keep Sunnydale on an even keel, with nothing more than a distinctly fragile Buffybot for protection.[5] Following a long line of philosophers from Plato onwards, you can't know something that's not true. You might believe it, but you can't know it. So, Buffy probably didn't *know* that the people she loved were safe. Nonetheless, in the place she was at, she did feel very strongly that they were safe. And that's why she thought it might be heaven.

Then she was dragged back to the terrestrial plane, a place that was now for her the epitome of hell: somewhere so hard and violent, as she puts it. And, of course, this point gets hammered home by the arrival of a pack of Hells Angel demons – *hellions* – who physically transform Sunnydale into a vision of hell.

Buffy, like the rest of us presumably, defines her heaven in terms of what troubles her most on earth; more precisely, in terms of the *absence* of that thing. And what troubled Buffy most was the

---

5. A robot Buffy, commissioned by Spike as a sort of deluxe blow-up version of Buffy, and built by the evil Warren. The Buffybot is strong, but distinctly fragile, and meets its demise at the hand of the *hellions* at the beginning of series 6.

immense weight of obligation she felt towards other people. Heaven, for Buffy, was the absence of this weight. But, even then, the obligation she feels towards her friends is such that she will not tell them how they've totally screwed up her life, or rather death. Instead, she puts on a brave face and actually thanks them: 'You gave me the world, and I'll never forget that.' Which is one way of saying you've made my life a living hell. A bittersweet, double-edged thank you if ever there was one.

The idea of Buffy being given the world is one way of bringing out the difference between modern and pre-modern concepts of obligation. If you're modern, then your overriding obligations are going to be you – specifically, to your self-development, realisation and fulfilment – all the stuff that we looked at in the introduction. This is the one and only non-negotiable obligation you have. You can't avoid it – the obligation is there whether you live up to it or not. All the other obligations you might have – to other people and the world around you – are all negotiable. They are obligations you might accept or decline, depending on how they fit into your over-all project of self-fulfilment. The obligation to fulfil yourself is one you can't avoid, but all the others are more or less optional extras.

We can develop this idea in terms of a distinction between what we might call *identity-constituting* obligations and *identity-reflecting* obligations. The distinction is a tricky but important one. What I am going to call an identity-reflecting obligation is one that is, in the above terms, an optional extra. It's an obligation that is nego-tiable, one whose existence depends on your choices. Suppose you choose to accept an obligation to something outside you, an obli-gation like, say, saving the world a lot (or at least when the opportunity presents itself). Then, accepting this obligation might – morally speaking – be a very good thing for you to do. If you accept it, then this might reveal something very favourable about you – you're a stand-up girl or guy. But, from the perspective of modernity, this obligation can never do anything more than *reveal* or *reflect* the sort of person you already are.

That is, it makes sense to suppose that you – the very same *you* – might, in different circumstances, have declined this obligation instead. If you had become a cheerleader rather than a Slayer, then the obligation to save the world a lot might have been, for you, distinctly negotiable. It might have been one of those obligations you accepted if you were an especially brave and noble cheerleader, for example, but it would still be numbered among your obligational optional extras. And, crucially, it makes sense to suppose you – the very same *you* – could have lived your life this way instead of as a Slayer. At least, it makes sense if you have a modern conception of obligation.

For modernity, the self or person exists *prior* to its obligations – at least, it exists prior to its obligations to others and things outside of it. These obligations are like a coat the self can put on and take off. Which coat you wear depends on your choice. Just as the same person can wear many coats, so too can the same self wear many obligations. And just as your choice of coat may reflect the sort of person you are, so too will your choice of obligations. But the coat does not constitute or make you the person you are. And neither, according to modernity, do your obligations to people and things outside you. With regard to these people and things, what obligations you choose to accept may reflect the sort of person you are, but they do not constitute the person you are.

However, according to modernity, there is one obligation that runs far deeper than that. This is the obligation to realise, develop or fulfil yourself. This is not merely an identity-reflecting obligation; it is an identity-constituting one. You cannot separate *you*, the self or person you are, from your obligation to fulfil yourself. For what you are, in all essentials, is a project of self-development or self-fulfilment. If you take away the obligation to fulfil yourself, you are not left with you. So, you do not exist prior to your obligation to fulfil yourself. This obligation does not merely reflect who you are – it makes you the person you are.

One central characteristic of modernity – and this is implied by the individualism that lies at its core – is that you have no identity-constituting obligations to people or things outside of you. But this is very different from the pre-modern perspective. Here, the character of your existence was determined or fixed by your place in the great chain of being – and the obligations you have would be similarly fixed by this place. Buffy's being *given the world* is, in effect, a matter of her being reintroduced to her place in the great chain of being. She has been reacquainted with her obligations to the world where these obligations are not merely identity-reflecting, they are identity-constituting. As The Slayer, her obligations to the world don't just reflect the person she is; they make her the person she is. The conclusion that gets forced on us is that when you're The Slayer, you can't be a citizen of modernity. What you are, in fact, is pre-modern.

Just look at the difference between Buffy and the rest of the gang. The rest of them are all into self-development and self-fulfilment. All except, maybe, Xander – but that seems to be the result of an intellectual failing rather than a general ideological rejection of modernity. Willow is, willy-nilly, developing the magical and lesbian aspects of her personality, no matter what the cost to the world – and we all know it very nearly goes pear-shaped at the end of series 6. Anya is developing the entrepreneurial side of her personality at the expense of the vengeance-demon side. Dawn is even worse: denying the very essence of her existence – basically, an interdimensional portal/weapon of mass destruction – in favour of what she chooses to be: a singularly unremarkable schoolgirl. Everyone is choosing who and what they want to be. Their overriding obligation is to themselves – the only identity-constituting obligation they have is to fulfil themselves in whatever way they see fit. As long as they get on with the general requirement for self-fulfilment, then, within that, they all have *options*.

And options, basically, are what Buffy doesn't have. For Buffy, modernity never got its arse in gear. Saving the world a lot is not an optional extra. You can't take away this obligation and be left with The Slayer. Saving the world is what Buffy *is* as much as what she *does*. Buffy isn't a post-modern icon. She's not even modern. She's pre-modern.

Death is your gift

The difference modernity makes is not the difference between having no obligations and having lots of them. You can have just as many obligations today as you would have had in pre-modern times. The difference lies in the connection between your obligations and who you are. Modernity claims that you can have no identity-constituting relations to other people or other things. Any obligations to other people are identity-reflecting rather than identity-constituting: they don't *make* but, rather, *reflect* the person you are. For modernity, identity-constitution is solely a matter of a relation that you bear to *yourself*. Your sole identity-constituting obligation is to fulfil *yourself*. For modernity, identity-constitution is, as we might put it, a wholly *internal* affair.

Buffy, pre-modern that she is, is defined by her obligations to people and things outside of her in a way that no modern person can be. This all starts to become clear around series 4 – the series where she goes to college, drops out of college, and battles an evil military-industrial complex that has created Adam, a modern-day Frankenstein's monster type of thing. She eventually manages to dispatch Adam, but only by, in effect, becoming possessed by the long line of previous Slayers and temporarily inheriting their power. This leads to a sort of on–off relationship with the first Slayer, who pops up periodically to give Buffy veiled hints about her real nature.

The most important of these hints surfaces in series 5. 'Death is your gift,' the first Slayer tells her. Buffy, at first, understands this way too literally and interprets the idea of *gift* as *talent*. So, she takes the first Slayer to mean that the only thing she is good for, the only thing she can ever give to anyone, is death. This is, itself, a claim about her essential nature, about what she is – her nature is to be a bringer of death. But the reality is, as always, far more complicated.

Death is her gift, in fact, turns out to mean two things. First, she is going to die in order to save the world. So, her death is a gift to the *world*. Secondly, death releases her from the crushing weight of obligation that is slowly but surely destroying her. Her death is also a gift to *her*. The first sense in which death is her gift reveals something about what she can *do*; the second sense reveals something about what she *is*. She can save the world a lot – that is what she can *do* – and she *is* the being whose destiny is to be crushed under the weight of obligation that this power brings with it.

This brings out just how close is the connection between who Buffy is and her obligations to other people. The claim that death is her gift, on the first interpretation, denotes an obligation that she has to other people. She is obliged to die so that others may live. But, in the second sense, she is the being whose nature, and therefore destiny, is to be crushed under the weight of obligation that accompanies her power. In the second sense, her death is a gift to her, and also the fulfilment of her destiny – apart from the whole resurrection thing at the beginning of series 6, of course. You combine the two senses and you are left with the idea that Buffy is defined by her obligations to others. In finally working out the meaning of 'Death is your gift', therefore, Buffy is discovering who and what she is.

We're all vampires now

The novelist Milan Kundera once wrote a book called *The Unbearable Lightness of Being*. It's all about the relation between lightness and weight in a person's life. Disappointingly, Buffy doesn't figure in it, though, to be fair, Kundera wrote it in 1984, and Buffy presumably wasn't even a glint in Joss Whedon's eye in those days. But it could have easily been written about Buffy. What makes your life light, according to Kundera, is the absence of attachments to other people (or, for that matter, other things). Attachments tie you to people, they bind you to things outside of you – they *weigh* you down. Obligations are, of course, a form of attachment – perhaps the most serious form. For us moderns, any obligations we have are freely chosen by us, and can be revoked just as easily as they were initially endorsed. Modern existence is, in Kundera's terms, essentially *light*.

Buffy's existence, on the other hand, is unbearably heavy – defined by her obligations to others. So, from the perspective of modernity, Buffy has a problem. She is being denied something that everyone else has: the freedom to choose who and what she is going to be. A typically modern way of understanding what Buffy is missing appeals to the absence of an *aesthetic* dimension to Buffy's life.

The ideas of self-development, self-realisation and self-fulfilment were certainly around long before modern times. But modernity gives them a new twist. Self-development now becomes not a matter of *discovery* but a matter of *creation* – it is no longer the realisation of something that was already there, but the creation of something that was not. Buffy has been denied, in effect, the element of creativity that is bound up with the modern worldview. And in modernity, the idea of self-creation is closely associated with the idea of artistic creation. An eighteenth-century German philosopher, Johann Gottfried von Herder, got the ball rolling on this when he put forward the idea that, as he put it, each person has his or her own 'measure'. Each person has a unique way of existing, but this is not something that simply is, but something that has to be created. And the type of creation involved is, basically, artistic. Or, as Nietzsche – the nineteenth-century prophet and critic of modernity – put it, you should 'Live your life as a work of art'.

But modernity can compare life to art in this way only because it also transformed the concept of art. Before modernity artistic excellence was understood in terms of the replication of a reality that was already there. A painting was judged as good or bad in terms of how well it depicted the way the world really is. But one of the features of modernity is the replacement of this idea of art. Art now becomes a matter of *expression* rather than imitation, the creation of something new and original, rather than the replication of something old and familiar. We get the same sort of shift with the idea of a person – a change from discovering what is already there to the idea of creating something new. What you are is no longer a matter of self-discovery; it is more a process of self-creation. Just as we got expressionism in art, so too we get expressionism in life. Express yourself! Perhaps the fundamental requirement of modernity.

Buffy's problem is that while everyone else is going around expressing themselves all over the place, this has basically been denied her – she was unfortunate to be the one from each generation who is defined by their attachments to others. In this, vampires are the perfect existential counterpoint to Buffy. Vampires are just so *modern*! Their lives are light, defined by the absence of that which defines Buffy's life: obligation. Vampires recognise no obligations, certainly not to others. Vampires just do what they want, when they want to do it. As long as it's dark, of course. And as long as they don't get that pesky soul thing back. If that happens, they're truly screwed. Then, not only will they be assailed by a barrage of annoying but insistent new obligations, they will also have all the obligations that stem from their not having any obligations before. These largely seem to involve the obligation to redeem themselves and stuff like that. When this happens, any prospect of happiness seems to go right out of the window.

Just look at what happened to poor old Angel. One minute he and Darla were happily terrorising their way around Europe. The next – some bitter and wizened old crone had given him his soul back, and condemned him to many lifetimes of unrelieved misery. Indeed, that he be miserable was explicitly brought into the whole having of a soul thing – any moment of 'true happiness' and off his soul goes again.[6] And so Angel's soul has the status of something like an addiction for him. He's got it and it makes him miserable. If he could get rid of it he would be happy, but he wants to keep it – and so misery it is. Similar problems afflicted Spike when he got his soul back. He's miserable and largely insane for an entire series, and then dies.

---

6. What this means is not entirely clear. It was, apparently, an ejaculatory emission involving Buffy that sent him all evil again in the first series. But will any ejaculatory emission do the trick? Or must it be into someone you love? Recent events in series 5 of *Angel* strongly suggest the latter – e.g. his antics with Eve in the episode where everyone was being unduly influenced by the enhanced telepathic abilities of a sleep-deprived Lorne. Or maybe he just didn't 'finish' then? In any event, the question, to me, seems of obvious importance. Also, if true happiness is not tied so strictly to the purely sexual, it becomes unclear whether other forms of happiness might also count. If Angel won the lottery, for example, would he turn evil again?

But what is this soul thing anyway? The fact is that the only grip we have on what people are talking about when they talk of Angel getting his soul back, or losing his soul, or whatever it is this week, is a *moral* one. When Angel doesn't have a soul, he does things we regard as bad and refrains from doing things we regard as good. When he gets his soul back, he does things the other way around. Talk of a soul here, is, basically, talk of a *moral sense* – a sense of right and wrong, a sense of *obligation*. This isn't simply a matter of what you *do*. Spike was making a reasonably good job of *doing* the 'right thing' before he got his soul back – courtesy of the chip implanted in his brain by the US government. But the chip only modified Spike's behaviour – it didn't change what he *wanted* to do, but only what he *did*. Having a soul is not only about *doing* the right thing, but also about *wanting* to do the right thing, and, indeed, doing the right thing *because* you want to do the right thing, which is what obligation is all about. That's what Angel and Spike's getting their respective souls back comes down to.

To do the right thing because you want to do the right thing is to recognise that there is something outside of you – something that transcends you and your fascination with your own self-fulfilment. It is to recognise that there is something important and valuable independent of your own project of self-realisation. That's what you get when you get your soul back. Getting your soul back transforms you from modern to pre-modern. To the extent that we are modern – we're all vampires now.

It would be difficult to defend the idea that getting their souls back makes Angel and Spike any happier – quite the contrary. Recognising that there are important and valuable things outside of you is often a pain in the arse. So why did they want them back in the first place? Well, Angel, of course, had very little choice in the matter. Some crone whacked his back into him without so much as a 'by your leave'. But Spike actively sought out his soul, undergoing a variety of painful tests and ordeals to get it back. Why bother? The basic reason seems to be that Spike recognised that without his soul – his moral sense – his influence on Buffy wouldn't be what he wanted it to be. Sure, he had been shagging her for the best part of a series by now, but he wanted more. And Buffy would never love him if he didn't have a sense of moral obligation. Pre-moderns prefer their own, apparently.

That's the problem with being truly light – other people tend not to give a toss about you. This is what we might call the *dark side of modernity*, and a recurring theme we shall encounter many times in this book. A life burdened with obligation has obvious drawbacks. But a life that is unduly light seems no better. The flip-side of being light is that you fail to have any impact, or leave any impression, on other people. A life free of obligation is the life of a ghost, who drifts through the world but leaves no trace on those he meets. And so, it seems, Spike voluntarily exchanged lightness for weight, a life of freedom for a life of *significance*. This makes it ironic, of course, that he is reincarnated in *Angel* series 5 as, in effect, a kind of ghost.

Understanding Buffy

From our modern, vampiric, perspective, where self-fulfilment is our only non-negotiable obligation, we have a hard time even understanding how the world must look to Buffy. Of course, like Buffy, we can have obligations to other people. But what we call obligations are not at all the same sorts of things that Buffy calls obligations. Our obligations ultimately come from us. You can have all the obligations to others you want; indeed these may be an important part of your self-fulfilment. But these obligations are things you choose to accept or decline. Obligations are not things objectively present in the world, moral truths that are out there to be discovered. Rather, your obligations are ultimately created by your choices. They exist only because you have chosen certain paths, certain courses of action, over others. You could have chosen other things, but you didn't. You make your obligations; they don't make you.

For Buffy, things are reversed. Obligations exist not as products of her choices, but objectively in the world. They are not the sorts of things that can be created by our choices, but, rather, things to be discovered and to which our choices, if we are good people, should conform. For us moderns, obligations are things created by choices. For Buffy, obligations are things to which choices must conform. We moderns make our obligations; Buffy's obligations make her.

It is really difficult for moderns like us even to *understand* the way Buffy sees the world. When you think about it, obligations that exist independently of our choices would be the strangest things. Obligations, for Buffy, are things to which we *should* conform – things that we *should* obey. If we understand obligation the way Buffy does, then there may be no more mystifying word in the English language than *should*, or its cousins *ought* or *supposed to*. We sometimes use the word *should* in an easy to understand way. If we drop a stone from a height, then it *should* accelerate at a rate of 9.8 m/s². But, when we say this, all we really mean is that it *would* accelerate at this rate if we dropped it – that's simply what's going to happen to it. So, we can easily replace the word *should* with the word *would*, without any loss of meaning. Saying that the stone *should* accelerate at 9.8 m/s² is exactly the same as saying that it *would* accelerate at 9.8 m/s² unless anything weird and unexpected happens.

But, in connection with human beings, the word *should* seems to work quite differently. It's pretty obvious that a person can do other than what they should. This happens to most of us – and for some of us it happens a depressing amount of the time. It is pretty obvious that people do what they shouldn't do, and don't do what they should. Unlike the case of the stone, when we say Buffy *should* do such and such, this does not necessarily mean that she *would* do such and such. And this raises difficult issues about exactly what we mean when we say that you should do this, or shouldn't do that.

Philosophers have a tendency in situations like this to talk about what they call *truth-conditions*. Truth-conditions are things that sentences have. The truth-conditions of a sentence are, basically, the way the world would have to be in order for the sentence to be true. Take a true sentence like 'Snow is white.' The truth-conditions of this sentence are the way the world would have to be for the sentence to be true: namely, snow would have to be white. Snow is, of course, white – the world is, in fact, that way – and so the sentence is true. Not all sentences are true. The sentence 'Snow is green' is false. But the sentence still has a truth-condition. This is the way the world would have to be in order for the sentence to be true. The world would have to be such that snow is green. If it were, then the sentence would be true. So, snow being green is the truth condition of the sentence 'Snow is green.'

Philosophers have been going on and on about truth-conditions for a century or so now. This is because of a very simple and plaus-ible principle: *to understand the meaning of a sentence is to understand its truth-conditions.* We can understand both true sentences like 'Snow is white' and false sentences like 'Snow is green.' Why? Well, the suggestion is that we can, in both cases, understand how the world would have to be for each sentence to be true. We understand that in order for the first sentence to be true, snow would have to be white – which it is – and for the second sentence to be true, snow would have to be green – which it is, of course, not.

Problems emerge when we think about the truth-conditions of sentences like 'Buffy should fight against the First Evil', or 'Buffy should stake Spike.' Or, what amounts to the same thing: 'Buffy has an obligation to fight against the First Evil' or 'Buffy has an obligation to stake Spike.' Contrast these sentences with one like 'Buffy, upon diving off the tower erected by the demented followers of Glory, should accelerate at a rate of 9.8 m/s².' The truth-conditions of the latter sentence are pretty clear: we know exactly how the world would have to be if this sentence were true: Buffy, upon diving off the tower erected by the demented followers of Glory, *would* accelerate at a rate of 9.8 m/s². Unless, of course, anything unforeseen happens – gravitational distortion produced by inter-dimensional openings, for example. In this sort of case, *should* reduces to *would* plus a few background assumptions.

But when we say, 'Buffy should stake Spike' (a sentiment endorsed by several people in the final series, including Giles and the new school principal), what are we saying? What are the truth-conditions of the sentence we utter? How would the world have to be in order for this sentence to be true? It's difficult to say. It's not at all like the case of Buffy falling from the tower. It's not simply as if Buffy *would* stake Spike, because, manifestly, she didn't. *Should*, in this sort of case, does not reduce to *would*. So, what are the truth-conditions of 'Buffy should stake Spike'? What would make this sentence true, if it is true?

Moderns that we are, we are going to explain *should* in terms of *choice*. If, for example, Buffy chooses to kill Spike, and she also believes that staking him is the best way of going about this, then she *should* stake Spike, unless she chooses differently in the intervening period. There's no problem understanding the concept of *should* in this case: *should* reduces to choice, plus the most efficient means of implementing that choice. But, as we have seen, Buffy explicitly rejects this conception of obligation. Obligation does not simply stem from what we choose. Obligation is out there – an objective feature of the world. The problem for us moderns is that we are going to have a really hard time understanding this.

If we can't make sense of what Buffy *should* do in terms of what Buffy *would* do, or in terms of what Buffy *chooses* to do, then how do we make sense of it? It's a problem. In fact, it's a problem with a history. David Hume, the seventeenth-century Scottish philosopher, talked about the problem as the *is/ought gap*. No matter how much we know about the world, no matter how detailed and comprehensive our knowledge of the way the world *is*, we cannot derive from this any claim about the way the world *ought* to be, or the way it *should* be. We cannot derive an *ought* from an *is*, no matter how much we know about the *is*. If Hume is right, then obligation can't be something that exists out in the world independently of what we choose, want or do. The world simply *is* – it is a collection of things that exist or *are*. It is not composed, not even in part, of the way things *should be*.

Take a slight variation on a classic example used by Hume. Suppose you come across a murder scene. The body is in front of you, lying on the ground. Appropriate investigation can reveal to you all sorts of things about the murder. You might, for example, be able to work out what the murder weapon was: neat surgical incision, looks like a scalpel. You might be able to work out the time of the murder: body is cold, it probably occurred some time the previous night. Various factors might allow you to ascertain the motive and identity of the murderer: heart is missing and you and all your friends have lost your voices – looks like the work of *The Gentlemen*, the demonic surgeons who harvest human hearts and who can be killed by a human voice. These are all facts about the way the world *is*. But one thing that you will never be able to work out, according to Hume, no matter how meticulous your investigation, is that the murder was *wrong*, and so *ought* or *should* not have happened. For this is not a fact about the way the world is at all – it is a claim about the way the world *should* be. And we can never get, logically, from a claim about the way the world is to a claim about the way the world should be. This is the is/ought gap. The problem modernity has in understanding the concept of obligation is a special case of this general problem.

Another way of looking at our problem is in terms of the *binding power* of our obligations. What force or authority do our obligations have over us? The way the world is can certainly have a force or authority over us. And this authority is easy to understand. Buffy is, among other things, a body with a certain mass (probably somewhere in the vicinity of 50 kg). In virtue of this, if she were to do something like, say, jump off a tower erected by the followers of Glory, she would be compelled by the laws of gravitational attraction – themselves facets of the way the world is – to accelerate at a rate of 9.8 m/s². This is relatively easy – we have a reasonable idea how natural laws such as those of gravitational attraction can bind us. The question is whether there is anything similar – any analogue – in the case of our obligations? We can understand how the way the world *is* can bind us. But how can the way the world *should be* bind us? This is the problem of obligation.

Glory and God

We're trying to understand, so far without much success, how the way the world *should* be can bind us, or have authority over us. A typical pre-modern strategy is to explain this idea in terms of the dictates of a higher power – usually referred to as God, but which Buffy might think of as the *powers that be*. The idea is that just as Buffy can be compelled by natural laws of gravitation, so too can we be morally compelled by another type of law – not a natural law, but a *moral law* created by the powers that be. It is this moral law that determines the way the world should be, and so what we should or ought to do. Will this idea work?

Of course, the whole idea of a God-made moral law does not go down too easily in these modern – and increasingly secular – times. But even discounting problems of believing in the existence of God, or the powers that be, or whoever, the suggestion has problems. Suppose, for the sake of argument, there were a God-made law. What would give this law its moral legitimacy? What would make it the sort of thing we *should* obey, or have an *obligation* to obey? There seem to be two possibilities. The first is that the law is morally correct precisely because, and *only* because, God creates it. That is: God creates what's right and wrong *by* creating the law. The second is that the law is morally correct independently of God creating it. In creating the law, that is, God doesn't create right and wrong but simply taps into an already existing moral truth. The problem is: neither of these suggestions is going to work.

The problem with the first idea is that it seems to confuse *power* with *legitimacy*. Suppose, at the end of series 5, Buffy fails, and Glory returns to her own hell dimension where she sets herself up as unrivalled ruler where she is, in effect, all-powerful, or pretty close to it. In her new capacity as ruler of her world, she creates, and more importantly enforces, various rules or laws. But just because she has the power to create and enforce various rules does not make those rules morally right. We cannot derive the legitimacy or correctness of rules, moral or otherwise, simply from the power of the being that creates them.

Of course, you might want to reply, God isn't like that. Glorificus's rules will all be rather unpleasant ones, stemming from the singularly unpleasant, if admittedly rather hot, creature that she is. But God is not at all like that. God, as well as being all-powerful, is *good*. But then we simply have the question of what makes God good. And this is, basically, the problem we started with. After all, God is supposed to create moral goodness when He creates His various laws. So how can He be good before He does that? And how can He be good independently of that? If God creates moral goodness when He creates His moral laws, we can't explain why those laws are good ones by appealing to God being good. That would put the cart before the horse.

This leads to the second possibility. Throwing His weight around, creating various moral laws that are supposedly good simply because He creates them is not, in general, the sign of a good being. Part of what's involved in being a good being is only creating laws that are good or just. So, God's laws must be consonant with, or reflect, an independently existing moral truth. It is not the fact that God creates the moral laws that makes them good but, rather, the fact that these laws are statements or reflections of a moral truth that exists independently of them. That is, God is good precisely because he only makes laws that reflect the independently existing moral reality.

But if this is right, then when we are trying to work out what our obligations are, we can simply jettison God as an unnecessary middleman. If the laws were there all along, as independent moral truths, ones that God simply reflects or acknowledges in the laying down his laws, then our obligations are determined by these independent moral truths. It is *these* we need to know if we want to understand what our obligations are. Of course, if God provided a good way of finding out what these moral truths were, things might be different. But God doesn't seem to give us much help anyway. Who knows what God thinks? In the Bible He seems to think one thing, in the Koran another. The Torah tells us a somewhat different story. And don't even mention the Vedas. Different, conflicting, and often contradictory messages about what God wants: that's what we get.

So we now have two problems. First, working out what the moral truths are. Maybe God knows, but He isn't saying. Or if He is saying, He's being none too articulate about it. Secondly, we still have the problem of working out how these truths could possibly bind us to our obligations – to make our obligations things that we *must* fulfil. But that's more or less the problem this section started out with. In other words, we've got nowhere. Appealing to God-made moral laws to explain our obligations just seems to lead us down a blind alley.

A wind blowing towards the world

Despite the difficulties that God has got into lately, what with people not believing in Him and all, some people remain attached to the idea of an objective moral code, one that will tell us how the world should be, and so inform us of our obligations. This tendency was ridiculed by the French existentialist philosopher Jean-Paul Sartre, who said that people like this believed in the God-made law, but not in the God who made it! In this secular context, the so-called God-made law would not be one literally made by God – since, by hypothesis, He is not around to make it – but some sort of analogue. Instead of the law having a supernatural origin, its genesis is purely natural. And so we get the idea that our obligations are determined by us: in virtue of the types of creature we are. Our obligations are determined by our *essential nature*.

We've already seen this line of thought emerge in connection with pre-modern Buffy. Death is her gift: she has the obligation to save the world a lot by dying at appropriate junctures. That's the sort of thing she is. It goes with the territory when you're The Slayer. Is this line of thought plausible? Can we have obligations in virtue of the sorts of creatures we are? If so, we might have gone some way to understanding the pre-modern concept of obligation.

Sartre's rejection of this idea provides one of the defining features of modernity. Sartre took a pretty dim view of the whole idea of obligation in this sense. In fact, he thought the whole idea was self-serving crap. The notion of obligation is something we make up in order to avoid having to face up to the unpleasant truth: that we are radically and irredeemably free to do whatever we want. And if someone who is pre-modern claims that it is our obligations that define us, that too is nonsense: we can never be defined. Each one of us is what we are not, and not what we are – and that's all that can ever be said of us by way of definition.

Sartre was one of the most important figures in the philosophical movement known as *existentialism*. Existentialism is one of the most important expressions of the modern view of human beings. Roughly speaking, it's the view that each one of us is absolutely free to make whatever choices we make. In any situation, we can always choose. In fact, the only thing we can't choose is not to choose. And so, as Sartre puts it, we are *condemned* to be free. The whole idea that we have to do something because of what we are, or can't do something because of what we are, is misguided: because, at the end of the day, we are *nothing*, nothing at all. Each one of us is *nothingness*. It is nothingness, rather than obligation, that pervades us to our core.

Pretty whacky stuff, admittedly. But Sartre had some good reasons for making these strange claims. The starting point is human consciousness. What does Sartre mean by consciousness? Well, we're conscious in the sense that we are aware of the world. You're The Slayer and patrolling and – oh look! – a vampire has just jumped out of the shadows at you. Who would have thought? You become aware of the vamp, whereas you weren't before: and that's all it means to say you are conscious of it. You can be conscious of lots of different things at any given time – you can see the vampire, smell it, hear it if it is one of those annoying talkative ones, and so on. This is basically what Sartre and others mean by consciousness: to be conscious is simply to be aware of things in the world.

But consciousness is unlike anything else in the world in at least one sense: consciousness can at least try to become its own object. That is, consciousness can at least try to become aware of itself. We can at least try to turn our awareness towards our own states of awareness. Not only are you aware of the vampire that has just jumped out at you, you can, if you are so inclined, turn your attention to your awareness of the vampire. Not a good idea, admittedly, since turning your attention to your own conscious states is, in this context, seriously taking your eye off the ball, and is probably going to result in him getting to stick you before you stake him. So Slayers, in the normal course of events, shouldn't be turning their attention to their own conscious states while in the process of hunting vampires. Common sense really. Nonetheless, it is possible. Consciousness can turn towards itself in this way. Consciousness can at least try to become an object *for itself.*

In this respect, consciousness is unlike anything else. Nothing else can try to become an object for-itself in this way. This is why Sartre distinguished two types of existence. There is the type of existence possessed by consciousness and conscious beings. This he called *être pour-soi: being for-itself.* Everything else has a different type of existence, *être en-soi: being in-itself.* Since we are conscious creatures, each one of us is characterised by a type of existence or being that no non-conscious thing has: being for-itself.

So far, so good; but now it starts getting tricky. Consciousness – being for-itself – is for Sartre *nothingness*. It is, in its very essence, nothing at all. As Sartre puts it, in his usual unhelpful way, *it is what it is not and is not what it is*. Why? Well, go back to the idea of turning your awareness on your own awareness. When you try to do this, there is always a part or aspect of consciousness that, so to speak, slips away from you. Not only is there that upon which your attention is focused or directed, but there is also your focusing or directing of attention. And the directing of awareness cannot, as a directing of awareness, be something upon which your awareness is directed. So, when you try to direct your awareness on to your awareness, the directing of awareness necessarily slips away, so to speak, from your conscious grasp.

So: the vampire has jumped out at you, and you are aware of him or her. Suppose you now try to make this awareness into an object of your awareness. That is, you try to become aware not of the vampire but of your awareness of the vampire. As I said, not advisable in the circumstances – but just suppose anyway. In one sense you can do it. But there is always something that slips away from you in this attempt: the *directing* of your awareness on to your awareness. You might indeed become aware of your awareness of the vampires, but your awareness of your awareness is something that, consequently, escapes you.

It is not clear how far this process can go. You might attempt to direct your awareness on to your awareness of your awareness of the vampire, for example. But no matter how far you go, how many higher-order awarenesses you invoke, there is always something that will necessarily evade your conscious grasp: your awareness of whatever it is you are aware of.

Sartre's claim that consciousness is nothingness, then, amounts to this. First, whenever we direct our awareness or consciousness towards something, there is necessarily something that slips away from, or evades, our conscious grasp: the directing of consciousness. Secondly, Sartre thinks that this directing of awareness is what is essential to consciousness. Whatever consciousness gets directed upon – even if that is itself – this is precisely what consciousness is not. Your awareness of the vampire, when it becomes an object of your awareness, is no longer consciousness: it is what consciousness *was*, but not what consciousness *is*. In general, objects of consciousness, no matter what they are, are not parts of consciousness – they are what consciousness is not. And so we get to Sartre's claim that consciousness is not what it is and is what it is not.

Why does this mean that consciousness is nothingness? Sartre's basic idea is that consciousness is something that can never be found in the world. No matter how hard you look, no matter how diligently and stringently you focus your attention on the world and the things in it, you will never find consciousness. And this includes the inner world – the world of your experience – as well as the outer world. For consciousness is always in the looking and is never among the things looked at. It's in the directing of awareness and not something upon which awareness is directed. It's real, but it's nowhere. It is a pure directedness towards objects. It is, as Sartre once put it, a wind blowing towards the world.

Faith and bad faith

Because each one of us is nothingness, each one of us is characterised by a radical existential freedom that makes the whole idea of obligation null and void. The idea behind obligation is that there are certain things you must do and/or certain things you cannot do. Obligations are compelling – that's why they impinge on your freedom. But things can compel you in this way only if you are a thing with properties: a being *en-soi* in Sartre's terminology. A falling object is compelled to accelerate at a rate of 9.8 m/s². It can do no more and no less. This is because a falling body is an object with certain properties, and in virtue of those properties, it is compelled to obey certain physical laws. The moral is that you can be compelled – obliged – to do something, or not do something, only if you are *something*. We are, of course, both physical bodies and centres of consciousness. But it is our consciousness that allows us to choose and act. The body doesn't choose or do anything. Things *happen* to it, but it doesn't *do* anything. But consciousness isn't something; consciousness is nothing. Therefore, Sartre argued, our choices and actions are absolutely free. They lie outside the natural order – the realm of compulsion – and, therefore, also outside the realm of obligation.

Often you will get philosophers at this point accusing Sartre of confusing *obligation* with *compulsion*. If obligations bind us, these philosophers argue, it is not at all in the same sort of way that natural laws compel us. But actually, I think this sort of objection misses Sartre's point. Basically, what Sartre is getting at can be put in the form of a challenge. We want to think that obligations bind us in some way; that we must do certain things, or must refrain from doing other things. But what does 'bind' mean in this case? Alternatively, what does 'must' mean here? Is it that there is a powerful supernatural entity who is going to ream us if we don't do what He or She wants? Probably not. Is there some natural law that compels us to do certain things in virtue of what we are? If Sartre is right, no way. We are ultimately nothing, and so fall outside the domain of natural law. But then what can we mean by saying that our obligations bind us? It's all very well for the critic to say that Sartre is confusing obligation with compulsion – but without an account of what obligation is, and its power over us, the critic's objection looks pretty hollow.

Since we have no plausible account of the binding power of obligation, Sartre thinks, we are absolutely free to do whatever we choose. Since we are nothing, we are outside the causal order. Since we are nothing, we do not have the features that would allow us to fall into the grip of the realm of necessity. We cannot be compelled – for there is ultimately nothing there for the compulsion to take hold of. Therefore, since we have no independent conception of obligation, any obligations we may feel we have are simply the results of our choices, and can be undone with a new choice just as simply as they were acquired with a previous choice. We are free, and there is absolutely nothing we can do about it. That is, we are *condemned to be free*: the only thing we cannot choose is not to choose. To suppose otherwise is to be guilty of what Sartre calls *bad faith* (*mauvaise-foi*).

Perhaps this is why Joss Whedon, the genius behind *Buffy*, decided to call Buffy's Slayer friend/nemesis Faith and, of course, make her *bad*. Faith provides a classic example of someone engaging in *mauvaise-foi*. Admittedly, she was unfortunate to lose her watcher to the old gnarly vampire at the beginning of series 3. But to think that this compels her down the nefarious and duplicitous road she took later in that series would be to engage in bad faith. Faith is always free to choose what she does at any moment in her life. Even if it is her fear that propelled her along the path she took, she was always free to ignore her fear, or at least to choose not to let it overcome her, at least according to Sartre. Faith is always, ultimately, responsible for what she does. To suppose otherwise is to commit the very mistake that Sartre cautions against: to think of her as something – as an object in the world – that has various properties by virtue of which she is compelled – by fear, anger, shame, or whatever – to do various things or not to do various other things. The mistake that underlies bad faith – and bad Faith – is to suppose that Faith is something, when she is in fact nothing. In this, she is no different from any one of us.

Why do we do this? Why do we engage in bad faith? What is its allure? If Sartre is to be believed, we do it because we don't want to face up to the unpleasant truth – that we are free to do whatever we want – for that truth brings with it awesome responsibility. We can't use anything about us, any facet of ourselves or our role in society, as a psychological crutch to lean on when we choose how to act. Everything we do is our choice, hence our responsibility. And, if Sartre is to be believed, we find this radical existential freedom deeply unsettling. *Angst* or *dread* is its likely accompaniment. And angst or dread is not something we want to feel. So, we hide behind our obligations like the existential pussies that we are (or are *not*, if you see what I mean).

The me that will be when I am no longer

Sartre provides a classic expression of the modern worldview. From Sartre's modern perspective, Buffy is simply mistaken if she thinks she has obligations. Buffy can have no obligations to others, or the world at large – at least not in the sense in which she thinks she has them. Buffy's obligations, if they existed, would have to be the sorts of things that could bind her – that could compel her to do things in a way akin to, if not precisely the same as, the way in which natural laws compel her. But, there is nothing that can compel her in this way: her freedom is absolute because she is, when all is said and done, nothingness. Therefore, she can have no obligations to other people – not in the way she thinks herself to have them.

There is still a sense in which Buffy can have obligations; but this is only a weak, modern, sense. Buffy, like everyone else, is ultimately nothing rather than something, and so free to choose whatever she wants. If she wants to save the world a lot: all well and good. If not, if she would rather do something else – say go back to cheerleading – that's her choice. If she decides that saving the world is her bag, then she is obligated to do certain things if she wants to endorse this choice. She has to be out there slaying things that want to destroy the world – otherwise, she didn't really make the decision that saving the world was what she was going to do. In other words, she is obligated, on basic grounds of consistency, to do certain things in order to endorse, or back up, her choice. But her obligations, in this sense, are simply functions of what she happens to choose. And they can be revoked or even reversed simply by making a new choice.

But there is one thing that neither Buffy nor any of us can avoid – choice. We are condemned to be free, as Sartre puts it. Our only obligation, but this is a non-negotiable one, is to *choose*. To choose not to choose is to choose the unchoosable. In choosing, Buffy develops, realises or fulfils herself in one way rather than another. So, self-realisation or fulfilment is unavoidable – we are committed to it. It is, in effect, obligatory: as unavoidable as any obligation is supposed to be. So, according to Sartre, while our obligations to others are non-existent, our obligations to ourselves are unavoidable. And this is a classic statement of the modern worldview.

Modernity needs two things to make its account of obligation, or lack of it, complete. First, it needs an account of the weak sense of obligation to explain how we can have obligations to ourselves. Secondly, it needs an explanation of why many of us – like Buffy – think of ourselves as having obligations in the stronger, pre-modern, sense when, in fact, there are no such things.

In explaining the weak modern sense of obligation, the typical modern strategy is to emphasise the aesthetic character of life choices we encountered earlier. We moderns can distinguish *being* something from *aspiring to be* something. If Sartre is right, each one of us is essentially nothing. But this doesn't mean that we can't aspire to be something. In fact, even for Sartre, we shall all, in fact, one day be something: we shall die. Of course, when we die we are no longer around to be this thing that we have become. But what Sartre is getting at is that when we die, our properties become fixed once and for all. We become what we have done. In effect, we are no longer *être pour-soi* but *être en-soi*; no longer *being for-itself* but *being in-itself*. When we die, we become an object in the world just like any other. Our birth as a being *en-soi*, as something rather than nothing, is achieved by our death. And, in this sense, death is our gift, our gift to ourselves: it allows us, for the first time, to be something.

The choices we make when we are nothing, therefore, shape the person we shall be when we are no longer around. This is what I am doing through my choices: building the me that will be when I am no longer. Some of us may want to keep this in mind when we choose. Of course, we don't have to keep this in mind. It's not like we can be compelled to care about the person we will eventually become, nor can we be obligated to care about this person. To care or not care is a choice we must make. But some of us do care, and for a very simple reason. The person you will be when you are no longer is your legacy to the world. It is the only thing that remains of you. Indeed, if Sartre is right, it is the only thing you ever truly were (as opposed to were not). Your death is not only your gift to yourself – in the sense of that which makes you something – it is also what you bequeath of yourself: it is your gift to the world.

The face of your Watcher

The other thing modernity needs is an explanation of why people like Buffy – and presumably many more of us too – take themselves to have obligations in a strong, pre-modern, sense, when there are, in fact, no such things. The typical strategy is to try and explain away these apparent obligations in terms of something else. It is this strategy that, in part, explains the reverence modernity has for the work of Sigmund Freud.

Modernity tells us that obligations can't bind us. We make them in the first place through our choices, and we can revoke any choice just as easily as we made it by choosing something else. So, what we need, from the perspective of modernity, is not to explain our obligations but to *explain them away*. We need to explain not why we actually have obligations – for we don't – but to explain why we *think* we have them. It's an attempt to explain not *actual* obligations but *perceived* ones. This is where Freud comes in. And this leads us nicely into a Freudian interpretation of the Giles–Buffy relationship. But, unfortunately for the sickos among you, since this is the late Freud we're talking about – the Freud who wrote *Civilization and its Discontents*, rather than *The Psychopathology of Everyday Life* – there's not going to be any sex in it.

Giles is, of course, Buffy's Watcher. He's also the closest thing she has to a father. The function of the father, or, in this case, Watcher, in Freud's scheme of things, is to inculcate in you the sense of moral obligation that is going to be required for your assimilation into civilised society. The process starts off with basic human feelings: love, affection, the desire to please, to desire to be loved, and so on. Buffy, of course, being a normal healthy cheer-leader, has these in abundance. These are all very well, but they're really not going to cut it when push comes to shove and the demons are at the gates. When the going gets tough, The Slayer is going to need more than these: she is going to need a strong sense of obligation. Otherwise the basic human feelings might be outweighed by other basic human feelings – such as the one to run like hell from any gnarly demons she happens to meet. And the function of The Watcher is to work on, to discipline, regiment, and ultimately transform, the basic human emotions into a sense of obligation, one that will always be there no matter what.

In doing this, Giles works with The Slayer's fear of forfeiting his love. Buffy's desire for love and approval is used against her to instil in her the moral sense that will, one day, get her killed (at least twice). When she does things that exhibit a sense of obligation, Giles praises her. When she does things that betray a failure of obligation, or a lack of concern, he scolds and admonishes her. In this way, her desire to be loved is used against her, and a sense of obligation is trained into her. Eventually the voice of Giles becomes internalised; it becomes her moral compass, her conscience. Now she is a fully functioning Slayer – someone who will put up with all the shit that this obligation brings with it.

In later years, fathers die, and Watchers shag off back to England. But they are still used as the templates against which we measure our actions. What would the face of her Watcher be like if she were to do such and such? Would it be smiling in approval? Or frowning in disgust? The face of our father is the criterion according to which we classify actions as right or wrong.

So, if Freud is right, the whole idea of moral obligation stems from this primitive sense of moral conscience instilled in us by our parents (or Watcher). Different parents lead to different senses of obligation. For example, just think how differently Angel's son Connor might have turned out if he hadn't been raised by that psycho Holtz. We have no choice in the obligations we accept. Early in life, we are trained, like the salivating dogs that we are, to feel and accept certain obligations. And the ramifications of these early events are felt throughout our lives.

Who knows? This story may be plausible; it may even be true. We'll look at Freud a lot more closely in the next chapter, where we'll examine the contribution he has made to the north New Jersey mob. But what you should realise is that the Freudian story doesn't even begin to explain actual or real obligations – not in the strong pre-modern sense. It only explains why we *take* or *understand* ourselves to have various obligations. It doesn't explain how we could *actually* have obligations. We have got to be careful to distinguish two very different things. On the one hand, there is a story of how we come to be such suckers for obligation. This is the story of how we come to *feel* or *believe* that we have certain obligations. On the other, there is the story of how we *actually have* obligations. The first story is not the same as the second. We can believe or feel we have certain obligations, even if we don't in fact have them. And we can actually have certain obligations that we fail to recognise or refuse to believe.

The Freudian story gives us an account of why we come to feel obligated in the way we do. But it doesn't tell us how we are in fact obligated. If the Freudian story is true, and I grew up raised by, for example, *Der Kindestod*, then I might feel a very different sense of obligation from the one I feel now. The sucking of the life force of babies and children might be high up on my list of *perceived* obligations. But I can hardly *really* be obligated to suck the life force of babies and children. And this is characteristic of accounts like those of Freud. They can explain why we *perceive* ourselves to be obligated in certain ways – why we *think* we have certain obligations – but they don't tell us what our obligations *in fact* are. Of course, this limitation of Freud's view is not a problem from the point of view of modernity. From this point of view, there is no such thing as obligation, not in the pre-modern, choice-independent sense. So we shouldn't expect an explanation of how we have *these* sorts of obligations – because we don't have them.

Modernity and the meaning of life

Modernity, remember, is not so much something that we are, but a tendency that is in all of us to some extent or other. This tendency whispers to you that your fundamental moral obligation is to yourself – to develop yourself to the best of your ability, to fulfil yourself, to be the best you can be. All other obligations are secondary, and therefore less *real*. But there are, I think, certain spheres of our life where we just can't bring ourselves to be modern. And this is a really good thing. It would be a poor parent who regarded obligations to her or his children as secondary and less than fully real. And those whose obligations to their partner always come off second best are going to find themselves in relationships that are, at best, fragile. Whenever we want to safeguard the idea that there are things in our life that are valuable, over and above ourselves and our fulfilment, we always find ourselves retreating from the modern to the pre-modern. Modernity's thing is freedom; it can't handle value.

When the attachments – including the obligations – you have to things outside yourself are identity-constituting ones, when you wouldn't be the same person without them, then it is easy to see how those things can be valuable. They are part of you. To have identity-constituting attachments to other people or things, or maybe to the world as a whole, is to have things that are worth dying for. Buffy has things that are worth dying for – on more than one occasion, in fact. Our lives inherit the significance of the people and things in the world around us. Therefore, our lives each have the capability of being *big* lives; they are capable of having a grandeur bequeathed to them by the greatness and majesty of the world in which they exist and of which they are constituted.

One of the dangers of modernity is that it takes away from us this sense of the grandeur. In the absence of identity-constituting attachments to things outside of us, any sense that we share common purpose and also common fate with the world around us is in danger of being lost. The meaning or significance of our lives shrinks with the shrinking of the boundaries of the self. Things outside us no longer form part of who and what we are; and we cannot understand our meaning, purpose or value in terms of the meaning, purpose or value of the world. And so we busy ourselves with *little* things. We work in crappy jobs with little or no significance and even less satisfaction. Then we go home and watch *Pop Idol* – basically as a way of killing time before we go back to the crappy job again. Our lives are a fascination with the facile. We kill time. And then we die.

In such a life, it seems, there is little that is *big*. There is little that seems to have meaning or purpose. That is a danger of modernity. Very few things are worth dying for any more. And our lives, accordingly, are the poorer. In fact, their poverty threatens to undermine the very idea of self-fulfilment that lies at the core of modernity. If the choices we make that shape our lives do not correspond to things that have real significance or value, if one choice is no better than another, then the idea of self-fulfilment becomes null and void. In this way, the danger *of* modernity is also a danger *for* modernity: a danger that it will erode its own foundations and eventually be swept away in the tide of history.

two
THE SOPRANOS

Modernity and morality

One of the most striking characteristics of the modern world is a tendency to think about morality in a peculiar way. We have already had glimpses of this in the previous chapter. Modernity's attitude towards the idea of *moral obligation* is to suppose, in effect, that it is not what we think it is. Modernity, as we have seen, has a hard time understanding the idea of obligation to others. The modern view of human beings – where self-fulfilment is the overriding obligation – leaves little room for the idea that we can have genuine obligations to things outside of us. Because of this, there is a strong modern tendency to suppose that such obligations are not real, but only *apparent*: they are really something else masquerading as obligations. So, obligations to other people are not things to be explained; they are things to be explained *away*.

This tendency to think of morality as something less than fully real is a pervasive feature of the modern worldview. It manifests itself not just in modernity's attitude towards moral obligation, but towards morality in general. In particular, it is a crucial facet of modernity's attitude to the idea of moral *evil*. Modernity has a hard time accounting for moral evil. To the extent it exists, we moderns tend to suppose, it must really be something else. In fact, this idea didn't spring into existence fully formed with the birth of the modern age. What is characteristic of modernity is the *emphasis* it puts on this idea. If we want to pinpoint its origins, we will have to look back much further: to the ancient Greek philosopher, Plato. That's not surprising, really, as much of what we think of as philosophy today began with Plato.

Footnotes to Plato

Alfred North Whitehead was a philosopher who did most of his work in the early twentieth century. Some of his stuff actually wasn't bad at all. He co-wrote a book with Bertrand Russell, called *Principia Mathematica*. It was on the foundations of mathematics and attempted to show, among other things, that mathematics could be reduced to logic. Apparently this is important. Unfortunately, they failed; but it was a very impressive failure all the same: very complex, very sophisticated. It took them over 80 pages to prove, using only the logical apparatus of set theory, that $1 + 1 = 2$. So you can imagine how big the book was. And you can't help being impressed – if you like that sort of thing. And in his own work, he developed what he called a *process* view of reality, a view according to which change, not objects, is fundamental, and where purpose should be understood as something out there in the world. Very interesting, very Zen – again, great if you like that sort of thing. Unfortunately, due to the vicissitudes of philosophical fortune, no one is all that interested in Alfred North Whitehead any more. If people know about him at all, it's largely because of a famous claim he made, not about reality or mathematics, but about philosophy. Philosophy he said, and by this he means philosophy as practised in the West, is a series of *footnotes to Plato*.

Whitehead meant that what people think of as philosophy turns on a series of questions, problems, issues and disputes identified by Plato. What philosophy should be doing, the sorts of problems it should answer, and even the sorts of questions it should ask: all this comes directly from Plato. Plato, if you like, made up the rules of the game, and we're still playing by those rules today. It is in the questions he asked, and the ways of addressing these questions, that Plato's importance lies. It's certainly not in the answers he gave: in these Plato was most likely wrong on just about everything. Much of what Plato said was, I think, pure fantasy. If we just focused on the answers he gave, philosophy might as well be a series of footnotes to *Lord of the Rings*.

Nowhere is Plato's influence – good and bad – more noticeable than in *The Sopranos*, a tale of the modern mob, and, what is less well known, an exploration of various philosophical themes instigated by Plato. The main theme: what is the relation between what we are and what we do? Or, more specifically, *is it possible for a good man to do bad things?* And in *The Sopranos* we find the same acting out of various problems, disputes, contradictions and confusions that so exercised Plato. If anything is a series of footnotes to Plato, it is *The Sopranos*.

The Sopranos

Tony Soprano is a worried man. More precisely he's an *anxious* man. He suffers from severe anxiety attacks, and these can result in him passing out. So, he's seeing a shrink. No biggie, you might think. But the problem is Tony is also *capo* of a New Jersey crime syndicate. And his associates are not going to take kindly to him blabbing anything to anyone – shrinks included.

Part of the problem is, presumably, because Tony works so hard for a living. As well as busting balls, he has to spend much of his time juggling them. First, there is his family – his unhappy wife Carmela, his son Anthony Junior, and his daughter Meadow. Then there is his psychotic mother, Livia. And let's not forget the succession of mistresses, beginning with the Russian in series 1. Then there is his *family*, his outfit: Christopher, Paulie, Pussie, and Silvio (and later Furio), and several more distant associates. In addition, there is a man both family and *family* – his uncle Corrado 'Junior' Soprano. Then there are his business activities, an impressive portfolio. First, there is Bada Bing, his strip club, where he seems to spend most of his time, and plans his other activities. These include money-lending. Not a philanthropic enterprise for Tony – he lends money so he can either make lots and lots of interest or, more typically, so he can get his hooks into the business – shop, restaurant, etc. – of whoever he has lent the money to. He combines this with an interest in card games, which are often associated with money-lending of the sort outlined above. In addition, there is his interest in the waste management business – he owns a waste management company, which he inherited from his father. And then there are the general pies any self-respecting crime boss would have his thumb in: extortion, larceny, armed robbery, racketeering and, when the occasion calls for it, murder.

These activities allow Tony to live very comfortably. He has a huge house in the New Jersey suburbs, and a huge yacht on the New Jersey shore. Carmela spends much of her time buying things – material comfort serving as proxy for the lack of emotional comfort she gets from Tony. Meadow is going to go/is going to a very expensive college. You get the picture. But he also, as I mentioned, has a problem: he's sick.

You're sick!

There is a way of thinking about morality that is peculiar to modernity. Whatever morality is … it must really be something else. We saw this idea at work in the previous chapter in connection with the idea of moral obligation. At most, our obligations are the narcissistic ones of self-realisation and self-fulfilment. Our obligations to others are not what we take them to be: they are functions of our choices, and not objective features of a reality to which our choices must conform. We're confused because we can't tell *inside* from *outside*: we mistake the internalised voice of our parents (or Watcher, for that matter) for moral truths that exist objectively in the world outside us. We think of moral obligation as something that stands outside us when really it is something that comes from within us.

It is characteristic of modernity to apply this general idea not just to moral obligation but to moral right and wrong in general. Moral right and wrong must ultimately be an expression of us, and our inner natures, and not something that stands outside us, or over and above us. And, in probably its most recent influential version, this idea takes the form of what we might call a *medical* model of morality. Moral right and wrong reduces to mental health or sickness.

Take one of the ubiquitous expressions of recent times: 'You're sick!' What does it mean when someone says this to you? Well, assuming that there's nothing obviously wrong with you in a physical sense, they probably mean that your sense of right and wrong is severely warped – perhaps, that you have no standards of moral decency at all. They mean much the same thing when they tell you that you 'need help'. Why all the medical metaphors? We do this all the time – run together the ideas of right and wrong, good and bad, with the ideas of health and sickness. Every time we come across a case of serious moral depravity, we seem almost compelled to wheel out a medical metaphor or two. Hitler was sick. Saddam is sick. When we condemn someone morally by calling them *sick*, is this just a figure of speech, or is there more to it than that? Is it simply a metaphor, or is there a deeper truth underlying it?

Tony Soprano is an interesting case, since he is arguably sick in both a moral and a medical sense. Tony is a ruthless man – he's had to be to get where he is today and to hang on to what he's now got. 'Sick' is an epithet many would willingly fling at Tony. In the very first episode of the first series, he sets the tone for the entire programme quite nicely by running over a guy who owes him money. Then, when the guy's lying on the ground, with bone sticking out of his leg, Tony punches him – and even now my eyes water thinking about this – in the nuts, and then repeatedly in the face. And this is just a gentle warning. Tony wouldn't think twice about having the guy whacked if he doesn't start producing the lucre soon. Murder, extortion, racketeering, vice – these are just some of the impressive items you would find on Tony's CV. So, if someone likes the illness metaphor for gross moral turpitude, they would probably have no hesitation in calling Tony sick.

But there's also a clear sense in which Tony is a good man. In the same episode, we find him at his daughter Meadow's volleyball game, gently talking to her afterwards about her relationship with her mother, and so on. Indeed, he's a regular at all of Meadow's sporting events. He presumably would be too at Anthony Junior's sporting events, except for the fact that Anthony Junior is a fat kid who is crap at sports, at least until the third series when he ditches the weight and becomes a football hero. In many ways, then, Tony is the epitome of a good family man. He loves and protects his children, and, although he screws around on his wife, Carmela – frequently – he is still very fond of her in his own way.

So, morally speaking, Tony is a strange mixture of the good and the bad, the healthy and the sick. And, interestingly, his good side seems to win out in our affections over his bad. Very few people are rooting for the Feds to make a case stick against Tony – quite the opposite, in fact. We have no similar fondness for his uncle Corrado 'Junior' Soprano, or even some of Tony's lieutenants, like Pussy or Paulie, even though they are in the same business as Tony and employ the same sorts of methods. Clearly, Tony has something that they don't.

But Tony, of course, is also sick in another sense. He's psychologically unwell. Tony has blackouts. He's undergone tests, and it seems there is no straightforward physical cause for these – no lesion in the brain, for example. The cause is psychological rather than physical: the blackouts are brought on by severe anxiety attacks. He's worried enough about it to be seeing a shrink – a hazardous enterprise for someone in his line of work.

Is there any connection between Tony's moral sickness and his medical sickness? This brings us back to Plato.

Being good and doing bad

One simple and obvious explanation of why Tony Soprano can be both good and bad is that good people can do bad things, and bad people can do good things. So, perhaps Tony is a good guy – *goodfella*, actually – who does some bad things. Or maybe he's a bad guy who does some good things. Either way, none of us is wholly good or bad; we have our best side and our worst. And we should distinguish what a person *is* from what a person *does*.

Plato would say that this is all wrong. We cannot separate what a person is and what a person does in this way. In order to *do* good things, in anything other than an accidental or fluky way, you have to *be* or *become* a certain way. And when you become that way, you really will not be able to do what's bad. What you are and what you do are tightly connected in this way. Plato talked about the *soul* here. But what he really had in mind was what we would, today, call the *personality*. If you are to do good things, then your personality has to be a certain way. Your personality has to take on a certain *form* or *structure*. And when it has this form or structure, you will automatically do good things – because that is the sort of person you are.

In this idea, Plato did something that, to this day, dominates the way we think about morality: he *medicalised* it. When someone does something we don't like, why do we call him sick? It all stems from Plato: it's from him we get the idea that moral transgressions are a form of sickness. If you do something that's morally wrong, this is because your personality does not have the right structure. You are suffering from a personality defect, a psychological deficiency – a *medical* problem. You are both morally and medically sick. In fact, your moral sickness is an expression of your medical sickness.

You may think I'm mistaken about Plato's influence on us. We don't really think about morality like this, do we? After all, aren't we very *forgiving* of moral transgressions today? Don't we all think that everyone makes mistakes, and everyone deserves a second chance? This is all true, but misses Plato's point. Tony doesn't regard his murdering, extorting and racketeering as a mistake at all. On the contrary, he regards it as a necessary and important part of his job, and as something that he must carry out rigorously, professionally and intelligently. Mistakes can be made, but only when the activities necessary to the flourishing of his *family* are not carried out professionally or intelligently – for example, when Christopher's meth-head friend Brendan rips off one of Junior's trucks (a mistake that eventually results in his being shot through the eye by Mikey, Junior's right-hand man, whom Tony later has whacked). From Tony's point of view, these are not mistakes in the activities themselves – Tony does not (generally) question the legitimacy of the activities themselves – but mistakes in the way the activities are carried out or executed.

And this is Plato's point. Tony cannot see or understand what's right and wrong; he has not learned to distinguish properly between the two. And he cannot properly distinguish the two because his personality has not yet taken on the correct form or structure that would allow him to do so. His personality is an *unhealthy* one. The question is: what, for Plato, is the correct form or structure for the personality? What is the healthy personality like?

Capos, soldiers, and strippers

Everyone's personality, Plato claimed, is made up of three distinct parts: *reason*, *spirit* and *appetite*. However, different people have these things to different degrees. In some, the appetites may be very strong. In others, it may be the spirit. In others, it may be reason. The result is that different people have different personalities because of the different ways that reason, spirit and appetite combine within them. And Plato's claim is that a personality can be healthy only if this combination is just right.

Reason, as you might have gathered if this part of your personality is at all prominent, is the rational part of you. This is the part of you that allows you to think logically or rationally about issues, problems and choices that you face and to come up with a workable option or solution. The province of reason covers many things, from your ability to engage in abstract mathematics and logic, at one extreme, to the homespun practical wisdom that allows you to work out that if you want to drink the beer in the can, you'd better pop the top first.

Spirit, for Plato, means something like *will*. It's that part of you that allows you to 'force your heart and nerve and sinew / To serve your turn long after they are gone, / And so hold on when there is nothing in you / Except the Will which says to them "hold on"', as Kipling once put it. But spirit is more than just will. It's also made up of various emotional capacities; ones that are involved in the way the will works, and which even allow the will to be so effective in the first place. It might be your anger, for example, that allows us to come through a testing time. Or maybe your fear, or your shame. Or maybe it's that stubborn streak you've always had that manifests itself as a certain dogged determination to keep on going. Spirit is this powerful amalgam of will and emotion.

When Plato talks about *appetite*, he means something like what we would call *desire* – but not just any desire. There can be all sorts of desires, and appetites, for Plato, are more restricted than that. There can, for example, be desires of reason – the desire to prove Fermat's last theorem, for example, or to prove that history did, in fact, come to an end when Hegel put the last full stop to the last sentence of the *Phenomenology of Spirit*. There can also be desires of the spirit – the desire to show that you do have the balls and the ruthless dedication necessary to be a *made* man is a particular favourite of Christopher's, for example, or, at least, it was before he actually became a made man. The desires that make up what Plato calls the appetite are far more basic than this. If you think of what biologists call the four Fs – feeding, fighting, fleeing and fucking – then you're pretty much on the way to understanding what Plato means by the appetites. These are what we might call basic or *primitive* desires: ones that we have because of our biological nature – because of the type of creature we are – and which we share with many other animals. To understand what Plato means by the appetites, we just have to construe the four Fs broadly enough. So, feeding should be understood as *consumption* in a more general sense – the taking in of what is outside you, including not just feeding, but the acquisition of wealth and power also. And fucking can be understood both in its literal (screwing someone) and metaphorical senses (screwing someone *over*).

Each one of us has a personality made up of all three parts. But there are, according to Plato, some personalities that are healthy, and some that are not. Consequently, there are some personalities that are good and some that are not. The key to being healthy and good is getting all three parts to behave in the right way. Each part has its place and its role to play, and in the healthy and good person the parts all know their place and all play the right role.

Plato's baseline position is that reason must be in control. Spirit must support reason. And the appetites must go along with what reason and spirit tell them to do. There are various subtleties, but that's the baseline. So we have reason telling us how to demonstrate mathematical proofs and open cans of beer. Spirit assists reason by providing the necessary emotional qualities like a sense of self-respect, self-control, dignity and strength of will, and stuff like that. And, through their combined efforts, reason and spirit control the rather unruly feeding, fighting, fleeing and fornicating aspects of our personality. At least, that's the way it goes in a healthy personality.

It's not like reason has got to dominate totally. Absolute suppression of everything below reason isn't going to get anyone very far. If your rational capacities aren't motivated by emotions and desires, for example, then life would become pretty meaningless. Why would you bother doing anything if there was no emotional satisfaction involved? Emotions, just as much as rational capacities, point out to us what we need to do and why we need to do it. When this happens, the main job of reason is to supply the *how*. And, of course, a life where none of the appetites was satisfied would be a very short and miserable one. The key to a healthy personality, for Plato, is not obliteration of everything by reason, but, rather, that all parts should have their place. Appetites are to be satisfied to an appropriate extent, but no more. Emotions and higher desires are to be allowed appropriate free rein, but no more. And it is reason that decides what counts as appropriate. In the healthy personality, reason has always, ultimately, got to be the boss, the *capo di tutte capo*.

The healthy personality also provides the model for Plato's model of the ideal society. Society, Plato claimed, has essentially the same structure as the personality – it is made up of analogous parts, and can be healthy or sick, depending on how these parts are arranged. In a healthy society, the parts are arranged in the same way as they are in a healthy personality. Corresponding to reason, we have what Plato called *philosopher-kings*. These are backed up by *auxiliaries* – the soldiers and police – who defend society from external threat and internal disarray. And then we have the plebs – corresponding to appetites – doing their plebby things: feeding, fighting, fucking and watching *I'm a Celebrity, Get Me Out of Here!* The philosopher-kings decide what to do, auxiliaries enforce their policies, and the plebs going on fighting and fornicating but, crucially, producing enough to keep society going.

Most people object to this vision of society on the grounds that Plato was a fascist bastard, which is, of course, true. There's probably also a more basic problem: there's really no evidence whatsoever that any philosopher – king or otherwise – could organise a piss-up in a brewery. But while it may not be a very convincing model for society as a whole, it may, strangely enough, provide a pretty good model for Tony Soprano's *crew*. Running things you have Tony Soprano, the *capo di tutte capo*, the crew's version of the philosopher-king. Supporting him are his loyal auxiliaries or soldiers: Pussy, Paulie, Christopher, Silvio and Furio, who enforce his will and implement many of his money-making schemes. At the base of the operation are his minions or plebs – the people who collect the garbage, the ones who wrap themselves around the poles in his strip joint, the people who serve the beers to people who watch the people who wrap themselves around poles in his strip joint. And so on.

However, there is one important difference between Tony's operation and a perfect society. The problem lies with Tony. He's fucked up! In him, reason, spirit and appetite are all over the place. So, he's not a plausible example of a philosopher-king, and so everything below him is messed up too. In Plato's model, if you don't get it right at the top, then everything below is going to be wrong too.

Tyrants and madness

The assimilation of moral goodness to a type of health is absolutely central to Plato's philosophy. Morality isn't about the way things *are*, but the way they are *supposed* to be. But when we talk about health, we are also talking about how things are supposed to be. Philosophers often put this by saying that the concept of morality and the concept of health are both *normative* concepts. A normative concept is one that concerns how the world is *supposed* to be, or how it *should* be, and is opposed to a purely *descriptive* concept, which concerns only how the world is. In the previous chapter, we looked at another normative concept – *obligation* – and found it incredibly difficult to work out what this concept actually meant. Thus is it generally with normative concepts. Plato has a general line on normative concepts such as *right* and *should* and *ought*: he tries to explain the normative character of morality in terms of the normative character of health.

To see how this works, take the concept of physical health first. This concept is closely associated with the concept of *function*. Physical health occurs when a person's bodily organs are all performing their proper functions – they are all doing what they are *supposed* to do, or what they *ought* to do: the heart pumping blood at a certain required rate, the lungs providing a certain required amount of oxygen to that blood, the kidneys removing waste products from that blood, and so on. So physical health is a matter of the body and its parts all doing what they are *supposed* to do.

The same is true, Plato thinks, of psychological health – the health of the personality. This is a matter of reason, spirit and the appetites all performing their proper function – doing what they are supposed to do: reason is *capo*, and spirit sides with reason to control the appetites. To the extent that this doesn't happen, the personality is diseased or disordered: it is not the way it is supposed to be.

One form of disorder that will ring a bell with many of us is what Plato calls the *tyrannical* personality.[7] In the tyrannical personality, certain of the appetites – 'lawless desires', as Plato sometimes refers to them – have got away from us. In the healthy personality, these would be kept under control – repressed – by the reason/spirit coalition. In the tyrannical personality, they're on the loose. The consequence of this, according to Plato, is that one of these appetites will eventually set itself up as a 'master passion', a passion that acquires total dominance over the mind, and the other desires subserve it like worker bees feeding the queen. Finally, Plato

---

7. The fact that he describes this sort of person as *tyrannical* is part of his project of thinking about society along the lines of the person or personality. The tyrannical role of the master passion is mirrored by that of the tyrant who has usurped power without lawful authority. In fact, when the ancient Greeks talked about tyrants, that's all they meant: someone who had usurped power without lawful authority. Tyrants, in the Greek sense, don't necessarily have to be vicious bastards. Some of them can be quite sweet.

claims, 'the master passion runs wild and takes madness into its service ... all discipline is swept away and madness usurps its place'.

We all know what Plato is talking about. Madness is actually a pretty apt expression. Suppose, for example, you're out with the lads/ladettes, and, quite frankly, you've had one *Staropramen* too many. Most of the time, you may be a perfectly healthy and not at all tyrannical personality type. But now your discernment – itself the province of reason – is lost, and you want to get yourself some action no matter what the consequences. The desire to get laid sets itself up as a master passion and the evening veers towards its depressing but inevitable conclusion. In the morning, when reason has, if a little groggily, reasserted itself, you will quite happily gnaw off your arm if you judge that's what's needed to escape from this person who, last night, seemed the paragon of attractiveness. Madness, indeed.

An unbalanced – and therefore, unhealthy – personality is, for Plato, the source of all moral wrongdoing. Take, for example, the sort of wrongdoing typically committed by Tony. Having people clipped, for example. Tony doesn't do this very often, nothing compared to, say, his hotheaded Uncle Junior before he became ill, and when he does have people whacked, he's usually got a very good reason – from his perspective anyway. But he does have people clipped when it is necessary to protect his interests, and he'll clip someone himself if they've done something to really piss him off – for example, if they've tried to clip his nephew Christopher. And what are his interests? The business, and its associated activities: larceny, embezzlement, gambling, extortion, racketeering – the whole gamut of criminal activity. But why would anyone want to engage in these sorts of activities, and in the whacking necessary to ensure their continuance, in the first place? According to Plato, they are almost always the result of a tyrannical personality type, where a master passion has set itself up in control and the function of other desires serve this passion.

Precisely which master passion is involved can vary from person to person. The most obvious one, for example, can be unchecked greed. Or, more subtly, the greed itself can simply be a symptom – a passion that itself serves another master passion. For example, greed might be a symptom of an underlying feeling of insecurity, and the desire for safety or security might then be the master passion. Or the feeling of insecurity might itself be the symptom of something more basic – unresolved self-hatred, and associated desire for self-destruction, for example. The desire for security would then be a reaction to the underlying master passion: the appetite for self-destruction.

So, there are various possibilities. But the underlying idea is that when people do bad things this is because their personality is diseased or disordered. The wrongdoer is, in effect, *sick*.

Why Tony isn't happy: Plato's story

According to Plato, a healthy, balanced personality is not only needed for you to be moral, it is also needed for you to be *happy*. You can't be happy unless you're healthy. This applies not only to physical health, but also the health of the personality.

Men don't reckon that life is worth living when their physical health breaks down, even though they have all the food and drink and wealth and power in the world. So we can hardly reckon it worth living when the principle of life breaks down in confusion, and a man wilfully avoids the one thing that will rid him of vice and crime, the acquisition of justice and virtue in the sense that we have shown them to bear.

The principle of life, as Plato puts it here, is the balance between the three elements of the personality. You can't be happy without this sort of psychological health any more than you can be happy without physical health.

Tony's basic problem, Plato would think, is that he has allowed certain of his appetites to run away from him. He has a tyrannical personality type, and certain of his desires are all vying to set themselves up as master passion. It is, therefore, no coincidence that his main symptoms are anxiety attacks. The typical cause of such attacks is the feeling that you're not in control of your world, that things are slipping away from you and there is nothing you can do to stop it.

The basic problem, of course, is that his mother, the highly dysfunctional Livia, has, at least unconsciously, wanted him dead his whole life. Who knows why? Presumably she's sick too. This unconscious desire of his mother's keeps surfacing at various points, and culminates in her, in effect, giving Junior the go-ahead to have Tony clipped. But the desire itself has been around since Tony's childhood. The effects on Tony are fairly predictable – even if they largely manifest themselves only as unconscious wishes. Most obviously, the desire for security and protection sets itself up as a master passion, one that other desires will come to serve. Tony's problem becomes exacerbated, however, because his master passion – the desire for security and protection – becomes served by two sub-passions, and these are, in a variety of ways, incompatible.

One thing that serves Tony's master passion is his desire for money and power. The other is his passion for his family – that is, his family not his *family* – even his wife Carmela. The problem is that the passion for money and power requires him to do things, and also to embrace certain sorts of emotions and psychological attitudes, that are incompatible with his love of his family. His master passion can be served in two ways. But the first way requires him to become the sort of person who would have a lot of trouble being successful with the second way. The result is that the more he follows his appetite for money and power, the greater the chance of his family slipping away from him.

There are various reasons for this – running a strip joint can't be good for marital accord, for one thing – but the deepest problem is the dissonance between the violence and callousness he has to employ in his public persona and the feelings and emotions that are necessary for a happy family life.

A very good example of this comes in the episode in the first series when Tony takes Meadow on a tour of New England colleges. As luck would have it, while stopping in a gas station in Maine, he sees a former colleague turned snitch who is living there on the witness protection programme. So, Tony decides to combine his role of devoted father showing his daughter around some of the most expensive private universities in the North East with the whacking of the former colleague. Note also that he makes this whacking as personal as possible. He doesn't shoot him; he strangles him. He didn't just whack the guy out of duty; he also enjoyed it. Imagine the dissonance between the kinds of feelings he would have to have in order to enjoy strangling the snitch and the kinds of feelings he would have to have in order to enjoy taking his daughter on a tour of colleges. It is difficult to see how the two sets of feelings could reside in the same person.

Later in the episode, while waiting for Meadow at Bowdoin College, he sees a quotation from Nathaniel Hawthorne, one that perfectly sums up Tony's situation: 'No man can wear one face to himself and another to the multitude without finally getting bewildered as to which may be true.' Tony is an essentially *fractured* man. It's not just that the face he shows to the world is different from the one he shows to himself. Often, he shows two incompatible faces to himself. His personality has become split – bifurcated – into two incompatible and semi-autonomous components. He has, that is, a *schizoid* personality.

His schizoid personality type, Plato is going to say, is the result of a deeper tyrannical personality type. The master passion for security manifests itself in two incompatible ways: as a desire for money and a desire for family. And given the way he makes money – given the means he has to employ – the two desires are very difficult to house within the same person. The result is Tony's schizoid personality and partial dissociation from himself. This is the sort of thing that can happen when you have a tyrannical personality.

With his tyrannical personality, Tony can never be truly happy. The master passion manifests itself in various ways, ones over which Tony has no control. Any happiness that he thinks he feels is the happiness of the addict – the temporary cessation of a gnawing desire that can never be permanently slaked. He is enslaved to his appetites and the master passion underlying them; he is not master of them, but they of him. Tony is the *capo* of his crew, but he's not *capo* of himself.

Freudian footnotes

An important set of footnotes to Plato can be found in the work of Sigmund Freud. To those of you familiar with Freud's work, Plato's account of the personality will probably sound very familiar. Freud was, in fact, deeply indebted to Plato in the sort of way you are deeply indebted to someone whose ideas you've nicked.

In Freud's version of Plato, *reason* gets replaced with the *ego* and the *appetites* get replaced with the *id*. And Plato's *spirit* makes a somewhat transmogrified appearance in the form of Freud's *superego*. Ego and id correspond pretty closely to what Plato meant by reason and appetite. The id consists of primitive drives and urges, many of which you would get locked up for if you displayed or acted on them in public. And because of their rather disgusting and shameful nature, these drives and urges are often relegated to the realm of the *unconscious*. The introduction of the idea of the unconscious was one of Freud's most famous innovations, and it is an important departure from Plato's account. In contrast to the largely unconscious instincts and drives of the id, the ego is the conscious, rational, part of the personality.

Freud's idea of the superego, however, is somewhat narrower than Plato's idea of spirit. The superego corresponds, very roughly, to conscience, and it is created by the internalisation of parental authority. We came across this idea in the previous chapter when we looked at how Giles might have inculcated a sense of obligation in Buffy. When you are a child, your parents tell you to do various things. Most of the time you will do what you're told – but not because you want to. Instead, you are worried about forfeiting your parents' love. I'd better do this, or they won't love me any more, or so you are supposed to think. This is the origin of your moral sense: your sense of what's right and what's wrong. Originally your moral sense is an *external* voice – the voices of your parents scolding you for doing something or praising you for doing something else. In the process of growing up, this external voice becomes internalised. Your parents' commands, their scolding and their praising, become internalised, in the form of an inner moral voice that we call conscience. The superego is, in essence, the amalgamated and internalised voices of your parents.

The superego is both a good thing and a bad thing. It's a good thing because it is an essential prerequisite for living in any sort of society. The id is made up of instincts and desires that, if we were simply to act on them, would undermine any possibility of living in a harmonious society. In his earlier work, Freud famously emphasises the sexual instincts and desires. And if everyone was constantly acting on these, then, admittedly, it would be difficult to run society on anything like efficient and harmonious lines, what with people having sex all over the place. In his later work, however, Freud began to emphasise another type of instinct, or rather group of instincts, contained in the id. He grouped these together under the general heading *Thanatos*, from the Greek god of death. Thanatos makes up what we might call, combining Plato and Guns N' Roses, our *appetite for destruction*. And 'destruction' refers both to destruction of other people and yourself. Aggression, for example, is one of the primary forms of Thanatos, and your aggression can be directed both towards other people and towards yourself.

Men are not gentle creatures who want to be loved, and who at the most can defend themselves if they are attacked; they are, on the contrary, creatures among whose instinctual endowments is to be reckoned a powerful share of aggressiveness. As a result, their neighbour is for them not only a potential helper or sexual object, but also someone who tempts them to satisfy their aggressiveness on him, to exploit his capacity to work within compensation, to use him sexually without consent, to seize his possessions, to humiliate him, to cause him pain, to torture and to kill him.[8]

Homo homini lupus – man is a wolf to man – is one of Freud's more famous pronouncements and, despite being inaccurate and unfair to

---

8. Freud, *Civilization and its Discontents* (Penguin: London, 2002), chapter 5, paragraph 8.

wolves, you know what he means. So, whereas in his earlier work, Freud regarded the id as composed primarily of one type of instinct – the sexual instinct – in his later work he came to think of it as made up of two competing sorts of instincts and desires. The former, the erotic ones, he now called *Eros*, and the latter, the destructive ones, he called *Thanatos*. Either way, the id has all sorts of negative ramifications for the possibility of living together in a social group, what with all the humiliation, theft, torture, murder and non-consensual sex. So, pretty clearly the id has to be controlled. In fact, it has to be given a good kicking; and to the extent that this is the function of the superego, the superego is a good thing.

But the superego is also potentially a danger, and the danger is an obvious one, or at least it's an obvious one today after Freud did so much to highlight it: *repression*. And repression is a constant danger, for Freud, precisely because of the aggressiveness that's involved in the formation of the superego. Initially, as a child, you will go along with the commands and cajoling of your parents because you are scared of forfeiting their love. As you grow up, however, their commands and cajoling start to be felt as commands and cajoling coming from within you. However, these commands and cajoling that you sense coming from within you usually conflict with your own wishes. And so there are two forms of aggression involved in this process. First, there is the aggressiveness with which the superego combats the petitions of the id, coming up with a firm and repeated 'no' to its constant demands. Secondly, this aggression is reinforced by the hostility that you, as the growing child, will feel towards this inner voice that constantly frustrates your desires and instincts. This hostility has nowhere to go but *inwards*; it is turned against the demands themselves and against the person who both makes and refuses them: *you*!

What means does civilisation employ in order to inhibit the aggressiveness which opposes it, to make it harmless, to get rid of it perhaps? ... His aggressiveness is introjected, internalised; it is, in point of fact, sent back to where it came from – that is, it is directed towards its own ego. There it is taken over by a portion of the ego, which sets itself over and against the rest of the ego as super-ego, and which now, in the form of 'conscience', is ready to put into action against the ego the same harsh aggressiveness that the ego would have liked to satisfy upon other, extraneous, individuals.[9]

The result can be an agonising sense of guilt and self-loathing, one that, ultimately, can be traced back to the ambivalent feelings of love and hostility you have towards your parents. Worse than that, repressed feelings of this sort can manifest themselves in entirely unexpected and seemingly unconnected ways, often manifesting themselves in physical forms such as hysterical paralysis, for example, or, as in Tony's case, blackouts.

Freud's emphasis on the aggression involved in human relationships, aggression directed both towards other people and towards oneself, allows us, I think, to paint a somewhat different account of Tony Soprano and his problems. One thing that Plato's account of Tony did leave out was the insistent aggressiveness that pervades every fibre of Tony's being. We see eruptions of it in just about every episode – whether directed towards Jennifer Melfi, his psychiatrist; Carmela, his wife; the fat guy who serves beer in his strip joint; or, in fact, just about anyone who crosses or questions him in any way. His aggression is almost palpable; it hovers all

---

9. Freud, *Civilization and its Discontents* (Penguin: London, 2002), chapter 7, paragraph 2.

around him like a physical presence. And it is this aggression that will provide the basis of the Freudian explanation of Tony.

And who can blame him? His own mother wants him dead and has done, at least unconsciously, ever since he was a boy. This is, of course, a lot to cope with. So, how does the little Tony cope? He places both his realisation that his mother wants him dead, and his resulting hatred of his mother, deep in his unconscious. Not an easy thing to do – and we would have to think that the superego is at its most aggressive in forcing little Tony to do this. And there the realisation and hatred sit and fester – like sores. And psychic sores, according to Freud, are precisely what they are. And like a buried physical sore, their poison slowly leaks out, impinging on Tony's life in a variety of ways. They are at the root of his panic attacks, and they are what lie behind his frequent outbursts of anger.

Modernity's medicalised morality

In medicalising morality, Plato paved the way for the peculiarly modern way we think about morality and moral responsibility today. Morality comes from within us. Moral right and wrong reduce to psychological health or disease. It would be impossible to overestimate the staggering influence this idea has had on modern society. Evil isn't really evil, it's illness. And someone who is apparently evil, in reality needs help. But it is, I think, far from clear that this idea is correct. It's not that someone who is apparently evil *can't* be sick. Sometimes they are, and that's precisely why they do bad things. But the assumption that if someone is morally repugnant they *must* be sick is one that isn't supported by a shred of evidence.

There is one basic and clear flaw to the whole approach begun by Plato. The analogy between mental health and physical health is a dubious one. When we talk about someone being physically healthy or unhealthy, then there is an objective physical criterion to which our talk may be held accountable. Does someone have coronary heart disease? Open him up and have a look – see how much fur is on those major blood vessels. We can make sense of the idea of physical health, and ill health, because there are objective features about the way the body is supposed to be and what its parts are supposed to do. So we understand, more or less, what we are talking about when we say someone is physically healthy or unhealthy.

How about when we say someone is psychologically healthy or unhealthy? What is it that justifies our claim that someone is psychologically healthy or ill? There are two cases that we have got to distinguish. Often, when someone is said to be mentally ill, there is an identifiable physical problem involved. They're depressed, for example, because their brain isn't producing enough serotonin. No problem – what they are then is *physically* ill. And our talk of their being ill has a reasonably clear meaning – it means that their body is not functioning physically in the way that it is supposed to.

But in Tony Soprano's case – and this is quite common – there is no identifiable physical cause. So, Tony, as far as we know, is not physically ill at all – he is only *mentally* ill. What does this mean? The problem for Plato's enterprise of medicalising morality is that a judgment that someone is mentally ill in the absence of an identified physical cause is often a *moral* one, at least in part. Of course, with Tony, there are other problems beside moral questionability – he keeps passing out. But often there are no other problems – the sole basis on which we say someone is sick is because they do horrible things. It's in this sense that Jeffrey Dahmer is sick, or Charles Manson, or Ian Huntley is sick or, for that matter, Hannibal Lecter is sick. But in cases like this, we can't understand moral illness in terms of medical illness – because someone counts as medically ill only because of the immoral things they do, or because of the immoral feelings they have.

The problem with this is that it makes the attempt to explain moral evil in terms of medical illness *circular*. It would be like explaining, to use an example made famous by Molière, why opium puts you to sleep in terms of its possessing a 'dormitive virtue'. To say that something has a dormitive virtue simply means that it tends to put you to sleep. So the explanation would be that opium puts you to sleep because it tends to put you to sleep. And this is what is known as a *circular* explanation. Similarly, if the only grip we have on the idea of mental illness involves moral evaluation – we say that someone is mentally ill precisely because they do morally repugnant things – we cannot explain moral wrongness in terms of mental illness. Such an attempt would be as circular as the claim that opium puts you to sleep because it has a dormitive virtue.

This leads to another, related, problem. You might have noticed that we have come up with two different interpretations of Tony Soprano – a Platonic one, and a Freudian alternative. The Platonic interpretation sees Tony's behaviour as the result of his being a tyrannical personality type, and consequently in the grip of a 'master passion', probably the desire for security. And when you have a mother who wants you dead, this is entirely understandable. This master passion is, in turn, served by two conflicting passions, the desire for money and the desire for family. But as we have seen, these just don't go together – not given the way Tony makes his money. The result is that Tony is a schizoid, or fractured, personality, and his panic attacks are a manifestation of this. The Freudian interpretation, on the other hand, sees Tony's problems as a result of the aggressiveness with which he has had to repress the hurt caused him by his mother and his resulting hatred of her. His panic attacks and angry outbursts are a result of this repression.

So, we have two different interpretations, both of which say quite different things about the cause of Tony's problems. But the proliferation of theories doesn't stop here. There are almost as many schools of psychoanalysis as there are members of the New Jersey mob – Freudian, Jungian, Reichian, Lacanian, the list goes on – and each one would tell us a different story about Tony and his problems. They can't all be right. So how do we work out which one, if any, is?

This has always been the problem with psychoanalysis. There is no real way of testing any psychoanalytical theory. More precisely, there's no way of proving any psychoanalytical theory *wrong*. Consequently, there's no reason for thinking that any psychoanalytical theory is *right* either. Take, as a case in point, the Freudian explanation of Tony's problems. His panic attacks and anger are a result of his unconscious realisation of the fact that his mother wants him dead and his resulting unconscious hatred of her. A good story, elegant even. How do we know if it's true?

You can't look inside Tony's brain and inspect the contents of his id or the operations of his superego. Nothing remotely like ego, superego or id has ever been discovered by neuroscientific investigation of the brain. If they're somehow in there, it's not in any straightforward sense. So we can't work out if the Freudian explanation is correct by any sort of direct means.

So, maybe we could show that the Freudian explanation is correct by indirect means? For example, suppose Jennifer Melfi bases her treatment of Tony on the Freudian interpretation of his problems. If Tony improves under her care, isn't this at least some evidence that the Freudian interpretation is correct? Maybe – but this line of argument is going to prove very embarrassing for the Freudian. In fact, not just for the Freudian psychoanalyst but *any* psychoanalyst. Because what studies that have been done on the effects of psychoanalysis tell us that there is no evidence that psychoanalysis does *any good whatsoever*! Many people do improve when given psychoanalytical treatment. But as many people improve *without* psychoanalytical treatment – say from talking to their friends, or even doing the thing that psychoanalysts tell us they shouldn't, under any circumstances, do: putting things to the back of their minds and getting on with our lives. Time, it is sometimes said, and I think truly said, heals all wounds. Or maybe not all – but a lot. And psychoanalysis takes time. So, even when someone does improve under psychoanalysis, we can't disentangle the beneficial effects of psychoanalysis from the beneficial effects of time. So, there's no firm evidence that psychoanalysis has ever done anyone any good.

Suppose, on the other hand, Tony doesn't improve. And, of course, we all know that he doesn't. Does this show that the psychoanalytical interpretation is wrong? Well, psychoanalysts have been reluctant to accept this, for obvious reasons. And usually they'll come up with some explanation for why the treatment hasn't worked. Most types of explanation blame the subject in some way – so if Tony doesn't improve, it's his fault, *unconsciously*, of course. So, Tony might be employing some sort of psychic *resistance*, a sort of *blocking* – an irrational reluctance to accept the correct interpretation. Indeed, when this happens, it's a *good* thing: it shows the analyst is on the right track. If the interpretation of Tony's problems were not correct, why would he be trying to block or resist in this way? So treatment is going well, and just another $10,000 or so and we should be able to work our way around the block. Or maybe not, but at least we will have tried.

In this way, the psychoanalytical interpretation becomes immune to just about any objection you can raise to it. If Tony improves, it shows the interpretation is right. If he *doesn't* improve, it still shows that the interpretation is right. So, there is no way that you can show that the interpretation is wrong, since whatever Tony does the theory is going to be proved right one way or another. But any theory that can't be proved wrong – any theory that is right come what may – is no theory at all.

Models and metaphors

Underlying the whole idea that we can medicalise morality, in the way that Plato, Freud and their intellectual descendants tell us we can, is, I think, a philosophical mistake. What Plato and Freud provided us with were, I think, *metaphors* or *analogies*. There's nothing wrong with that. We use metaphors and analogies all the time, usually without realising it, and some metaphors and analogies are *good* ones. But what they mistakenly thought they were doing was providing us with a theory of the mind, a scientific account of the structure of the person or personality. And there's no way they were doing that.

The philosophical mistake Plato and Freud make is a failure to recognise that there are two different sorts of metaphor and analogy. One sort is used in building scientific models of things; the other isn't. For example, sometimes we talk about sporting events in the same sorts of terms as we use to talk about life. A defensive lapse in a football game, for example, might be talked of as a *tragic* mistake, of which a certain player is *guilty*. And the guilty player's markedly improved later game might be talked of as a *quest* for *redemption*, and also for *reconciliation* with his teammates. There is absolutely nothing wrong with these metaphors. We use them all the time, and they can increase our enjoyment of the spectacle. Also, they can allow us to see aspects of the game that would otherwise remain hidden if we didn't know how to employ these metaphors. We might call them *aspect-seeing metaphors*.

This sort of metaphor is perfectly legitimate. But we have to distinguish it clearly from the sort of metaphor employed by science – a type of metaphor that we might call *model-building*. Take, for example, a certain metaphor used to explain the nature of atoms, particularly in the first half of the twentieth century: the solar system model. The structure of an atom was conceived of as something like a tiny solar system, with electrons, understood as negatively charged point particles, orbiting a positively charged central core of protons and neutrons. We now know that this is largely wrong. But the crucial point is that this sort of metaphor led, with a little bit of work, to testable predictions. For example, if the solar system model was correct, the orbit of electrons should decay over time. So scientists were able to test the model to see if there was such decay. If there wasn't, then we would need an explanation of this, and one possible explanation would be that the model was simply wrong.

Aspect-seeing metaphors, on the other hand, lead to no new predictions. That is not their function at all. Their function is to allow us to see aspects of things that would be invisible to us if we didn't have the relevant metaphor at hand. When we describe a football game in terms of concepts like tragedy, guilt and redemption, various aspects of what is going on in front of us thereby become lit up, and we see the game in, to employ yet another metaphor, a *new light*. But what we are not doing is coming up with a *theory* about the nature of the game. We are not digging beneath the surface of the game to uncover its essential core. That is the sort of thing that scientific model-building metaphors do; but it is not how aspect-seeing metaphors work.

To reiterate: there is absolutely nothing wrong with aspect-seeing metaphors. They are an important part of how we understand the world. What an aspect-seeing metaphor does, in essence, is provide us with an invitation: *why don't you look at things this way?* Sometimes the metaphor works, and you see things in a new and helpful way; sometimes not. But an aspect-seeing metaphor is not a model-building metaphor – it does not provide us with a way of getting beneath the surface of a phenomenon and discovering its hidden nature or structure.

Suppose we weren't clear on the distinction between the two. Then we might take our use of aspect-seeing metaphors to be a way of discovering a hidden truth about whatever we apply the metaphor to. So, we might come up with certain metaphors about the nature of the personality – it's made up of reason, spirit and appetite, for example, or ego, superego and id – and think that we had discovered something about the hidden nature or structure of the self. But this would be to confuse two different kinds of metaphor, and two different kinds of understanding that the metaphors provide.

Cunnilingus and psychiatry brought us to this

In one of the all-time classic lines from any TV series, Tony, at the end of series 1, rues his predicament: 'Cunnilingus and psychiatry brought us to this.' His Uncle Junior has tried to have him clipped because (a) he has discovered Tony is seeing a shrink and is worried about the Feds finding out what he's been telling her, and, more importantly, (b) Tony has been ripping the piss out of Junior for his cunnilingual proclivities. Apparently they are a distinct no-no among the circle of *friends* to which Tony and Junior belong – on the grounds, apparently, that if you eat pussy you will eat anything!

While I'm not in any position to make a comparison, I'm pretty sure that eating pussy is, in fact, not anything at all like sucking dick. This is a good example of how dangerous a mistaken analogy or metaphor can be: Tony nearly got whacked because of one. But almost as dangerous is mistaking the *status* of the analogies or metaphors you employ. This is arguably what many forms of psychiatry, psychoanalysis and psychotherapy do. They take themselves to be making discoveries about the nature of the mind and the structure of the personality. But what they are really doing is issuing invitations: why don't you look at things like this? They think they are in the business of model-building analogies, but are really only in the business of aspect-seeing metaphors.

There is nothing wrong with aspect-seeing metaphors. But the big difference between them and model-building analogies is that the latter can actually be true, whereas the former can't. Aspect-seeing metaphors can succeed or fail; but they can't be true or false. Aspect-seeing metaphors succeed if they allow you to think about or understand a situation in a way that you find useful – perhaps because it helps you overcome certain problems you are having. They fail if they don't elicit such understanding. But aspect-seeing metaphors are not the sort of thing that can be true or false. The only issue is whether they help you or not.

Who is in the best position to decide whether a model-building analogy is a good one? It is a good one if it's a true one – and often an expert is the best person to decide this. Experts in quantum physics had to decide whether the solar system model was a good way of thinking about the structure of the atom. But aspect-seeing metaphors are good ones if they help you – and you are the best person to decide that. If the guilt and redemption analogy allows you greater enjoyment of a sporting event, then the analogy is a good one. No expert can tell you this. Or, to put the same point another way, with aspect-seeing analogies *you* are the expert.

Many branches of psychiatry, psychoanalysis and psychotherapy are based on a confusion of model-building with aspect-seeing metaphors. The psychiatrist, analyst or therapist supplies you with certain metaphors about yourself and your personality. She presents these as model-building metaphors – theories about the hidden structure of your personality, a structure that analysis can slowly, but surely, uncover. As such, these metaphors lie in the province of truth, and she, the expert, is best placed to decide whether they are good ones. But, in fact, she is mistaken: the metaphors are aspect-seeing rather than model-building. The criteria for whether they are good metaphors is whether they help you think about yourself in a new and useful way – new in the sense that you've never thought about yourself like that before, and useful in that this new way of thinking helps you cope with the world better than you did before. It is you who is in the best position to decide whether these metaphors are good ones.

The medicalisation of morality that begun by Plato, and has its modern-day expression in such activities as psychoanalysis, consists in a series of *invitations* masquerading as *assertions*. Invitations to think about yourself in a certain way are presented as assertions or statements about your hidden nature. Whenever this happens, there is a clear danger. Truth is a lot more difficult to obtain – and therefore more expensive – than usefulness. Many aspect-seeing metaphors may be useful to you in that they help you think about yourself in a new way, one that enables you to cope with the world or some aspect of your situation better than you did before. You can sort all that out for yourself. But truth is often the domain of experts – and for experts you have to *pay*.

And this, I suppose, is one of the deeply ironic features of *The Sopranos*. The psychoanalysis industry could teach the New Jersey waste management industry a thing or two about *rackets*. This is not to say that psychological counselling is a criminal activity. It is not. Nor is it to say that psychological counselling will never help. Sometimes it will. But in seeking such help, it is probably best to bring with you the healthy scepticism of the experienced gangster. First of all, *trust no one*. Your friends may not be your friends. One thing, and only one thing, you can be sure of: *everyone wants a piece of you*. Anyone you bring in to help you deal with your problems has vested interests of their own, and, in all likelihood, issues of their own. The interests are probably largely financial. But who knows what the issues are? For example, when Jennifer Melfi, in series 3, sends Carmela to see the shrink she recommends, is this because she – consciously or unconsciously – knows what he is going to tell her? Does she know that he will tell her to leave Tony? After all, Jennifer has just been raped, and has come to see Tony as a protective figure in whose company she feels safe. Remember, for example, her dream where the rapist gets driven off by the big, and morally ambivalent, Rottweiler. Perhaps she would like to see more of him, perhaps a lot more? By her own principles, Jennifer is probably not going to be sure of the answer to that one: she will need analysis to work out her own motives.

One thing the sceptical wise guy will always bear in mind: when we are talking about the mind, *truth is the biggest racket of them all*. A truth about yourself has a certain cash value that a mere invitation to think about yourself in a certain way doesn't. Anyone can invite you to think about yourself in a certain way – why should you pay for that? But not just anyone can come up with the truth. The truth is always worth paying for.

Modernity and evil

This chapter has looked at modernity's attitude towards the idea of moral right and wrong in general, and moral evil in particular. A pervasive theme running through the modern worldview is to suppose that moral evil is really something else. I focused, in fact, on just one development of this modern theme: the attempt to reduce moral evil to psychological illness, an attempt begun by Plato, and receiving a definitively modern expression in Freud. But a similar pattern emerges in all of the so-called human and social sciences. Take any markedly evil occurrence – the holocaust provides a good example. Then you will find just about all human and social scientists trying to explain this occurrence as, in reality, something else. The eventual explanations will invoke factors of the social situation – economic, cultural, historical, anthropological, and so on. But what these explanations will not involve is the idea that things like the holocaust happen because some people are evil. Evil is not to be taken at face value. It is something to be explained away – it is really something else. So what we have to do is explain why people hold evil beliefs without presupposing that there is such a thing as evil. Why? Because there really is no such thing as evil. *Evil is always something else.*

I seriously doubt whether any of this is right. But you can see how this idea would contribute to the sort of scaling down of the grandeur – the *bigness* – of life, something whose outlines began to emerge in the previous chapter. Evil people are simply deluded or ill. They are to be pitied or helped. And, of course, whether you choose to pity or help is entirely a matter of your personal lifestyle choices – it depends entirely on whether it coheres or conflicts with your overriding goal of self-fulfilment. Any obligation you have to fight 'evil' is an identity-reflecting rather than identity-constituting one. And, as such, the obligation is simply not important enough. The struggle against 'evil' is not the sort of thing that could imbue your life with a higher meaning or purpose. Not any more.

three
SEX AND THE CITY

WHAT IS HAPPINESS?

Small and vulgar pleasures

The core of modernity is, as we have seen, the principle of individualism: your overriding moral goal is to realise, develop, or fulfil yourself. In the previous two chapters, we developed this idea in terms of the distinction between what I called identity-constituting and identity-reflecting attachments. For modernity, you have no identity-constituting attachments to anyone or anything outside yourself. The only identity-constituting attachment is, so to speak, an *internal* one, a relation you bear to yourself – the obligation to fulfil yourself. All attachments to things outside of yourself are only identity-reflecting ones.

Bound up in all of this is an implicit view of the nature of the self or person – a view about what you essentially are. The self or person is the sort of thing that can be complete in itself. Your identity as the person you are does not, in any essential way, depend on your relation to things outside of you. These relations do not make you the person you are; at most they reflect the person you are or have become because of other factors.

This view of the self has a long and distinguished history, and it's still with us today. It is a view that has important implications for the way we think not only about ourselves but also about something we regard as crucial to our lives: our *happiness*. Laying my cards on the table – I think this is unfortunate. For not only is this concept of the self untenable, it also leaves us with a unworkable conception of happiness. And this is, in large part, the reason why so many of us are unhappy.

Think about it. What sort of thing could happiness be in such an age? If you are what you are independently of anything else, and if self-fulfilment is your ultimate goal and value, then what sort of thing could happiness be? The sort of happiness that stems from having something so important in your life that without it you wouldn't be the same person? Modernity has no room for such happiness. The modern world is a *disenchanted* one, where the possibility of something being this important has largely been removed. The sort of happiness that stems from doing the right thing, because it's the right thing, even though the heavens fall? There is no right thing. The sort of happiness that stems from fighting, even dying, for something whose value transcends you? But, for modernity, value is all relative or subjective. Value depends on your choices, not the other way around. So what sort of thing can happiness be? The answer is, as Alexis de Tocqueville put it nearly 200 years ago: *small and vulgar pleasures*. Similarly, Nietzsche talked of the 'last men', the ultimate products of modernity, as aspiring to nothing more than a 'pitiable comfort'.

And you know what they're talking about. If we are not careful, our lives become made up of little more than distractions – things we use to pass the time while we get on with the far more important business of doing absolutely nothing worthwhile. We sit at home and watch *Big Brother*, or *Pop Idol*, or *I'm a Celebrity, Get Me Out of Here!* Or we go out with our mates and get pissed. Such distractions may be all that is left to us after modernity has taken away the sorts of things that might have made our lives significant. The consequence of a disenchanted world is a disenchanted life – a life of small and vulgar pleasures. And what are pleasures? Pleasures are *feelings* – what makes something a pleasure is the way it feels to have or undergo it. And so we arrive at modernity's recipe for a fulfilled life. Happiness is the sign that your life is fulfilled, and happiness consists in *feeling* a certain way.

There is an excellent philosophical exploration of this modern conception of self-fulfilment. It's called *Sex and the City*.

Sex and the City

This show, which began in 1998 and ended in 2004 after its sixth season, has everything that, I'm told, a woman could want: sex, sex talk, colourful cocktails, shoes – Jimmy Choos in the earlier series switching to Manolo Blahniks later on – and, of course, the existential *angst* of post-industrial woman. Carrie, Samantha, Charlotte and Miranda have great lives – or so it seems. They have interesting jobs – respectively, sex columnist, publicist, art gallery manager and lawyer – and spend all their time in fashionable bars and restaurants or buying ridiculously overpriced shoes. Of course, in the real world, in order to drink, as they do, enough cocktails to keep a small battleship afloat, they would have to be on salaries that would keep a small country afloat. Believe me, I know. But they never seem to be working – for the simple reason that they spend all their time in fashionable bars and restaurants, only stopping off on the way home to buy some shoes. You would think Joseph Heller had never written *Catch 22*.

Anyway, while dropping several hundred thousand a year on shoes and cocktails, they meet interesting people, have interesting sex with them, and, afterwards, have interesting bitching sessions about the quality of this sex in interesting bars or restaurants. Surely, it doesn't get much better than this. But scratch a little beneath the surface, and none of them seems particularly happy. And that's one of the reasons they spend so much time in fashionable bars and restaurants: they have so much complaining that they need to get done. With Carrie, for example, we might get 'Big did this, and Big did that, and Aidan is too possessive, and I hate his house in the country and … my boyfriend broke up with me on a Post-it!' etc.: an impressively consistent record of discontent for most of the six series. The others are not much better, and Miranda, if anything, is worse.

Of course, the girls are no different from most of us. Why the unhappiness? The answer, I think, is that their lives, like ours, are embodiments of a great philosophical mistake. As usual, a man is to blame. A seventeenth-century French man with a big nose. Looks a bit like Carrie's Mr Big actually – and you can't tell me *that* is a coincidence. But first something else.

When are you happiest?

Happiness is big business nowadays. Rainforests in much of the Amazon basin and significant parts of Indonesia have laid down their lives just so we will know that men are from somewhere and women are from somewhere completely different. The British government has decided to get in on the act too: recent studies confirmed that we're apparently no happier now than our parents or grandparents were in the 1950s, despite our cars, dishwashers, PCs, microwaves, Manolo Blahniks and the appreciable improvement in the quality of TV offerings. So, the government has decided to make us happy, whether we like it or not. Professional academics, who will do more or less anything for money anyway, smell a gravy train, and have been desperately trying to jump on board. The upshot is that some time in the near future you may well find a total stranger with a clipboard coming up to you and asking you impertinent questions like:

'When are you happiest?'

Apparently, the most popular answer to this, so far anyway, is:

'When I'm having sex.'

Clearly, much of the great British public identifies with Samantha who, except for that short period, at the end of series 1 and beginning of series 2, when she had managed to acquire a boyfriend with a risibly small penis, would wholeheartedly endorse that sentiment. What does this tell us about our conception of happiness? What must we think happiness is if we answer 'When I'm having sex' to the question 'When are you happiest?'

The answer is that we must be thinking of happiness as a *feeling*, or collection of feelings. That's what sex does, if you're doing it at all correctly – it produces various feelings in you.

The same studies usually also ask:

'When are you unhappiest?'

And to this, apparently, the most popular answer is:

'When I'm talking to my boss.'

It's not clear what happens if you're talking to your boss while having sex with them – maybe we should ask Samantha. The feelings associated with talking to your boss – and it will of course vary from boss to boss, but often include uncertainty, insecurity, vulnerability, anxiety, fear, boredom and/or outright contempt – are taken as classic manifestations of unhappiness. So, probably the most common view of happiness and unhappiness takes them to be feelings.

So conditioned are we today to thinking of happiness as a feeling that we have a hard time understanding any distinction between *feeling* happy and *being* happy. But this distinction was absolute to a more ancient way of understanding happiness; a way associated with, among others, the ancient Greek philosopher Aristotle.

Being happy: Aristotle on happiness

In philosophical terms, Aristotle was *The Man*. He dominated the intellectual world for around fifteen centuries, which, when you consider that the average philosopher of today's notoriety lasts about fifteen minutes, is a pretty impressive gig. Plato got him started – Aristotle studied and worked at Plato's school in Athens, The Academy, for around 20 years, until Plato died in fact. Then he went off and taught a young Alexander the Great. And after Alexander had headed off on the whole world-conquering thing, Aristotle returned to Athens, where he founded his own school, The Lyceum.

Aristotle, like most philosophers of his time, had a lot to say about happiness. First, there's the obvious stuff: happiness is the ultimate goal of human life. The whole point of our existence is to be happy. In this, Aristotle is pretty close to what most of us think. I mean, what else is there apart from happiness? We want lots of things – money, sex, success, material possessions, more sex – but we only want these things because they'll make us happy. Or because we think they will. We don't go around wanting things we think are going to make us unhappy. So, happiness is what it's all about. Duh!

Here's something less obvious: happiness isn't a feeling at all. Not for Aristotle. He would have no time for some nerdy little academic coming up to him today and asking him when is he happiest. The question, for Aristotle, would make little sense. Being happy isn't a matter of feeling a certain way. Happiness is a way of *being*, not a way of *feeling*. 'Happiness' translates as *eudai-monia* – and this has a meaning far closer to *well-being* rather than any sort of pleasurable feelings. Today we equate our happiness, or lack of it, with the way we feel. But this is a modern idea, and has no echo in Aristotle's thought. To be sure, being happy often goes with having pleasurable feelings of a certain sort. But not always. And these feelings, whatever they may be, are tangential to what true happiness is.

This, of course, is not going to help us very much, unless we know what a *way of being* is. For Aristotle, a way of being is living a certain life. Specifically, it consists in acting in accordance with reason. A life lived in accordance with reason is a happy life. It is not simply that such a life *makes* us happy – as if it produces in us an inner feeling of happiness. Rather, for Aristotle, acting in accordance with reason is precisely what being happy *is*. This might help us if we knew what living a life in accordance with reason is. And understanding this is one of the hardest parts of understanding Aristotle.

A good way into this issue is by way of Plato's account of the healthy personality that we looked at in connection with Tony Soprano. Remember that Plato had this idea that someone's personality could be divided up into three parts: *reason*, *spirit* and *appetite*. Tony's problem, if you remember, at least according to Plato, was that he was at the mercy of lawless desires – basic instincts, desires and urges gone amok. In particular, there was his desire for security, instilled deeply in him by his psycho mother's wanting him dead, which has set itself up as master passion. This master passion has two conflicting expressions – one his love for his family, and the other his love for his *family* (and the wealth it provides for him). The feelings, emotions and attitudes necessary for the first expression of his master passion are incompatible with those necessary for the second expression of that passion. The result is that Tony has become an essentially schizoid personality.

Tony's appetite control problem is not unusual. According to Plato, the appetites are usually the problem, in one way or another. They have to be kept in their place. Reason has to be boss, and if the appetites don't like this, then spirit, like the good soldier it is, has got to keep them in line. The model of psychological health advocated by Plato, then, is basically one of suppression and, in severe cases, even repression. The desires or appetites have to be strictly controlled, kept in line, ordered and regimented by the combined forces of reason and spirit.

Repression of this sort can take various forms. Samantha, on the face of it, seems to be someone who is admirably free of repression: a sort of anti-Plato, at least when it comes to sex. Most of Samantha's appetites, of course, seem to be sexual ones. She doesn't seem to be doing much repressing of those, and so, on the face of it, would count as unhealthy on Plato's standards, but healthy by our post-Freudian liberal standards. But, in fact, what she does is repress something else – any sort of emotional attachment that might, in other people, typically go with the sexual appetites. That is, she represses not the appetites themselves but the feelings that often go with those appetites.

In effect, this is a way of allowing her sexual appetites free rein, but making sure that their consequences will be strictly limited. You don't often find Samantha Jones falling head over heels in love – only three times in the entire six series by my counting. And so it's only very occasionally that she has to suffer the devastation of betrayal that goes with, for example, finding your boyfriend eating another woman's pussy. Most of the time she wouldn't care. Only when she's in love does it hurt.

So, whatever benefits Samantha might, according to Plato, get from repression of her sexual appetites, she gets from repression of the emotions that, in other people, typically accompany sexual appetites. That's the way it sometimes goes with repression. We think we are being admirably non-repressed, uninhibited, when we do various things – or in this case various people – but, in fact, a deficit of repression in one area of our lives will show up as a surfeit somewhere else. Indeed, often, repression in one aspect of our lives may be a precondition of lack of inhibition in other aspects. So, you can't get around being repressed simply by being as uninhibited as you can. That's way too simple.

Aristotle, however, provides something that is quite unusual in the history of thought: a model of mental health not based on the idea of repression and the associated imagery of a controlling part and a controlled part of us. Aristotle's idea was that in the healthy – and therefore happy – person, the desires or appetites could somehow *themselves* be rational. Not because they are controlled by some rational power or agency outside them (reason in Plato's view, the superego in Freud's view) but because they somehow directly embody rationality. Their rationality was internal to them and not, as on Plato's and Freud's view, external. That is, some desires or appetites could be rational because of what they were in themselves and not because of their relation to some rational power or agency that had control of them.

So what we have to do is understand how appetites or desires can be intrinsically rational. Aristotle's answer for this is both famous and widely misunderstood. It's known as the *doctrine of the mean*. Many people misunderstand this, and see it as some sort of depressing counsel of moderation: *never go to extremes*. Don't do extreme things and don't feel extreme emotions. Rather, let your actions and emotions fall in the middle range of what it is possible to do and feel. Be neither greatly elated nor greatly dejected. Fall neither violently in love nor out of love. In everything you do, be neither too enthusiastic nor too apathetic.

Neither I, nor you, I suspect, would want such a person as a friend. Such a person is basically on the philosophical equivalent of Prozac. They are average, middle-of-the-road, B-O-R-I-N-G! And they would never get invited to any good parties. Far better, I think, to be like Jack Kerouac's description of the 'mad ones', who 'burn, burn, brightly like fabulous yellow roman candles exploding like spiders across the stars'. The problem is, of course, that when you burn, burn brightly and all that stuff you tend to burn out quickly (as, in fact, did Kerouac). So you've got to learn to pick your moments. And this, I think, is what Aristotle was really getting at.

People often misunderstand Aristotle because they fail to distinguish something that Aristotle himself definitely did distinguish: two senses of the mean. On the one hand there is what he called the *mean in relation to the thing* and, on the other, the *mean in relation to us*.[10] The mean in relation to the thing would be the mid-point between two extremes. Instead of drinking ten Cosmopolitans or drinking none, you take the middle option – the mean in relation to the thing – and drink five.

If you were looking to Aristotle for support in this policy, you can look again. If you had read him properly you would realise that his doctrine of the mean is a doctrine of the mean in relation to *us* not in relation to the *thing*. Understanding this, however, is no easy matter. This is Aristotle's attempt to explain what he's on about:

> *It is possible, for example, to feel fear, confidence, desire, anger, pity, and pleasure and pain generally, too much or too little; and both of these are wrong. But to have these feelings* at the right times on the right grounds towards the right people for the

---

10. Just to prove I'm not making this up, the distinction can be found in Aristotle's *Nichomachean Ethics* (Penguin: London, 2004) at II.6, especially 1106a 26. So there!

right motive and in the right way *is to feel them to an inter-mediate, that is to the best, degree; and this is the mark of virtue.*[11]

Not exactly crystal clear, admittedly. But what Aristotle is getting at is that what you should feel, and so what you should do, is dependent on the circumstances you find yourself in. So, your best friend has just called you to go Cosmopolitan drinking because her boyfriend has just broken up with her on a Post-it. A pretty harrowing event, or so we're led to believe. In these circumstances, the doctrine of the mean might legitimately – indeed *rationally* – call for a record-breaking intake of Cosmopolitans. On the other hand, you may be going not because of any harrowing event in particular, but simply because a window has opened up in your shoe-buying activities, one that you can't think of any other way to fill. The doctrine of the mean, in this case, might call for you to restrict yourself to one or two Cosmos, tops, or even mineral water!

The doctrine of the mean, as Aristotle intends it, calls for us to feel the right things at the right times on the right grounds towards the right people for the right motive and in the right way. Now all we have to do is work out the meaning of: 'the right things', 'the right times', 'the right grounds', 'the right people', 'the right motive', and 'the right way', and we're laughing. And on these points of, apparently somewhat vital, detail, Aristotle, like the true philosopher he is, gives us absolutely no help whatsoever. Great philosophers are like that.

For our purposes, what's important to take from Aristotle is the idea that happiness is not primarily a way of feeling but a way of being. And the specific way of being is living your life in accordance with reason, where reason is identified in terms of the idea of the

---

11. *Nichomachean Ethics* (Penguin: London, 2004), II.6, 1106b, 18–23.

mean in relation to us. It's not a matter of having the sort of warm fuzzy feelings that most people think of as happiness. Rather it is to learn to deal with life in such a way that we feel the right things, and so do the right things, in the right circumstances. Happiness is not, in essence, a way of feeling, but a way of dealing with the world where feeling and action cannot be separated. And, for Aristotle, both are essential components of happiness.

Descartes and Mr Big

Many people seem to think that all of Carrie's problems, at least up until the end of the final series when he does a U-turn, stem from Mr Big – as if it was as simple as that! If only the prick had married her instead of the stick insect with no soul then Carrie would now be happy. This is probably too simplistic: Carrie was arguably fucked up long before Big came into the picture. On the other hand, I think there is something in the idea that Big lies behind her problems. However, he is not, I think, the *cause* of Carrie's problems but, rather, a *symbol* of them. Because Big is clearly modelled on the seventeenth-century French philosopher René Descartes, and Descartes, I think, has a lot to do with Carrie's tribulations.

Just consider the evidence. Big has a big nose, Descartes had a big nose. Big went to live in France, Descartes was from France. Big (series 1) was harassed by a woman who demanded more than he was able to give at the time; so too was Descartes.[12] Big, a corporate raider, is a financial mercenary, Descartes was an actual mercenary. OK, Big's name, we eventually discover is John, not René, but no

---

12. Respectively Carrie and Queen Christina of Sweden; the latter, after giving Descartes an apparently cushy job teaching her philosophy, forced him – an habitual and recidivist late riser – to get up at 5.00 a.m. to begin lessons. Descartes died soon afterwards.

comparison is ever perfect. Given this moderately overwhelming evidence, who can deny that Candace Bushnell modelled Big on Descartes? And it is indeed Descartes who, I think, lies behind Carrie's problems. It was Descartes who was responsible for the big change in our conception of happiness, from Aristotle's notion of happiness as a way of being, to the modern notion of happiness as a way of *feeling*. He did this by separating mind and body in a way that had no reflection in Aristotle's thought.

Descartes's big thing was the mind. Indeed, many people credit him with inventing, virtually single-handedly, the modern concept of the mind. Here's how it went. First of all, the mind is an object. In some respects, it's just like other bodily organs: the heart, the liver, the eyes, and so on. Just as these have their own particular functions – the eyes to see, the liver to process waste, the heart to pump blood – so too does the mind. This, according to Descartes, is to *think*. That's what the mind is: a thinking thing. However, there's one big difference between the mind and these other bodily organs – at least according to Descartes. The mind is a *non-physical* thing.

This means that the mind and the brain, for Descartes, are quite different. The brain is physical, the mind isn't. Of course, they can communicate with each other in various ways. The mind gets the body to do various things by way of the brain – it tells the brain what to do, and the brain then goes on and tells the body what to do. You want to go to the new cocktail bar on 53rd and Broadway? Wanting is something that, according to Descartes, your non-physical mind does. So it sends a message to the brain saying something like 'Get me to 53rd and Broadway', and then the brain goes about its business of getting the body to make the appropriate movements in the appropriate direction. When you get there, various arrangements of electromagnetic radiation impinge on your retina. The message is sent on to your brain, via the optic nerve. And your brain is activated in a certain area (the visual cortex). Your mind then interprets this activity as meaning there is a *Cosmopolitan* on the table in front of you.

So, the mind and brain are connected in various ways, and this allows a constant flow of information from one to the other and back again. Nonetheless, the mind is a non-physical thing, and so quite distinct from the physical brain. This sort of view is known as *dualism*. It sees each one of us as made up of two different parts or components – hence *dual* in the title. There is the physical part of us – the body (and the brain), and there is the non-physical part – the mind, soul or spirit.

Where exactly is the mind, this non-physical part of us? Well, it's not exactly clear in Descartes's scheme of things. The mind is a non-physical thing, and, for Descartes, part of the deal in being a non-physical thing is that the mind doesn't take up any room. It doesn't occupy space. It doesn't, as Descartes put it, have any spatial *extension*. But, wherever it turns out to be, it is somewhere *inside* of us. Descartes's own favourite hypothesis was that the mind resided somewhere in the vicinity of the pineal gland: a small gland in the centre of the brain. Admittedly, this was probably only because he didn't know what the pineal gland did, but there you go.

The result was a fracturing of the person into an inside and an outside: the mind within and the body without. The body is part of the ordinary physical world, on a par with tables and chairs and other ordinary physical things. That is not the special part of us. What is special is what's on the inside. For Aristotle, thinking of the person in this way would have made little sense. Each one of us is a psychophysical whole. We cannot separate our inside from our outside in any useful or meaningful way. But Descartes won out, and his way of thinking about us has taken hold and it is now the way most of us think about ourselves. The real me is what's on the inside, the special part that no one else can see.

For Aristotle, happiness was a state of the person as a whole, a psychophysical unity maintained by a complex web of feeling and action. Once we split the person into two components, we face the question: when I am happy, which part of me is happy? Is it the outside, the body? Clearly not: the body, on Descartes's view, is just meat. Its essential feature is simply taking up room, occupying space. It is not the sort of thing that can be happy. Happiness, when we have it, must belong to the inner, non-physical, special part of us: the mind. Happiness is a state of the mind rather than the person as an Aristotelian psychophysical whole.

What sort of state of mind would happiness be? Descartes's view of the mind was, actually, quite restricted. What the mind did, for Descartes, and pretty much all the mind did, was *think*. The mind was the rational part of us. However, other people – dualists who inherited Descartes's basic idea – extended the role of the mind, understood as a non-physical inner essence. Its role was now not simply to think, but also to *feel*. The mind now became not only the rational part of us, but also the *sensitive* part, the part that feels.

And so with Descartes was born the modern view of happiness. Happiness consists in certain feelings. And feelings are things that exist inside of us. The obvious upshot is: if you want to know whether you're happy: look inside. That's where your happiness, if you have it, is to be found.

The result of this modern view is what we might call a *compartmentalisation* of happiness. Happiness, as a way of feeling, is restricted to the part of us that feels – the inner, special part of us that no one else can see. Descartes severs the close connection that Aristotle saw between happiness and action by relocating happiness inwards. For Descartes, the connection between the two is only a *causal* one: acting in certain ways can make us happy – cause us to have the relevant feelings – and being happy can cause us to act in certain ways. This is very different from Aristotle's view of the relation between happiness and action. For him, happiness, in part, *consists in* acting in certain ways. That is, being happy is not simply caused by acting in certain ways. Rather, acting in the appropriate ways is precisely what happiness, in part, *is*. Happiness is a feature that belongs to all of you – the whole person – rather than some small part of you that does the feeling.

This modern understanding of happiness, initiated by Descartes, will probably sound very familiar. This is because Descartes's view, which was in his day a controversial philosophical hypothesis, has by now evolved into common sense. Controversial philosophical hypotheses have a nasty habit of doing that.

The rampant rabbit and the experience machine

Is happiness a way of being or a way of feeling? Is it a state of the entire person, or simply of the part of the person that feels? A way of being can include ways of feeling, because feeling is one way of being. But it includes much more than that. In particular, it includes action in the world as well as feelings produced by the world. Aristotle's version of this was the idea that happiness consists in acting in accordance with reason. Happiness is a way of dealing with the world where we both *feel* and *do* the appropriate things in the appropriate circumstances. The modern conception subtracts the doing part of the equation and sees happiness simply as a way of feeling. The question is, as Carrie might put it: which is best? Is the ancient or the modern conception a better account of happiness?

To work out which conception of happiness is best, we would have to imagine a situation where what we do and what we feel can come apart. More precisely, we need imaginatively to compare two situations. In the first, you are able to choose exactly what you feel but, other than this, are not able to do anything at all. You are able to feel but not to do. In the second situation, you are able to both do and feel, but you have no more control over these than you do in the real world. Would you prefer to have absolute control over what you feel, at the expense of not actually being able to do anything? Or would you like things the way they are – to have control over what you do at the expense of control over what you feel?

You may find it difficult to imagine what you're being asked to imagine. If so, look to Carrie, Samantha, Miranda and, in particular, Charlotte for a little bit of a pointer. In series 1, the girls were, in one episode, extolling the virtues of a new vibrator known, apparently, as a rampant rabbit. Charlotte, in particular, became very attached to her rabbit, and it took an *intervention* by the others to persuade her that she needed help and that cold turkey was the only answer. The idea behind the rabbit is, of course, to reproduce whatever feelings of sexual pleasure are normally produced by a man. Or, more realistically, the function of the rabbit is to produce whatever feelings of sexual pleasure men are supposed to produce, but, sadly, often do not. So, imagine some man who is just as good as the rabbit in producing the relevant feelings. It may be difficult for some of you women to imagine this, but just suppose. Then we are on the way to imagining what we have to imagine in order to adjudicate between the rival conceptions of happiness.

When philosophers talk about what they call the *experience machine*, they are talking about something that is, in effect, a souped-up version of the rampant rabbit.[13] We can think of the

---

13. The experience machine, minus the rampant rabbit, is a famous imaginative device associated with the Australian philosopher Jack Smart. A more familiar modern version might be the matrix from the film of the same name. See my *The Philosopher at the End of the Universe* (2003, London: Ebury Press) for a discussion of the philosophical issues bound up with this idea.

machine as a complex virtual reality device that is completely under your control. The hardware is hooked up into your brain, but the result of this hook-up is a rich, detailed, virtual world indistinguishable from the real world. The idea is that the machine could produce in you any feeling or experience you wanted. If, like Samantha, your interests inclined towards the carnal, you could use the machine to produce the experience of having sex with a well-hung man, and the various forms of sexual pleasure that go with it. If your interests were more diverse, you could use the machine in more varied ways. Charlotte, for example, might want to use the machine to generate the experiences, and associated feelings, of being married to the man of her dreams, who comes from Old Money and has an apartment on the Upper East Side. Carrie might want to use the machine to create a world where Big does in fact love her, marries her, and where they both live happily ever after. But, there again, who knows what Carrie wants? The idea is that whatever experiences you can have in the real world, and whatever feelings go with these experiences, these can be duplicated by the experience machine.

Now for the crunch. The complicated neural hook-up involved with the machine means that once you are hooked up, you can never be detached. So, you have a choice to make. You can renounce the real world in favour of a world where all your feelings and experiences are under your control, but where you never really *do* anything. Or you can stay with the real world, with all its mess and complexity and misery, but where you do retain the ability to act on the basis of how you would like your life to be. Feeling versus doing, that's what the experience machine comes down to. Any feelings you could ever want you can have – but only if you are willing to sacrifice the ability to ever really *do* anything ever again. What would you choose?

It's not like anyone is going to invent an experience machine any time soon. But, that's not the point. The experience machine scenario is what philosophers call a *thought experiment*: an imaginative device whose sole purpose is to crystallise your thinking on a particular matter – in this case the relative importance of feeling versus doing. So suppose someone could invent such a machine – just for the sake of argument. Would you choose to be hooked up to it?

Most academic philosophers tell us that you wouldn't and shouldn't choose to be hooked up to the experience machine. There are two possible reasons for this. One is that the academic philosophers are right. The other is that they're all a bunch of joyless, deracinated geeks who wouldn't know a good time if it sat on their faces and wiggled. Who knows?

Anyway, far be it for me to tell you what you should or shouldn't do. What you would or should choose to do in an entirely imaginary situation is up to you. But what I can do is point out some of the consequences *if* you would *not* choose to be hooked up to the machine. Think of what this choice reveals about what you value. Basically, it shows that you value more than mere feelings. In addition to *feeling* certain things, you also want to *do* certain things. You don't simply want the pleasurable feelings that go with doing certain things – shagging a well-endowed partner, marrying the man of your dreams, living happily ever after with Big – it shows that you actually want to *do* those things too. If you wouldn't choose to be hooked up to the experience machine, this is because you must regard feelings without actions as in some way a sham. There is more to life, more to happiness, than feeling, there is also action. If you think this, you are, it seems, an intellectual descendant of Aristotle.

Carrie's Cartesian confusions

For Aristotle, the distinction between feeling and doing is irrelevant to understanding happiness. Each one of us is a psychophysical whole, where feeling and action are connected in various complex ways, each supporting and being supported by the other. It was Descartes who changed all this – relocating feeling to the realm of the inner, and seeing it as, in principle, independent of what we do. Carrie clearly embodies this Cartesian way of thinking about feeling and its relation to happiness.

Her treatment of Aidan provides a classic example of this sort of Cartesian way of thinking. First she cheats on him with Big. Then, in the next series, she gets engaged to him. Then she begins scrupulously and systematically to exclude him from just about every aspect of her social life. Out with her girlfriends one night, out with her gay friends the next. OK, it is, admittedly, partly Aidan's fault – him being so boring and all. But she really does rub his nose in it a little by constantly hanging out with Big, and even inviting him up to Aidan's house in the country – after it was her shagging of Big that made Aidan dump her in the first place. Even when Aidan asks to be allowed to go along with her sometimes, she won't let him. I'm not concerned with the moral evaluation of Carrie and her relationship, nor am I going to rag on Aidan for being such a pussy. Far more interesting are the assumptions – the philosophical presuppositions – that underlie Carrie's behaviour and attitudes.

Aidan has, of course, been compartmentalised. He has his place, and he's definitely been put in it. There's a little bit of her life that Carrie's set aside for Aidan, and that's all he's going to get. Meanwhile, Carrie can carry on living her life just as she used to. But this compartmentalisation of Aidan – this separation of him from the bulk of Carrie's life – is based on a prior separation of what Carrie *feels* from what Carrie *does*. Carrie assumes that whatever feelings she has for Aidan, she can have those feelings irrespective of the way she lives her life, and irrespective of what else is going on in that life. What she feels is one thing, what she does is quite another. And this is an expression of the Cartesian idea that feelings are internal states of a person, and as such can exist independently of our actions. If she were more Aristotelian, Carrie might realise that feelings and actions are not independent of each other in this way, and that you cannot expect to have certain feelings for someone if you systematically exclude him from just about everything you do. Feelings and actions, from an Aristotelian perspective, are either mutually supporting or mutually undermining. And without the appropriate actions, feelings will wither and die.

So, of course Carrie is not going to have the appropriate feelings for Aidan. She has set up her life in such a way that she cannot possibly be expected to have them. Any nascent feelings she might have had were bound to wither and die given the kind of desert landscape she had set up for them. There could, of course, be various reasons for this. One is that deep down, despite her claims to the contrary, she didn't really love Aidan at all, and was determined to sabotage the relationship. We've seen these sorts of psychological interpretations before – and their problems – and there's no point going down that road again. What we are interested in is the possibility of a *philosophical* rather than *psychological* interpretation of Carrie: we want to uncover the philosophical assumptions that must underpin the way she behaves. So, we'll take Carrie's behaviour at face value – if she tells us she loves Aidan, we'll take her word for it, just for the sake of argument. And, if she's telling the truth, this presumably means she has assumed a Cartesian separation of feeling from action. Her compartmentalisation – and indeed marginalisation – of Aidan is a result of this separation.

But there is a yet deeper philosophical assumption that Carrie seems to have made. Uncovering this is the key to understanding not only her problems but also those of Samantha, Miranda and Charlotte. The issue of happiness, and the issue of the precise relation between feeling and action, all these were just symptoms of something more fundamental: a metaphysical problem about the nature of the self or person.

Psychic monads

Monad was a term introduced by the seventeenth-century German philosopher Gottfried Wilhelm Leibniz (1646–1716). The term 'monad' originally meant 'unit' or 'unity'. A monad, for Leibniz, was something that couldn't be divided or broken down into anything else, and whose essential nature did not depend on its relations to anything else. It's something like what we used to think atoms were like, before we found out they could be broken down into more basic particles like protons and neutrons. On the old way of thinking about atoms, each atom is indivisible in that it can't be broken down into any smaller parts. And each atom is what it is entirely independently of its relations to other atoms. The identity of each individual atom depends only on what that atom is in itself and not on the relations it stands in to other atoms.

Descartes's view of the mind is, in many ways, similar to Leibniz's views on monads. First, each mind is, according to Descartes, indivisible – it has no parts, and so cannot be broken down into anything more basic. This is in contrast to all physical objects that can be divided into progressively smaller and smaller pieces. Secondly, each mind is what it is irrespective of its relations to anything else. What determines the identity of the mind is what's going on inside it, and nothing else. For Descartes, minds happen to find themselves in bodies, but things don't have to be

that way. Minds, as non-physical things, can also exist in disem-
bodied form. Your mind, at the present moment, happens to find
itself in a body – yours – but when you die, the mind will continue
existing in its non-physical form. So, your mind is what it is independently of its relation to your body. And, in fact, your mind is
what it is independently of its relation to the world. Even if the
entire physical world were destroyed, indeed, even if it never
existed in the first place, your mind could, according to Descartes,
still exist. It is not a physical thing, and so does not depend on the
physical world for its existence or essential nature.

But remember that, for Descartes, the mind is the essential you.
The body can come and go – as it came when you were born and will
go when you die – but the mind remains. So, this non-physical mind
is what you really are. We put all this together and we end up with
the idea that you – the essential and enduring you – are what you are
independently of your relations to anyone or anything else. What
makes you the person you are is solely a matter of what is going on
inside you – inside the non-physical mind that you are. What is going
on outside you – your relations to the world around you and to the
people in it – has no bearing on who and what you really are.

The idea of the mind or person as a non-physical thing has fallen
out of favour in recent years, what with the rise of modern science
and all. But the idea that what you are is determined solely and exclusively by what is going on inside you remains. Your relations to other
people, and to the world at large, have no bearing on what or who
you are. You are, in effect, a sort of *psychic monad*. The world and
the people in it can causally affect you – they can make you think
certain things, feel certain things, and do certain things – but they
cannot have any effect on your identity as the person you are. That
is all down to you – the inner you – not anyone or anything else.

This idea still virtually dominates the way we think about

ourselves today. And the girls are no exception. There's a scene, early in series 3, when they are sat in a coffee shop, discussing some doomed relationship or other, when Charlotte ventures the opinion that one of the functions of the perfect partner is to complete you – the familiar old Jerry Maguire shit. Miranda interjects critically, 'This means you must see yourself as needing completing.' And so we get a debate about whether boyfriends or partners or whatever should complete you or whether you should first be complete and then go looking for a boyfriend or partner. But this whole imagery of completeness versus incompleteness is just a bad metaphor that rests on the idea, introduced by Descartes, of the mind as the sort of thing that can be complete in the first place. It's like the mind is a sort of coffee mug, or cocktail glass, and when it's full it's complete, otherwise it's incomplete. Then, the question is whether you need a boyfriend to fill the mug/glass for you or whether it's best to do it yourself. All this sort of imagery rests on the idea of the mind as a thing, or an object, whose essential nature is independent of anything outside it. And this idea we inherited from Descartes.

We have encountered this idea before. In the Buffy chapter, we saw that modernity's conception of life was essentially *light* – we have no constitutive attachments to other people. You have no attachments that fix the identity of the person you are. Whatever attachments you have towards other people are identity-reflecting rather than identity-constituting. These attachments reflect the person you are, but they do not constitute that person. This is a modern conception of the self or person. And it is a conception we find very much to the fore in *Sex and the City*.

What this modern conception means, basically, is that all your relations to other people are inessential to you. You are, first and foremost, you, irrespective of who else is around, and what you think or feel about them. So you have to carve out your own space, and do the things you want to do – where both of these will be a reflection of who you are. Other people never touch you in your innermost being. They may have a place in your life, but you have to choose what that place is. Carving out your space, and fitting other people into the space you have carved out, this is all part of the defining project of the modern age: self-fulfilment. And so the Cartesian idea of the self or person as a sort of thing or object whose essential nature is independent of anyone else leads to the characteristically modern obsession with self-fulfilment.

It also leads to the overwhelming sense of loneliness and frustration that we find in *Sex and the City*. Or at least, I find it there. Manhattan becomes a city of one million isolated souls – a million psychic ships in the night. No real intimacy is possible; no real connection with anyone else can be made. Everyone else is always irredeemably *other* to you. You are your own country, and everyone else is always *alien* to you. Sure, when the loneliness gets too much, you can always cling to your friends for support. But this is a futile spasm, an idle gesturing towards the togetherness that is not possible in the modern Cartesian world inherited by Carrie, Samantha, Miranda and Charlotte.

Going shopping

So, there you are in the process of buying your new Manolo Blahniks. A shoe is what philosophers call a *relational* entity. It is defined by its relations to things outside it – namely feet. A shoe counts as a shoe only because it is meant to be worn on a foot. That is, it is part of the essence of a shoe that it be the sort of thing that is worn on a foot. Moreover, in a world where there were no feet, there would be no shoes either. So both the essence and existence of shoes involves something that is not shoe. So shoes are relational entities. You pay for your shoe with your credit card – which you hope and pray won't be refused. Your card is a relational thing too. It counts as a credit card only because of complex relations it bears to things outside it – to your bank account, to shops that will accept it, and the international banking system that makes it all possible. On your way home, you stop off for a well-earned cocktail. This too is a relational thing. Something counts as a cocktail – as opposed to simply a bunch of molecules – only because of various human practices that involve drinking liquids with certain types of molecular structure.

In fact, in your life, almost everything you ever encounter is a relational thing: it will involve, in its essence or for its existence, something other than it. Coming up with examples of non-relational things is not easy. A rock, for example, is arguably non-relational. It's just a bunch of molecules put together in the right way. It doesn't matter what anyone thinks of it or how they use it; it doesn't matter where it is. It's a rock. But most things are not like rocks at all. Most things we encounter, especially in our highly structured modern world, are relational things.

And yet, despite almost everything we come across being relational, we persist in thinking of ourselves as non-relational psychic monads. What are you? What makes you *you*? Well, probably, you are lots of things: you could be a lawyer, or publicist or gallery manager or newspaper columnist, or whatever. You could be female or male, and son, daughter, mother, father, brother, or sister. You could be black, or white, or somewhere in between. You could be bubbly and vivacious – or so you think – or a stick insect with no soul. There are as many things you could be as there are ways for anyone to be. And so there may be all sorts of things you *are*. The question is: which of these things are essential to you? Which go in to making you the person you are?

The answer we get from Descartes, remarkably enough, is: *none*, or, at least, *hardly any*. All these things are inessential, or accidental, features of you; they do not get to the essential core of what makes you the person you are. What you are, in all essentials, is a mind, a thinking thing. And all the sorts of features listed above are what we might call features of your *embodiment* and *embeddedness*. Your physical *embodiment*, your possession of the physical body you in fact have, accounts for features like whether you are male or female, black or white, and so on. Your social *embeddedness*, your position in a certain place in society – your being a Manhattan yuppie who happens to be in love, for example – accounts for most of the other features. The mind, the thinking thing that you essentially are, just happens to be embodied and embedded: it has become associated with a body that you call your own, and this body occupies a certain position in society. Bur neither your embodiment nor your embed-dedness get to the essential core of you. Why? Because the mind that you are is not an embodied or embedded thing. In all essen-tials, you are what philosophers have called an *unencumbered* self.

So, you're female. But you might not have been. You could still have been you if you turned out to be a man rather than a woman. You have no children, but things might have been different. If only Mikhail Baryshnikov hadn't had that vasectomy. You could still have been you even if you had produced loads of little baboushkas with him. You're not rich – but you might have been, and you might yet be. If so, it would still have been/will be you. You're white, but you could still have been you if you had turned out black instead. You're in love with Big, and you've never been in love before, but you could still have been you if you didn't love Big but loved lots of other people instead.

This is what is meant by saying that you are an *unencumbered* self. Most of the features you have, ones that seem so central to

your life, you have only inessentially, or *contingently*, as philosophers like to put it. These are features you happen to have, but they
don't define you. You could just as easily have turned out not to
have those features. What is each one of us essentially? According
to Descartes, just a thinking thing. According to his descendants,
just a thinking and feeling thing. Each one of us is a centre of
consciousness, and nothing else besides: a psychic monad.

There is a straightforward entailment of this conception of
people. The relations we enter into with other people – loving,
hating, adoring, despising, respecting, fearing, liking, dreading –
do not define us as the persons we are. These relations are like a
coat that we can slip on or off. Sometimes the coat may be
comfortable or cosy; other times we might find it stifling. No
matter, it's just a coat, and it doesn't in any way define us or penetrate us to our core. We can take it off or put it on whenever we
like. The real me, and the real you, is always inside, always separate
– always *alone*. And if ever there was a symbolisation of the essential loneliness of human beings, it is this theory that derives from
Descartes. Each one of us is a psychic atom clothed in an alien
material cladding; always estranged from other people, always
essentially separate from other people. Each one of us is like a ghost
to the others, a ghost shut away inside a bodily machine. We never
really leave any mark, any *trace*, on the other. We are never really
affected by anyone else, nor can we ever really affect them. We pass
each other as ships in the night.

Philosophers have a term for this separation of self from other:
alienation. To be alienated is to be alone and separate. It is to be
alien to other people, and for other people to be alien to you.
Sometimes, maybe, our alienation from other people hits us. At the
beginning of the first series, Carrie reacts strongly to Big's claim, in
his limo, that she had never been in love. On the one hand, you

just want to tell her to get a life: never really being in love is not that big a deal; it happens to most of us unless we are really, really lucky. But, on the other hand, there's this suspicion that there's something deeper underlying her reaction, something *metaphysical*. Maybe, at some level or other, she senses the essential loneliness, estrangement, *alienation* of the modern human psyche. The alienation consists in the feeling of isolation that goes with being a ghost in a city of other ghosts. Of being so light you can never leave any trace on the other, nor have them leave any trace on you. This all stems from the idea that you are a *ghost in a machine*. Maybe it's time to get out Carrie's laptop again – *are we all too Cartesian for our own good?*

Modern relationships and why they don't work

In painting us a certain picture of what the self or person is like, modernity has also provided us with a certain model of what a successful relationship would be like. It's a model that, I think, is consistently championed by *Sex and the City* – at least officially. As we have seen, modernity sees people as distinct and logically isolated egos. Each ego is complete in itself, and its identity is constituted only by what is occurring inside it, not by its relations to other people or other things. Given this view of the self, relationships basically come down to this: a relationship is a coalition or an alliance of people who band together for the purposes of mutually supported pursuit of interests. The interests pursued will vary from relationship to relationship. But one important interest that runs through most is what we might call *self-validation*. One of the central functions of most relationships is to support and reaffirm the identity of each person in it – an identity that was formed prior to, and independently of, the relationship. Modern relationships have the function of reassuring, supporting and encouraging the self in the identity it has established independently of the relationship.

So, in *Sex and the City*, Carrie is the introspective, analytical one of the group. Samantha is the go-getter, Miranda the cynic, and Charlotte the romantic. These characteristics form part of their identity, part of what they are. Their friendship with each other has been so successful, I think, because it allows, and even accentuates, this identity. Their relationship is a kind of *indulgence* that confirms or accentuates the self that is already there in each one of them, the self that is formed independently of those relationships. Self-validation is, to a considerable extent, the function of modern relationships, and any relationship that does not successfully fulfil this function is not going to last long.

Sure, they'll be disagreements from time to time. Carrie, Samantha, Miranda and Charlotte are all very punctilious in telling each other when they think one of them is making a mistake. If Carrie is making a mistake by seeing Big again, Miranda is going to let her know about it. If Charlotte is being hopelessly prudish in some way or other, and she usually is, Samantha is going to let her know about it. Sometimes these little disagreements can lead to tiffs, and the respective parties might not talk to each other for a few days. But they are all pretty minor spats. Whatever disagreements the gang have, these are all founded on a far greater background of agreement, agreement about why the relationship exists and what it is supposed to be doing: validating and even accentuating the self that each one of them is. The possibility of disagreement is *parasitic* on this wider agreement, and no disagreement can be allowed to challenge this wider foundation of the relationship without ending that relationship. And so the tiffs are soon over, and the self-validation can begin again.

So, modernity gives us this sort of recipe for the successful relationship:

SELF – identity fixed by what's going on inside
RELATIONSHIPS – affirmation and encouragement of
    what is going on inside

The self is fixed first. Successful relationships validate that self. The problem is that while this may work, at least to some extent, for the sort of relationship the girls have, it's not clear that it's going to work for lifetime partnerships of the sort pre-modern marriages were supposed to be. Self-validation is the foundation of the modern relationship, but various things can easily happen in the course of a lifetime that will quickly turn self-validation into self-demoralisation.

Here's an obvious one. Have you ever been jealous of your part-ner's success? Jealous, for example, in the sort of way Carrie's boyfriend Berger – of Post-it fame – was jealous of her success? If so, your relationship is a modern one. The greater success of your part-ner casts doubt, at least in your mind, on your own value. And the self-validation that was the basis of your relationship quickly turns into self-doubt. You can tolerate, at least within certain limits, the greater success of your friends. Your relationship with them is a modern one, and doesn't in any way define you – it merely validates the definition you have already arrived at independently of the friendship. The fact that you might not be able to tolerate the greater success of a lifetime partner says two important things about.

First of all, at one level, you have taken the modern recipe for the successful relationship and applied it to your supposedly lifetime partnership. You have a taken a model for the successful relationship that you learned from your dealings with your friends, and now applied it to your relationship with your lover. Secondly, on some other level, deep down, you realise that lifetime partnerships are not like that at all. Lifetime partnerships are an entirely different ball game. They are not about self-validation, still less self-accentuation. In lifetime partnerships, the identity of each person cannot be independent in the way modernity claims they are. A lifetime together is more like a musical composition that begins with two unrelated melodies. Slowly these grow together, reinforcing each other at various points. Sometimes the melodies harmonise; sometimes the strength is to be found in the dissonance. But the strength of the relationship is always a matter of the relation between the two. Eventually, these two melodies merge into one.

A lifetime partnership will work not because it provides you with self-validation – the affirmation or even accentuation of a self that existed prior to the partnership. Rather, it will work when it provides you with something quite different: *something outside of you so important that without it you would not be the same person.* But if successful lifetime partnerships provide you with this, it is easy to see why they are so difficult to pull off in modern times. If there is something outside of you – something other than you and your quest for self-fulfilment – that is so important that without it you wouldn't be the same person, then you cannot be the sort of thing modernity says you are. You cannot be a distinct and logically isolated ego whose identity is fixed solely by what's going on inside. Your identity is bound up with someone else. Successful lifetime partnerships are based on you *not* being modern. Modernity has the cards stacked against lifetime partnerships.

So, we have a choice to make. One option is for us to take a model of relationships we learned from our interactions with our friends and try to apply this model to our lifetime partnership – assuming we want one. This is, in effect, what Carrie does.

However, realising that she is not getting the self-validation she expected from the relationship, she then has to marginalise her different-sex relationships – her potential lifetime partnerships – and allow them to continue only against a background of self-validation and self-accentuation provided by her friendship with Samantha, Miranda and Charlotte. And so the only men who have lasted any time at all in Carrie's life are those that allow her to perpetuate her self-validating relationships with her friends. There is, of course, nothing wrong with Carrie doing this: quite the contrary. But the problem is her attempt to take a model of relationships she learned from her friends and apply it to her potential lifetime partners. And that just isn't going to work.

Carrie is, I think, ultimately hiding from her pre-modern self. Officially, she's modernity's poster girl. Just remember her parting words in the final episode. What has she learned over the past six seasons? *The most important relationship is the one you have with yourself.* I must admit, I was very disappointed in Carrie here. It seemed like she had learned nothing at all. But, in fact, I think she knew something all along – she just didn't know that she knew it. Because Carrie does have something in her life so important that without it she wouldn't be the same person. It's just not a man. It's New York City. That's why she couldn't live in Paris. That's why she hated Aidan's country house. That's why even a weekend in the Hamptons was challenging enough for her. Modern is difficult to be. If even Carrie Bradshaw can't pull it off properly, there's not much chance of the rest of us getting the hang of it.

four
FRIENDS

WHAT IS LOVE?

Modern love

With *Sex and the City*, we started looking at the implications that modernity – the philosophy of the modern age – has for the nature of relationships. For modernity, successful relationships are essentially associations or alliances of people who band together for the purposes of mutually supported pursuit of interests. And stable, thriving, relationships should be based on the validation, or even accentuation, of the self that was formed independently of the relationship.

However, as I also suggested at the end of the previous chapter, while this may be a workable recipe for success in friendships, it's not clear that it's going to work for lifetime partnerships. It's not clear that we can concoct a successful recipe for a loving relationship based on the idea of alliance and self-validation of a person that existed before the love began. Love, you might think, seems to involve more than this. The worry is that relationships based on nothing more than mutual gain and self-affirmation leave the related people just too estranged – alienated – from each other for the love to work out, at least in the long run.

It's no surprise, of course, that modernity is going to have a problem with love. Love is an attachment, something that binds you to someone else. But according to modernity, no attachments to anyone outside you can ever be identity-constituting. Such attachments do not, even in part, determine who or what you are. The only identity-constituting attachment you have is to yourself – to realise or fulfil yourself to the best of your abilities. But if self-realisation or self-fulfilment is the game, then love, as a merely identity-reflecting attachment, is something you're going to have to fit in around it. Your being in love is only going to be worth it if it contributes to your self-fulfilment – if it doesn't, well you just might as well forget about it. Love always comes second to self-fulfilment. At least, that's what modernity tells us. Love is, basically, a lifestyle choice, just one choice among the many others that go into realising or fulfilling yourself. We've encountered this sort of theme before on several occasions; indeed, it is one of modernity's constant refrains. The ties that bind us to others – whether these are ties of obligation, friendship, love, or whatever – always come off second best to modernity's first commandment: self-fulfilment. The problem modernity raises, therefore, is: how serious can love ever be?

As in the case of the other sorts of attachment, however, many of us have never really got the hang of being modern – we've never really managed to pull it off, not completely, not all the time. All of us are, to some extent or other, a blend of the modern and the pre-modern. It's no wonder we are so confused about love. A good way of exploring this issue is by way of the shifting relationships between the characters in the most successful sitcom of all time: *Friends* (ten seasons, 1994–2004).

Just look at the raw material *Friends* gives us. Monica and Chandler were friends. But in recent series, that has changed. Now, could they *be* any more in love? What's the difference between

Monica and Chandler when they were friends and when they were lovers? How does Monica change when she falls in love with Chandler? And how does Chandler change when he does the same with Monica?

Now, take Ross and Rachel. To begin with, they weren't even friends. Ross was Monica's geek brother, and if Rachel felt anything for him it was pity or even contempt rather than friendship. How did Ross and Rachel change when they became friends? Then Ross and Rachel fell in love. How did this change them? What's the difference between Ross and Rachel before and after they fell in love? That is, what's the difference between being a friend and being in love? Then, of course, due to Ross's jealousy and the well-documented, if hotly denied, break that they were on, they fell out of love and, eventually, became friends again. How did this change them? And were Ross and Rachel friends in the same way after their break-up as they were before?

The case of Joey and Rachel is more complicated. They were friends. Then Joey fell in love with Rachel, but it was, unfortunately, unrequited. Then Joey pulled himself together, moved on, only for Rachel to fall in love with him. So, after various twists and turns, they almost became lovers. Almost. They did their best – it just didn't quite happen for them, what with the slapping of the hands and the kneeing of the nuts and so on. But despite this failure to consummate, they still loved each other, apparently. At least that's what Joey said. So, Rachel and Joey raise various questions. How did they change when they, at different times, fell in love? And what is the difference between a love that involves sex and a love that does not?

The ancient Greeks would have known exactly what was going on in *Friends*. In fact, they would have loved it. Multiple rearrangements and renegotiations of the relation between *eros* and *philia* – that's what it's all about.

Eros and philia

How about a little pretentious philology – just for a sentence or two? Indulge me. In English, the word 'love' is derived from Germanic forms of the Sanskrit word *lubh*. However, it's not a direct translation. *Lubh* actually translates as the rather more broad term, *desire*. The ancient Greeks, conceptually precise race that they were, did a lot of useful work tidying up the concept of love. This concept, they thought, had at least three different meanings, ones that they expressed by way of the three terms *eros, philia* and *agape*.

The concept of *agape* is going to play no real role in this chapter, so I'll mention it briefly only to get it out of the way. When the Greeks talked about *agape*, they had in mind two things. On the one hand there was the supposed paternal love of God for man and man for God. On the other, there was the extension of this idea to include brotherly love that each of us is supposed to have for other human beings. So, when the later Judaeo-Christian tradition tells us that: 'You shall love the Lord your God with all your heart, and with all your soul, and with all your might' (Deuteronomy 6: 5), the sense of love in question was *agape*. And when the same tradition bangs on about loving 'thy neighbour as thyself' (Leviticus 19: 18), or even that you should 'love thy enemies' (Matthew 5: 44–5), again what they had in mind was *agape*. You get modern-day echoes of this in David Hume's idea of the social sentiments – natural feelings of affection and warmth that we have for other humans.[14] Also, the modern ideal of a universal moral law that applies equally to everyone might be regarded as a variation on this theme. But, forget about *agape* because it's not the right sort of love, and so not relevant to what we're going to look at in this chapter. What we're

---

14. We encountered David Hume in the chapter on *Buffy*, when we were trying to make sense of the idea of obligation. We'll come across him later on too.

interested in – and what *Friends* is interested in – are the two other senses of love distinguished by the Greeks: *eros* and *philia*.

We are going to take a good, long look at the concept of *eros* in this chapter. Working out exactly what it means is what a large part of this chapter is all about. But we can start off with a few preliminary ideas. When the Greeks used the term *eros*, they did so to refer to a type of love that involved a passionate and intense desire for something. That's the core part of the whole concept: a passionate and intense desire. In modern times, the type of desire involved has typically been regarded as exclusively sexual in nature – hence the modern notion of the term 'erotic', which derives from the Greek *erotikos*. Today if you have a passionate and intense erotic desire then you're, basically, gagging for it. It wasn't always like this, however.

For example, there was a, by modern standards, strange conception of romantic love that emerged in the early medieval ages – to be specific, eleventh-century France, and the French referred to it as *fine amour* – a sort of love peculiar to knights and damsels. This sort of love put you in a strictly shagging-free zone, since it was motivated by a deep respect for the lady in question, and so was to be expressed in the form of chivalric deeds rather than the bumping of uglies. Talk about sublimation (see the chapter on *The Simpsons*) and/or repression (see the chapter on *The Sopranos*).

In fact, this view wasn't original to the early Middle Ages – not surprising really, since no original idea was ever developed in early medieval times; people were really stupid back then. We don't talk of the Dark Ages for nothing. No, far from being original, the idea of *fine amour* actually derived from a view associated with our old friend Plato.

Plato argued that *eros* involved an intense and passionate longing or desire, but, unlike in its modern incarnations, this was a desire not for sex but for the *beautiful*. *Eros* provides us with a glimpse into a world beyond our senses, a world beyond the physical plane in which we live our everyday lives. He called this other world the world of *Forms* or *Ideas*. Beauty, true beauty, was a feature of this world of forms. And when we love – in the sense of *eros* – a beautiful person in this physical world, we do so because she or he reminds us of the beauty that lies in the world of forms. Understood in this way, *eros* is an intense longing for a world that lies beyond our own.

Philia, in contrast to the passionate longing of *eros*, is a sort of fondness and appreciation for the other person. *Philia*, for the Greeks in general, was somewhat wider than what we call friendship, since it incorporated not only friendship but also loyalties to one's family and also to one's *polis*, or local political community. The way the philosopher Aristotle used the term, however, corresponds very closely to the way we use the term 'friendship'. So, he writes: 'things that cause friendship are: doing kindnesses; doing them unasked; and not proclaiming the fact when they are done' (*Rhetoric*, II. 4). Amen to that.

More generally, Aristotle argued that the sorts of people we would like as friends are those who are similar to us in character, who don't bear grudges, who have the same sort of goals, desires and aspirations as us, who have a calm and moderate temperament, who are just or fair, who admire us appropriately as we admire them, and so on. It's no fun to hang out with someone who is quarrelsome or overly aggressive, or who will maliciously gossip about you as soon as your back is turned, or even put you down to your face. Nor is it any fun to hang out with people who are unjust or unfair – maybe because they expect far more from you than they are willing to offer in return. Or who are so self-absorbed that while they are quite happy to tell you about themselves and what's going on with them, will cut you short if you try to discuss what's happening with you. We all know people like this.

If there are two things that stand out from Aristotle's account of friendship it is (1) equality and (2) empathy. True friendship can only be between people who are equals, at least roughly. You can't be friends with the truly clingy; nor can you be friends with someone who sees you as beneath them. But it's more than just rough equality. It's the ability to put yourself in the place of the other person, understand what they are thinking and feeling, forgiving them when it is appropriate to forgive them, and speaking your mind when you think it is needed. All this is a delicate balancing act: there's a fine line between forgiveness and dereliction of friendship, and an even finer one between speaking your mind and being an overbearing meddler or bully. Balancing acts like this can be achieved some of the time – but it's very difficult to do it all of the time. That's why friendship can be so difficult. But one thing is clear. On Aristotle's account, the best sort of people produce the best sort of friends – that's why Aristotle devotes the bulk of his most famous ethical work, the *Nichomachean Ethics*, to the issue of how to be a person worthy of friendship or *philia*. Being an ethical or moral person, for Aristotle, is part and parcel of the project of becoming someone who people will want as a friend. That's one of the most important reasons for being a good person – a good person has good friends.

There are, admittedly, lesser kinds of friendships. And, for many of us, this may sound depressingly familiar. The lesser kind of friendship is based on the pleasure or usefulness that is derived from another's company. Maybe you need someone to go out on the tear with, for example. You can't put up with them for any length of time when you are sober, but liquor eases the annoyance. And, besides, you can always ditch them later when you have successfully pulled. Or maybe it's useful for you to be seen with someone – their status, you hope, will rub off, if only a little, on you. Lesser friendships are diversions – ways of killing time, or of getting something you want independently of the friendship. Lesser friendships are, in a word, means, not ends. And once the end has been achieved, or you realise that you will never achieve it, the friendship comes to an end.

Philials

The eponymous friends certainly do seem to meet Aristotle's conditions on *philia* quite well. For a start, they are all roughly equal. They are all of a similar age and similar stage in their careers. They all have roughly similar goals and aspirations – to meet someone with whom they can spend the rest of their lives, to be successful in what they do, and so on. For much of the time, they all have a similar income and standard of living – and when they don't it can lead to friction. Remember, for example, in the first series when a temporary schism had been set up between the rich friends (Chandler, Monica and Ross) and the poor friends (Rachel, Phoebe and Joey). The rich went off to dinner, a Hootie and the Blowfish concert, and a noticeable hickie on one of their necks, and the poor – well, they weren't very happy about it. But, for the most part, the friends are of a roughly equal social and economic standing.

Of course, there are differences between them. Chandler is the funny one, Monica the obsessive one, Ross the anal one, Phoebe the quirky one, Rachel the ditzy one, and Joey the hungry one. But these differences are all built on a far more significant foundation of similarity. It is the sharing of goals, aspirations and history that allows them to empathise with each other – to suffer when the others suffer and to forgive when the others transgress. Indeed, they are constantly forgiving each other various infractions, and so they clearly don't bear grudges – well, OK, they occasionally do bear grudges ('We were on a *break*'). But generally they admire and, more importantly, support each other when they do well, and console each other when they fail or are disappointed. They are not aggressive to each other; quite the contrary – they are generally calm and moderate in their interactions with each other. And even when they fall short of this, everything is eventually sorted out by a chat in Central Perk.

So, the sort of conditions Aristotle thinks you have to meet in order to qualify as a genuine friend, the gang all meet. So, it's easy to understand why they are friends. But then they go and fall in love with each other. The question we must look at is: what changes when this happens? When *eros* gets added to the equation, how do things change? Indeed, do things really change at all? And, if so, how?

Love or lust?

There is one basic question you can ask about love, and the answer you give to it will determine the sort of thing you think love is. The question is: does love reduce to lust? Is being in love with someone simply the same thing as being in lust with them? If you answer 'yes', you belong to a tradition that regards love as a purely biological phenomenon, one that exists alongside other purely biological drives. If you answer 'no', on the other hand, then you belong to a tradition that regards love as somehow special, as something over and above what we possess as part of our general biological nature. This tradition, as we have seen, has its roots in Plato.

Plato on eros

Plato's account of love is most fully presented in his book *The Symposium*, and also in *The Phaedrus*. For him, *eros* is essentially bound up with *beauty*.

Take a look at some beautiful people some time. It doesn't matter who; take your pick. Maybe you're Chandler in series 2, and have been caught in an ATM room with the latest bright young thing from the *Victoria's Secret* stable, for example. Take a long look. Then, when your former roommate Joey has Elle MacPherson move in with him, take another look. Then, have a look at Monica, Phoebe, Rachel and her sisters Reese Witherspoon and Christina Applegate. What do they all have in common? That is, what makes beautiful people beautiful? They must, it seems, have something in common – otherwise, how could they all be beautiful? What is this common element? Plato's answer was simple: *beauty*. Beautiful people are beautiful because they exemplify, instantiate or, as Plato often put it, *partake in*, beauty. But this, of course, doesn't get us very far. What is beauty?

While you are looking at Monica, Phoebe, Rachel, Elle, Reese and Christina, ask yourself: are any of them perfectly beautiful? Plato's answer is that none of them could be. Of course, most males around, it goes without saying, definitely *would*. But, according to Plato, no matter how fine they are, and no matter how much you *would*, there will always be some deviation from perfection – some flaw, some blemish, some imperfection that renders them less than perfectly beautiful. And it doesn't matter who we are looking at – take your pick: Giselle, Heidi Klum, whoever does it for you. And if you are a (straight) woman, you do the same thing for your males of choice. Even when we are talking about some of the finest ass that the world – the *physical* world – has to offer, there will always be some deviation from perfection. Therefore, Plato, concluded, beauty – true or perfect beauty – cannot be part of the physical world. While physical things, people and objects, can be beautiful, their beauty is always less than perfect. Therefore, perfect beauty must lie outside the physical world. A word that philosophers use for something that exists outside the physical world – the world of space and time – is *transcendent*. Beauty, for Plato, is a transcendent entity.

But is there any reason for believing in perfect beauty? I mean, if all we ever find are examples of beauty that are less than perfect, what reason is there for thinking that there is such a thing as perfect beauty? Plato thought there was a reason, one based on our ability to judge which things are beautiful and which things are not. We do this sort of thing a lot of the time, apparently. How many of us men have not ranked the three women in *Friends*? And although my female friends will tell me, initially, that they don't do this sort of ranking thing at all – when you push them they will, almost invariably, tell you that if they had to do one of the male cast it would be Joey. Ranking beauty is something that comes entirely easily and naturally to us. Any one of us can easily distinguish the *überbabe* from the minger, the stud from the geek. Some of us are very good at the intermediate grades too. How can we do this? What provides the basis for comparison? If we can rank people in order of increasing beauty, Plato argued, this must be because we have at least some sort of dim appreciation of what perfect beauty is. We may not know it well, but we have enough of an appreciation to be able to tell that one person is closer to it than another.

Some of you may have noticed a problem already, of course. What objective basis is there for ranking people according to their beauty? After all, isn't beauty in the eye of the beholder? Some of us, for example, might have a thing for Courteney Cox, perhaps because, when we were horny adolescents, we saw her in the Bruce Springsteen 'Dancing in the Dark' video. But what could we say to someone who thinks Jennifer Aniston is better looking? Maybe there is nothing we could say. Maybe beauty, after all, is just a subjective thing.

But, this rejection of Plato is just too quick. The problem in ranking Monica versus Rachel might just be that they are *so* close. So similar are they to the form of the beautiful that we can't really decide either way. Sometimes, you can't judge whether someone is bald or not – the amount of hair they have is indeterminate in this regard. But this doesn't mean that some people aren't bald and some people don't have a full head of hair. Sometimes a person might be neither tall not short because, obviously, they are of average height. But this doesn't mean that some people aren't tall and some people aren't short. The moral: just because you can't tell who of Monica and Rachel is the more beautiful doesn't mean that one of them isn't more beautiful than the other. At least, that's the sort of thing Plato would say. He wouldn't have any time for this 'beauty is in the eye of the beholder' stuff.

According to Plato, it is our at least dim understanding of what true beauty is like that allows us to rank people in terms of their level of beauty. And if there are some cases where we can't do this, this is only against a background of a much larger category of cases where we can do it. And this is why, Plato thought, we should believe in absolute beauty. If there were no such thing, then we would have no way of ranking people according to how beautiful they are. And so we arrive at the Platonic idea of beauty as something existing outside the physical world. He called this the *form* of beauty. We might call it *the beautiful*, or *beauty itself*. Beautiful things are beautiful because they resemble the form of beauty, beauty itself. Courteney Cox resembles the form of the beautiful. So too does Jennifer Aniston. We may not be quite sure who resembles it more but, as Plato would say: hey, nobody's perfect. But the general idea we get from Plato is that to be beautiful is to resemble the form of the beautiful, beauty itself. And people can resemble beauty itself to a greater or lesser extent. The greater the resemblance the more beautiful is the person.

When we love – in the sense of *eros* – a person, we love the beauty that is in them. That is what *eros* is, for Plato: a passionate and intense yearning for transcendent beauty itself. 'He who loves the beautiful is called a lover because he partakes of it,' Plato tells us. We love – erotically – a particular person when they remind us of this true beauty that exists in the non-physical world of forms. And they remind us of this true non-physical beauty because they, to a greater or lesser extent, resemble it. A beautiful person, like a beautiful thing, is, in effect, an *image* or *representation* of beauty, and, like all images or representations, will to some extent or other be flawed or inaccurate. And to love erotically is to love not a person or individual thing, but the Platonic form of beauty – the element the person or thing possesses of beauty itself.

So, for Plato, there is a clear distinction between (erotic) love and lust. You remember, in Chapter 2, when we looked at Plato's contribution to understanding Tony Soprano, that Plato talked about what he called the *appetites* – desires to feed, fight, flee and fornicate being, maybe, the principal ones. Lust counts as one of the appetites in this sense. Lust is always directed at a particular person. Love on the other hand, is directed not at a particular person, but to the form of beauty that they resemble or exemplify. Lust is firmly embedded in the physical world, and has things in that world as its object. Love, on the other hand, links us to another world, a world that exists outside space and time.

Plato's view explains something that many people claim to believe about love: that it is in some way ineffable or inexplicable. Plato argued that knowledge of the world of forms – the world where beauty resides – is very difficult to obtain. Years and years of training in mathematics and philosophy are required if we are to get even halfway to such knowledge. Without such training, we would not possess the intellectual capacities necessary to understand what true beauty is. Sure, we may gain glimpses of its essence – as Plato has Socrates argue in *The Symposium* – but its true nature lies beyond our intellectual grasp. Accordingly, beauty may be partially described, hinted at, or gestured towards, but not understood as it is in itself.

Plato, actually, has a famous analogy that he used to illustrate the tenuous nature of our grip on the nature of the forms. Imagine prisoners chained their whole lives in a cave. The cave is lit by a fire that casts shadows on the walls. The prisoners have never seen the outside world; their entire visual experience is confined to the shadows on the wall of the cave. Understandably, then, they have come to mistake these shadows for reality.

This, Plato thinks, is the predicament of the average person. The physical world that we discover through our senses is like a shadow cast by something more real – the world of forms. The physical world is a pale reflection of this world of forms, just as a shadow is a pale reflection of the object that casts it.

Imagine now that the prisoners escape from their chains, and make their way to the mouth of the cave. At first the light is simply too bright for them to see anything at all. Their eyes have evolved for a world of darkness and shadow, and they are simply not adequate to grasp the new bright world now presented to them. This is the predicament of the person who would learn about the world of forms. Our intellectual capacities have evolved for the physical world and are simply not adequate for understanding the world of forms – at least not without long and protracted training in philosophy and mathematics. Plato was somewhat equivocal on just how much this training could be expected to achieve. Sometimes he seemed to suggest that proper training would allow you to intellectually grasp the world of forms. At other times, he seemed a lot more pessimistic about this. But, in any event, the training required is of the sort that most of us never get.

So, at most, beauty is something that can be understood only by a small number of people. At worst, it can be understood by no one at all. But if we don't understand what beauty is, then neither can we be expected properly to understand what love – in the sense of *eros* – is. *Eros* is, to the extent that we understand it, a passionate and intense longing for beauty. But if we don't really understand what beauty is, then neither can we understand a passionate and intense longing for it. So, love, in Plato's view, may be as mysterious, ineffable and inexplicable as many people claim it is.

And this raises a further interesting question. Can we ever really experience something we don't understand? In one sense, I think we can; but in another sense, we can't. Understanding brings something to an experience that can often fundamentally change the nature of that experience. You hit middle C on your piano. Your dog hears it. Does he hear the same thing as you? Well, in one sense he does, and in another he doesn't. Even if what he hears sounds exactly the same as what you hear, there is still a sense in which you hear something different. You can hear the sound as a middle C. Your dog, it seems, can't. And think how much your experience changes when middle C develops into an entire sonata. Because of your musical training, let's suppose, you can pick out the harmonies, the subtle changes of melody, your dog can't detect. For example, you hear a certain passage of sound as a transition from a major to a minor key. Your dog cannot hear it in this way because he lacks the relevant *concepts*: that is, he does not have the ability to *understand* what a transition from major to minor key consists of. Understanding, it seems, can often fundamentally change the nature of an experience. This is not to say that your dog can't hear the sonata. Of course he can. But your understanding of what is going on means that your experience is very different from your dog's.

If this is right, then in what sense can we ever really have an experience of love if we don't understand what love is? And, on Plato's view, how can we understand what love is if we don't understand what beauty is? If Plato is right, most of us, and perhaps all of us, never fully experience love for the simple reason that we don't understand what it is we are experiencing.

Schopenhauer: love is blind

In these modern times, most of us are not too happy with the idea of transcendent realms of existence. And, I think, rightly so. Plato's account has lots of problems. Some of these he even worked out for himself. Take his explanation of why people, or things, are beautiful. Courteney Cox is beautiful because she resembles the form of the beautiful, or beauty itself. Ditto for Jennifer Aniston, Lisa Kudrow, Reese Witherspoon, Christina Applegate, and so on. So, you have all of these beautiful people resembling the form of the beautiful. More generally, all beautiful things, Plato would have us believe, resemble the form of the beautiful. And ugly things don't resemble it. What does that tell you about the form of the beautiful? I mean, if all beautiful things resemble the form of the beautiful and no non-beautiful things resemble this, what does that imply about the form of the beautiful? Basically, it seems to imply that the form of the beautiful must itself be beautiful. If not, how could all beautiful things resemble it and no non-beautiful things resemble it?

But if the form of the beautiful is itself beautiful, Plato's theory is up shit creek. The form of the beautiful, beauty itself, is supposed to explain what all beautiful things – Courteney, Jennifer, Reese, Christina, etc. – have in common. So, Courteney is beautiful because she resembles the form of the beautiful, so too for Jennifer, and so on. But if the form of the beautiful is itself beautiful then there is one more thing that needs explaining – what is it that makes the form of the beautiful beautiful? It seems we will need another form of the beautiful – beauty 2 – to explain what makes the original form of the beautiful – beauty 1 – beautiful. But it is difficult to see how beauty 2 could explain why beauty 1 is beautiful unless beauty 2 is also, itself, beautiful. How could resembling something that is not beautiful make you beautiful? Therefore, it seems, we have to allow that beauty 2 is also beautiful. But then it shares something with beauty 1 and Courteney, Jennifer, Reese and Christina. What is it they have in common? We are going to need as new form of the beautiful – beauty 3 – to explain what this is.

And now we're well on the way to what philosophers call an *infinite regress*. You are trying to explain something, but what you invoke to explain this presupposes the thing you are trying to explain in the first place. So, your attempted explanation gets you nowhere. Plato himself realised this problem with his theory; he talked about it in one of his books, *The Parmenides*. Unfortunately, he never came up with a convincing answer to the problem.

Therefore, maybe we can proceed to a more modern version of the nature of love in general, and the relation between love and lust in particular. Plato was one of those people who would answer 'no' to the question of whether love reduces to lust. And he instigated a whole tradition of thinking about love as, in some way, special, mysterious, and, perhaps, inexplicable. There is, however, an opposing tradition for thinking about love – one that regards it as simply one biological drive among others. On this tradition, love – in the sense of *eros* – is a form of lust: a biological drive whose function is to get you to copulate and propagate yourself or your species. Today, this line of thought is associated with what's known as *sociobiology*, the discipline that tries to explain human psychological characteristics in terms of their evolutionary role in furthering our fitness. However, the philosophical father of the idea that love reduces to lust was undoubtedly the nineteenth-century German philosopher Arthur Schopenhauer (1788–1860).

Love, it is sometimes said, is blind. Schopenhauer would totally agree with this. Love is indeed blind because it is the expression of a blind striving that Schopenhauer called the *will to life*. This is an inherent drive possessed by all living things to stay alive and reproduce. And this drive dominates humans just as much as it dominates all other living things. The will to life is why we do many, perhaps most, of the things we do.

For example, it's Friday night and you're out with your mates. Getting pissed is fun, admittedly, but you could do that far more cheaply at home with a few cans. Why are you out throwing away five quid a time on watered-down cocktails? It's your will to life, isn't it. Whether you realise it or not, you're on the pull, and it's your will to life that's making you do it. No, no, I just like hanging out with my mates, unwinding and stuff like that. Yeah, right! The will to life, on Schopenhauer's view, is pulling all the strings. As the night wears on, you may well be getting more and more drunk. Again the will to life is making you do it. You need to have a skinful before you have the bottle to make a move on anyone – and what you need the will to life makes sure you get. The alcohol will, of course, lower your normal levels of discernment and taste making it more likely that you will hit on any hunchback, heifer or wizened crone (if you are a man) or scumbag, sasquatch, or troll (if you are a woman), who happens to come within reach, thus increasing your chances of scoring. The will to life is not unambiguously happy about this – as we shall see, it has to consider not only that you produce offspring but how good they are too. Nonetheless, since it is Friday night, your will to life will probably let this slide, just for the time being. At all stages during the night, your will to life is calling the shots. And it isn't just when you're drunk that this happens. It happens all the time. The will to life, according to Schopenhauer, is the driving force behind virtually everything you do. You are, in effect, the will to life's bitch.

Of course, you don't realise this – at least not unless you're a fan of Schopenhauer. The will to life's dominance over you is hidden, clandestine, subterranean. It works covertly. It's all smoke and mirrors, and sleight of hand. Misdirection plays a big role in the authority the will to life has over you. In particular, part of its power lies in the fact that you think that you are the author of your own actions – the captain of your fate and master of your destiny. But this sense you have over your own authority and capacity to choose your destiny is, for Schopenhauer, an illusion. You're not really in control at all. What's going on, on your Friday excursion into town, has really nothing to do with you. Rather: 'What is decided is nothing less than the composition of the next generation … the existence and special constitution of the human race in times to come.'

Schopenhauer distinguishes between what is going on at the conscious level – the way things seem to you when you act – and the unconscious forces that are the real players in what's going on. When you're heading out on Friday night, the continuation of the species is probably not, unless you are seriously disturbed, at the forefront of your mind. But, in Schopenhauer's view, you are split into two halves – conscious and unconscious selves. The unconscious part of you is governed by the will to life, and it's all about staying alive and continuing the species. Of course, you have no inkling of this – it's all unconscious. The conscious part of you, on the other hand, thinks it's in control. But, in reality, it's totally subservient to the unconscious forces that are the real players in determining what you do.

The intellect does not penetrate into the secret workshop of the will's decisions. It is, of course, a confidant of the will, yet a confidant that does not get to know everything.

Rather then being the boss, the conscious part of you is the bitch – a largely unseeing and uncomprehending flunky of the dominant, sex- and survival-obsessed will to life.

In this game of misdirection, the whole idea of love is a big help to the will to life. If you are convinced you are in love, then you will pursue the second one of the will to life's demands – the propagation thing – with great vigour, indeed ardour. Love is precisely the sort of feeling that is going to make you and your partner do it like bunnies. All through this, the will to life may, unconsciously, be fucking with you – getting her to 'forget' to take her pill, or him to think that condoms are really only necessary in the middle of the month. Consciously, the whole charade is carried out against the background of this warm fuzzy feeling of love. More subtly, people are often very good at telling, at least unconsciously, when they are being conned. If you weren't in love, but only faking it, then your partner might be able to tell – from subtle signs you give – even if they didn't fully realise it. And this would make the whole indiscriminate sex thing less likely to happen. So, often, the unconscious will to life will convince you that you are in love in order for you to convince your partner that you are in love.

Plato or Schopenhauer?

If you were 'in love' with someone, and you hoped they were 'in love' with you too, which theory would you prefer to be right? Personally, I would hope that neither of them were. Consider, first, the problems you would have if Plato's story were true.

The first thing that jumps out at you on Plato's account is the strangely impersonal nature of love. When someone is in love, allegedly with you, it seems it's not really you they are in love with at all. What they are really in love with – erotically speaking – is the form of the beautiful. You get into the picture only because you happen to resemble this form, to a greater or lesser extent. So, you are, in effect, incidental to their love – you seem strangely peripheral to the whole thing.

Compare, for example, a situation in which we say, 'She/he only loved you for your money.' In this sort of case, the object of the love is the money, and the person gets in on the love only because they have a lot of money. A disappointing situation to be in – I mean, not the money aspect, but the only-be-loved-for-the-money aspect of the situation. However, the person who loves you for your money, popular, post-Freudian wisdom has it, might actually be unaware of this fact. They might be blind to their true motivation. Why? Schopenhauer would have a good explanation. By conning him or herself into believing they are in love with you, they stand a much better chance of conning you into believing they are in love with you. This is why money, like power, is supposedly an aphrodisiac. He or she might be greatly turned on by your money, and might genuinely believe they are in love with you. So now the question is: what's the difference between someone loving you only for your money and someone loving you only for your beauty? They may be greatly turned on by your beauty, just as others might be greatly turned on by your money. They may, in both cases, genuinely believe they are in love with you.

There are, of course, various acid tests that can be used to determine whether someone loves you simply for your money. People who love you only for your money are notoriously fickle. That goes with the territory. If they love your money, and love you only because you have a lot of it, then it follows that when some-one comes along with more of it, they are, all other things being equal, going to love them more. Even more worryingly, suppose you lose all your money. Then, since they only loved you for it in the first place, it follows, all things being equal, that they are not going to love you any more. The conclusion is, of course, that when we say that he or she only loves you for your money, what we are, in fact, saying is that he or she doesn't really love you at all. Their emotions consist in a pathological form of greed, but love doesn't come into it.

But what's the difference between this and the case of some-one who loves you only for your beauty? If what they really love is the transcendent form of the beautiful, then you are, it seems, as tangential to their love as if they loved you only for your money. What happens when someone more beautiful than you – that is, who more closely resembles the form of the beautiful – comes along? If they are genuinely in love with beauty itself, rather than you, then they should, it seems, love them more because of their more perfect resemblance to this form. And what happens when you get old and fat? The conclusion we should draw, I think, parallels that for the case of money. To say, as Plato does, that someone loves you for your beauty – because of your resemblance to the form of the beautiful – is the same as saying that they don't really love you at all. There isn't a well-known word in the English language, like greed, to convey what's going on. The closest is *aestheticism* – love of the beautiful. Someone who 'loves' you because of how closely you resemble the form of the beautiful is an *aesthete*. They are a lover of the beautiful, but not a lover of *you*.

I, of course, have no objection to someone loving me in the way Plato describes *eros*. Far from it – they can love me all they want because of how closely I resemble the form of the beautiful.[15] But I would sincerely hope that this is not the *only* way in which they love me. Any relationship based on this, it seems, just isn't going to last long. It will be as transient, and as fickle, as the beauty on which it is based.

But if you think Plato's theory of love provides a problem for the possibility of any sort of enduring relationship, just wait until you get to Schopenhauer! Love, you remember, reduces to lust. It is simply an expression of the will to life – and, in particular, that part of the will to life concerned with reproduction. That's the whole point of love – it's one of the ways the will to life has of conning you into reproducing. By making you believe you are in love with someone, and making the other believe they are in love with you, the will to life increases the likelihood of you doing it like you're on the Discovery Channel.

However, there is, as Schopenhauer noted, a clear difference between, on the one hand, what is good for reproduction, and, on the other, what is good for the person who reproduces. The whole point of the will to life, for example, is to produce children, and for these children to, themselves, produce children, and so on. There's no point simply in your producing children, if they can't go and produce children themselves. And what's the best way to ensure that the children you produce will go on and produce children themselves? Easy: make sure that your children are beautiful, intelligent and healthy. And so your will to life directs you towards people most suitable for producing beautiful, intelligent and healthy children. And it directs you away from people who are not suitable for producing such children.

---

15. And no, I don't care if this means they are blind, deluded or dangerously unhinged. I would also be delighted if someone loved me for my money – because that would mean I actually had some.

> *There is something quite peculiar to be found in the deep unconscious seriousness with which two people of the opposite sex regard each other when they meet for the first time, the searching and penetrating glance they cast at each other, the careful inspection of all the features and parts that their respective persons have to undergo. This scrutiny and examination is the meditation of the genius of the species concerning the individual possible through these two.*

Of course, when you go out on a first date with someone, you are not, unless you are a seriously scary person, consciously doing this. The will to life doesn't work this way. Its influence is clandestine – subtly pushing you in one way rather than another, making you find one person more attractive than another, and so on. And the criterion on which it bases all its covert efforts is whether the other person will produce beautiful, intelligent and healthy children for you.

Schopenhauer realised that this idea has somewhat bleak implications. First of all, the sort of person selected by the will to life because of their potential in the children-producing stakes may not at all be the right sort of person for you. Production of beautiful, healthy and intelligent children is one thing; compatibility is quite something else. But it's worse than this. The production of viable children may actually require that you seek out someone temperamentally unsuited to you. You've heard of the idea that opposites attract? Well, the idea was originally Schopenhauer's.

The theory behind the idea goes something like this. The will to life must ensure that the children you produce will be physically and psychologically fit enough to survive in a rather dangerous and demanding world. To do so, they must be both physically and psychologically suitable. Physically, they must be well proportioned – neither too tall nor too short, neither too fat nor too thin, etc.

But psychologically, they must also be well proportioned – neither too reckless nor too timid, neither too aggressive nor too passive, and so on. How does the will to life make sure this happens? Basically, it does it by way of the blending of opposites.

> *Everyone endeavours to eliminate through the other individual his own weaknesses, defects, and deviations from the type, lest they be perpetuated or even grow into complete abnormalities in the child which will be produced.*

Various breeding infelicities on the part of your parents – failures of the will to life, essentially – have left you too short, with a big nose, and a fat arse. What does the will to life do to rectify this? It makes you attracted to people who will cancel out these deficiencies in your children. That is, it makes you attracted to tall, small-nosed and slim-hipped people.

This is all statistical, of course. There is no guarantee that, in any individual case, this is what will happen. After all, sometimes beggars can't be choosers. You have to take what you can get – especially if you're a short, big-nosed fatty. But, as a general rule, Schopenhauer claimed, this is what will happen. This is all very well when we are talking about the physical characteristics of a person. But Schopenhauer applied the same theory to psychological characteristics. The general implication is that you will be attracted to people who are quite different from – and often incompatible with – you psychologically speaking. And you will be attracted to these people precisely because they are what is necessary to cancel out any psychological abnormalities you recognise in yourself.

> *Love ... casts itself on persons who, apart from the sexual relation, would be hateful, contemptible, and even abhorrent to the*

lover. But the will of the species is so much stronger than that of the individual, that the lover shuts his eyes to all the qualities repugnant to him, overlooks everything, misjudges everything, and binds himself for ever to the object of his passion.

Actually, not for ever, not these days. For what happens when the shagging stops, the children are produced, and the sexual instinct slaked? Staring right back at you is a person you don't really like or respect. And you're stuck with him or her – at least until you can get a divorce.

People today often express surprise at the rising divorce rates in the Western world. If they had read Schopenhauer, they would, perhaps, be less surprised. Reproduction, the production of beautiful, intelligent and healthy children, requires us to seek out sexual partners who would, typically, make poor life partners. They are partners who may supply us with good children, but, for precisely that reason, would not supply us with a good life.

Monica and Chandler: a Schopenhauerian analysis

The Platonic account seems entirely unsuited to explaining Monica and Chandler's relationship. It would be very implausible to think that they suddenly, in London, after all the years of being just friends, recognised the extent to which they each resembled the form of the beautiful. The form of the beautiful isn't like that. It doesn't sneak up on you; it hits you like a train. Whatever Monica and Chandler have for each other, it is not, I think, Plato's *eros*.

In fact, of all the love relationships in *Friends*, the one that seems to most closely fit Schopenhauer's analysis is that between Monica and Chandler. First of all, consider Monica's well-known idiosyncrasies. To begin with, she is, psychologically speaking, an extremely *masculine* woman – a not inconsiderable feat of acting given that Courteney Cox is such a cutie. Her masculinity has various typical expressions. First, there is her aggression. Most of the time, this remains beneath the surface. She isn't aggressive towards her friends in general – and a good thing too for they wouldn't stay her friends for long, at least not if Aristotle is right. But it does surface, typically in the context of sporting contests. Remember how much she enjoyed inflicting *foosball* humiliations on Chandler and Joey (You suck!). Moreover, her own family had, apparently, banned her from playing tag American football with Ross, due to the overly aggressive manner in which she prosecuted such activities. And look what happened when the attempt at resurrecting the 'Geller cup' led to the gang playing tag football in the park. This culminated in her and Ross lying on the ground for hours after everybody had left, each trying to claim ownership of the ball in the deciding play of the game. Or remember the table-tennis game with Mike in Barbados? Her aggression is, however, not limited to sporting contests. Monica is what some people call a Type-A personality – an ambitious, driven over-achiever.

In addition to her aggression, there is also her peculiarly anal approach to life in general, and to the tidying of the apartment in particular. Her friends have talked to her about this. Once she purposefully left a pair of shoes out on the living room floor when she went to bed – just to prove, to them and her, that she could do it. The result: she couldn't sleep a wink. This anal or obsessive side of her character may be a symptom of a certain sort of control freakishness that stems from the same source as her aggression, e.g. a desire to please grounded in insufficient love or approval from her parents. Who knows?

Monica's biological clock has been tick, ticking away for several years now, getting ever louder by the year. Given all of this, a marriage to an effeminate, passive and laid-back man is written all over her. And effeminate, passive and laid-back is, of course, precisely what Chandler is. These are pretty much his defining features. He's so effeminate he is constantly mistaken for being gay. This stemmed from earlier breeding infelicities on the part of his parents, Morgan Fairchild and … uh … Kathleen Turner – enough said? He's extremely passive, rather than aggressive. For example, he has no work-related ambitions other than to get a job – like advertising – that he enjoys. The whole idea of storming to the top of the career ladder is alien to him. And contrast his laid-back attitude around the apartment to Monica's. For several series, he and Joey kept ducks, and lived in a canoe.

So, Monica's will to life wants children, and Chandler is the closest thing there is to one who will provide her with suitable ones. He is, in effect, a sort of anti-Monica – and therefore someone who will help cancel out, in their children, the exaggerated masculinity, aggression and compulsiveness exhibited by Monica. And, of course, conversely: Monica would cancel out Chandler's excessive femininity and passivity.

The cosmic joke, of course, inflicted on Monica's will to life is that they seem to be incapable of having children. And having children, if they only knew it, is the entire reason for them being together. And so, I'm afraid, the future is somewhat murky for Monica and Chandler. Or at least it would be in the real world.

Ross loves Rachel: a Platonic analysis

Ross and Rachel's love – in the early series at least – seems to follow the Platonic model far more closely than the Schopenhauerian one. At least from Ross's side. Rachel has been the girl he lusted after all through high school, the beautiful friend of his fat sister. And she, presumably, came to resemble the form of the beautiful even more closely after she had the nose job. The adolescent Ross, therefore, fell in love, not with Rachel herself, but with the form of the beautiful that she closely resembled. With Rachel, on the other hand, I think there's something altogether different going on. But we'll get to that later.

Falling in love with the form of the beautiful is not a particularly rational thing to do. It's very difficult to come up with reasons explaining why you fell in love with beauty itself. Finding someone beautiful is, to a considerable extent, like preferring a certain flavour of ice cream. From your perspective, you either find someone beautiful or you do not. This is not because beauty is subjective. According to Plato's view, you can be wrong about whether someone is beautiful. The form of the beautiful, beauty itself, is a perfectly objective thing: beauty, for Plato, is definitely not in the eye of the beholder. Admittedly, with Jennifer Aniston you figure Ross is on reasonably safe ground in his judgment. But whether or not someone resembles the form of the beautiful, while it is an objective matter, is not the sort of thing you can give reasons for. You can't give reasons – not to other people and not even to yourself – explaining why someone resembles the form of the beautiful. They just do. Therefore, for the same reason, if your love for someone is Plato's *eros*, a passionate and intense yearning for the form of the beautiful, neither can you give reasons for loving someone. You just do.

Of course, this doesn't sit comfortably with Ross, at all – hyper-analytical pussy that he is. Therefore, he feels compelled to make the infamous *list* – detailing the pros and cons of Rachel versus the, then, incumbent of his affections, Julie. In the end, he simply acknowledges the inexplicable nature of his love for Rachel, by listing the biggest drawback of Julie as *not being Rachel*. This is all entirely consistent with the Platonic view, of course. Ross's love for Rachel is Plato's *eros*, a passionate and intense longing for the form of the beautiful she resembles. This is not the sort of thing you can rationalise or explain – you either see the form of the beautiful in someone, or you don't. Ross sees it in Rachel but not, alas, in Julie.

Joey and Rachel: all you need is philia?

I suppose the most notable thing about both models of love – the Platonic and the Schopenhauerian – is that we're screwed either way. If your love for someone corresponds to the Schopenhauerian model, then it's really all about producing healthy offspring. And the person you have picked to produce said offspring is one you have chosen to cancel out your own faults and shortcomings – both physical and psychological. For this reason, they are likely to be entirely incompatible with you. In fact, when the shagging stops, they are likely to make your life a living hell. And you were never really in love with them at all – your will to life was simply having its way with you.

In Plato's view, on the other hand, you are not really in love with the person you are supposedly in love with either. What you are in love with is the form of the beautiful, beauty itself. The person is a sort of gooseberry, a peripheral tag along, who gets in on the action only because they happen to resemble the form of the beautiful. This makes your relationship to the person – as opposed to their beauty – entirely unstable. Inevitably their beauty is going to fade – they will come to resemble the form of the beautiful less and less. And then, of course, you will have nothing. Your whole relationship was based on something that is no longer there.

So, either way, you're screwed. If you want a stable relationship with someone else, it's got to be based on more than love in either the Platonic or Schopenhauerian senses. What could this be? The answer is, in fact, staring us in the face all through the ten series of *Friends* – it's *philia*. That's why Monica and Chandler's marriage stands a chance of working, even though its Schopenhauerian motivation has been undercut. All you need, maybe, is *philia*?

The Rachel and Joey case is a good example of a relationship built on *philia*. They have known each other for ten years or so, so it's not as if they're going to suddenly get struck by just how much each resemble the form of the beautiful. That's the sort of thing you notice straight away. So, the Platonic analysis seems a non-starter. But the Schopenhauerian analysis doesn't seem to work either. It can't be about the will to life getting them together in order to produce beautiful, intelligent and healthy children – Rachel's already pregnant by Ross when Joey falls for her, and she's already had the baby by the time she falls for Joey.

So, in Joey and Rachel we have, in effect, an alternative to both the Platonic and the Schopenhauerian accounts of love. Their accounts may be true of some of the things we call love – but they can't be true of all of them. So, Joey and Rachel were pretty much our last hope – our only possible way out of the Platonic and Schopenhauerian accounts of love on which, as we have seen, we're screwed. But we all know, by now, that they don't stay together. Indeed, it's not even clear that they got together in the first place. It's tragic, truly tragic, that the writers of *Friends* have not read Aristotle.

According to Aristotle, the key to a loving relationship based on *philia* is *reciprocity*. This makes it very different from the passionate yearning of Plato's *eros*. Loving someone in Plato's sense does not require that they love you back. It doesn't even require that they be willing to piss on you if you were on fire. There's no reciprocity in *eros*; it often goes unrequited. But, as we have seen, *philia* is based around the notion of reciprocity. In particular, *philia* comes about because of two things. First, there is a considerable degree of *sameness* of the people involved. Aristotle claims that, to a considerable extent, for *philia* to occur, the two people involved must be similar in the way they behave, and they must want the same sorts of things. This distinguishes it from Schopenhauer's version of love that requires physically and psychologically dissimilar people so that their exaggerated features may be cancelled out in their children. Joey and Rachel seem to be similar in many ways. Neither, let's face it, is the sharpest tool in the box. Both like sitting around eating pizza and watching TV. And, of course, both have an interest, in somewhat different ways, in soaps.

No two people, of course, are exactly alike. And so, according to Aristotle, the other component of *philia* is the appropriate sort of *empathy* with the other person, and *toleration* of their foibles, quirks and failings. So, for *philia* to exist between two people, they have to be the sort of people who are not too aggressive, who don't bear grudges, who are not afraid to express their admiration for each other, who forgive the sorts of things that should be forgiven, who encourage when encouragement is necessary, and who caution when caution is required. Again Joey and Rachel fit the bill.

Conversely, *philia* is not going to be possible between people who are quarrelsome or aggressive towards each other. Nor will it be possible between people who never have a kind word for each other, who bear grudges, often seething away beneath the outwardly calm exterior. Nor will it be possible between people who cannot tolerate disagreement, or someone having a different opinion from them. It will not be possible between people who tend to put other people down, continually crapping on about their weaknesses rather than their strengths. Nor will *philia* be possible between people who simply *use* each other – whether this be for money, sex, company, emotional support or comfort. There's no problem with using someone – we all do it – but we had better be sure that's not the only reason why we keep them around.

The noticeable thing – and this was a point clearly emphasised by Aristotle – is that the sort of people who make the best friends – in the sense of *philia* – are the sort of people who are the best – period! One very good reason for becoming a good person, according to Aristotle, is because you have to be a good person in order to have good – and real – friends. It is only good people who are capable of *being* good friends. And for the very same reason, it is only good people who are capable of *having* good friends. Someone who uses other people, who constantly puts them down, who resents their weaknesses without appreciating their strengths, who never forgives – this is precisely the sort of person who will never have genuine friends.

Relationships based on *philia* are, Aristotle thinks, the best ones of all. However, I wouldn't be too quick to jettison the Platonic and Schopenhauerian alternatives. Each has a role to play in helping us with our relationships. On the one hand, there's a clear difference between love and simple friendship. You can be friends with stumpy trolls if you like, but there's no point in falling in love with them. Unless you're a stumpy troll yourself, of course. An intense and passionate yearning for the form of the beautiful never did anyone any harm. If you leave things at that, of course – that's when problems are going to arise down the road. But there's no harm in starting off there. The trick, then, is to fall in love with the person, and not simply their resemblance to beauty itself. And for this, what you need is *philia* – something that you might achieve if you are a good person, but won't if you are not.

What about Schopenhauer? Schopenhauer's view is also valuable – primarily as a cautionary tale. I, personally, think Schopenhauer is right. Our will to life – or as we say today, our genes – are constantly fucking with us. But we don't have to lie down and let our will to life walk all over us. We are not, necessarily, the will to life's butt monkey. To understand something is to be able to control it. When we recognise a motivation for what it is, we thereby acquire power over that motivation.

So, Plato's emphasis on beauty is something to be brought in to our loving relationships. Some people say that beauty is only skin deep. But, let's face it, what's under the skin is pretty nasty anyway! So: beauty – personally, I'm in favour of it! Schopenhauer's emphasis on the will to life and associated biological drives is, on the other hand, something to be recognised, but fought against rather than accepted.

Joey and Rachel, actually, seem to have absorbed the lessons of Plato, Aristotle and Schopenhauer quite well. As with all of us, I think, this is partly because of what they are, and partly because of what they've learned. Rachel is very attractive, of course. And, although I don't swing that way, I'm sure Joey is very handsome too. So they seem to have the Platonic angle covered. The Schopenhauerian angle is covered by, in effect, default: Rachel getting impregnated by Ross. She did fall victim to the will to life once, let's hope she learned from it. Rachel too, seems to have grown in the *philia* aspect of things. In earlier years, she was rather unforgiving and did hold grudges. And, as far as I, or any other man, is concerned, she and Ross clearly were *on a break*! But she definitely seems to have mellowed in recent years. And this would have boded well for the relationship – if the scriptwriters had bothered to read Aristotle.

All you need is philia – and a fine ass!

It's no accident that our exploration of the idea of love has brought us to the ancient philosophers Plato and Aristotle. Modernity – the philosophy of the modern age – was always going to have a hard time with love. Love – whatever else it might be – is an attachment to someone else, and attachments to other people, according to modernity, are second-class attachments. So, from the standpoint of modernity, love was always going to be something we had to fit in around more important things. Or, to put it another way, in modernity love is always a matter of *using* someone as a tool in your overall project of self-fulfilment. Plato's emphasis on love as directed towards something independent of our own projects – something valuable independently of whatever use we may have for it – helps moderate this *instrumental* view of love. This is further helped by Aristotle's insistence of the role that might be played in love by the sort of reciprocity that is characteristic of *philia*. If we want love in this modern age, we need a combination of Plato's *eros* and Aristotle's *philia*, and we should be ever wary of the nakedly instrumental view of love of the sort described by Schopenhauer. And so what can we learn from *Friends*? And from the wisdom of the ancients? Easy: as loving relationships go, *all you need is philia – and a fine ass!*

five
24

WHAT IS JUSTICE? AND HOW IMPORTANT IS IT?

Modern morality

Morality – haven't we done that to death already in the *Buffy* and *Sopranos* chapters? The sense of morality we are going to be looking at in this chapter – and in the next chapter on *Seinfeld* actually – is different. When we were talking about Buffy and Tony Soprano we were looking at what we might call *individual* morality. What does it mean for me, or some other individual, to have a moral *obligation*? What does it mean for me, or some other individual, to be evil, or to do something morally *wrong*? But there is another aspect of morality entirely, an aspect that focuses not on individuals but on society as a whole. Here the basic focus is not on what I should or shouldn't do in any given situation, but on society as a whole. What moral rules should we adopt to regulate the functioning of society as a whole? Philosophers often refer to these rules as rules of *justice*.

Modernity spawns a particular way of thinking about justice, one that really has no echo in anything that came before. As usual, it is modernity's individualism that lies behind it. Individualism tells us that self-realisation is what life is all about. Your only non-negotiable moral obligation is to develop yourself to the best of your abilities. However, if everyone sees their own fulfilment as their primary moral quest, then other people are going to appear to them as *means* – instruments that might help, or hinder, this quest. Each person is going to be motivated by different values – what is important to you is your fulfilment, and what's important to me is mine. And the value of everyone is going to be understood in what they can contribute to your fulfilment and not theirs. But no society can be run along those lines. Whenever disputes broke out, there would be no way of settling them – because what is important to you is not what is important to me. What we need, if society is going to work, is some sort of *impartiality*. And so we get the idea, characteristic of the modern age, that morality is all about impartiality. From your perspective, your fulfilment is what is important. From my perspective, it is my fulfilment that is crucial. What we need morality to supply us with, so the modern thought goes, is some way of counting all these as *equal*. We need a perspective from which my fulfilment is no more important than your fulfilment, and yours no more important than mine. This perspective is, precisely, the *moral* perspective.

And so, in the modern age, morality becomes equated with the concepts of *impartiality* and *equality*. These form the very essence of modern morality. To be moral is, precisely, to be impartial and, so, treat everyone as equal. However, the concepts of equality and impartiality are slippery ones – they are open to at least two different interpretations. And it is these two different interpretations, and the battle between them, that have more or less dominated the modern conception of justice. The debate between these two is cleverly brought out in the king of modern cliffhangers, *24*.

The life and times of Jack Bauer

It's not easy summarising 72 hours of blistering TV viewing. Thankfully, most of the philosophy I want to talk about in this chapter is contained in the first two series (2001–2). So, I'll just summarise 48 hours of blistering TV viewing. Easy. Or, rather, not. In fact, if you haven't seen the first two series, then, trust me, anything less than a hundred pages or so isn't going to make much sense anyway. And at the end of it all your viewing pleasure is going to be totally ruined by my giving away the endings anyway. So, if you've not seen them, (a) don't read this section and (b) go and buy the DVDs sharpish. If you have seen them, on the other hand, then there's no point you reading the summary anyway. Unless, like me, you're the sort of person who completely forgets the details of everything they ever watch. And the details – the twists and turns, the highs and lows, the happiness and the heartache – are what make *24* the great show that it is.

If the details are crystal clear to you, then here's the short version of series 1. Jack Bauer has to stop an assassination attempt on presidential candidate David 'the first black man with a realistic shot at the White House' Palmer. Jack wins.

The somewhat longer version: Jack Bauer is a man who works hard for a living – for the meagre salary he no doubt earns as Director of the US government's CTU – Counter Terrorist Unit. He has a habit of putting in very long days – not regularly, but at least three times. It's really not clear why he bothers. His marriage to wife Teri is on the rocks, and anyway he's been having an affair and even, for a short while, living with his colleague Nina Myers, who, let's face it, is marginally easier on the eye than Teri. You see, Teri has made the mistake that all wives make and has had her hair cut really short. Doesn't she know that longer hair is always better? Even when it sits on the head of a psychopathic terrorist-mercenary-spy? The main reason, it seems to me, why men don't want to get married is because they know that, as soon as they do, their wives will get their hair cut short.

And Jack's daughter Kim is not much better. Admittedly, her hair is not particularly short. But she is a total airhead brat whose one and only talent is getting kidnapped. Repeatedly. And even when she escapes, she always manages to find herself back in custody in no time at all. Kidnapping Kim is not a problem – it would be harder to *not* kidnap her. It's obviously some form of attention-seeking behaviour – a cry for help of some sort – perhaps because her father spends so much time at work.

Jack's first really long day in the office is the result of a plot to kill David Palmer, the presidential candidate, on the day of the California primary. Certain interests of a Serbian persuasion want Palmer dead. It's a long story, that doesn't emerge until about 13 hours into the first series. But, basically, a couple of years earlier, Palmer had authorised a mission into Kosovo to kill a fascist ethnic cleanser guy called Victor Drazen, played by Dennis Hopper. Hopper's recipe for success in this role apparently involves him playing exactly the same psycho he plays in every other thing in which he's played a psycho (which, come to think of it, is most of the things he's been in), and just adding a rather caricatured Eastern European accent. But – hey! – if people are going to keep throwing money at you … Anyway, Jack leads the mission. But it all gets fucked up. Jack's team is wiped out, and the only other people killed are Drazen's wife and daughter. So, he's out baying for revenge, his only impediment in this project being that he's a top-secret prison guest of the US Department of Defense. So, his sons, Andrei and Alexis, are running the show.

So, they commission a guy called Ira Gaines to assassinate Palmer. And in the bargain, they would also like Jack killed and/or disgraced. And Teri and Kim whacked too, of course. Gaines, being an imaginative hitter, comes up with the idea of getting Jack to assist in the killing of Palmer, and then taking the rap for it himself. So, he kidnaps Teri and Kim – planning to whack them later, thus satisfying desideratum three of the deal – and gets Jack to smuggle a gun into Palmer's breakfast press conference. Palmer is to be offed – desideratum number one – by a shooter who has had plastic surgery to resemble a photographer – the real photographer being in fact killed by an explosion on his plane initiated by the lovely Mandy, who makes another appearance at the end of series 2. (I told you this wouldn't make any sense unless you had seen the thing.) Then, Jack is to receive the gun from the shooter, and be disgraced and locked up – desideratum number two. Anyway, Jack cunningly manages to thwart the assassination attempt, and then save his wife and daughter, killing Gaines in the process. By now, we're a little over 12 hours down, and 36 to go.

The second half of series 1, hours 13–24, centres on the Drazen family. Not content with killing Palmer, framing Jack and killing Teri and Kim, Andrei and Alexis have been planning to bust their father out of a top-secret military prison. In this, they succeed. Or rather, Andrei does, because Alexis has been stabbed by one of the young – and slightly psychotic – female aides of Palmer who, unbeknown to her, he was shagging in order to get information.[16] But, anyway, Victor gets sprung, and in the process they have the bonus of capturing Jack, who they now plan to use to kill Palmer (again).

In the meantime, Kim gets kidnapped again. Jack gets sent off to kill Palmer, which he doesn't do even though he makes it seem like he does. Then off he goes to kill the Drazens, or what's left of

---

16. I mean, she knew he was shagging her, but she didn't know why. One of the penalties of a philosophical education is that one lives alone in a world of ambiguity.

them, because he thinks they have killed his daughter Kim. But, in fact, they haven't killed her – she's escaped! And the only reason Jack thinks they have killed her is because – shock, horror! – Nina Myers has told him that they have! Yes, Nina Myers, despite having marginally longer hair than Teri, turns out to be an evil terrorist-mercenary-spy-traitor. Actually, it's not clear what exactly she is, but whatever it is, it's not good. More than this: in her attempted escape from CTU, she whacks Teri, which pisses Jack off no end. End of series 1.

Then on to series 2! The short version. Jack has to stop Islamic terrorists detonating a nuclear bomb in downtown Los Angeles. Jack wins again.

The somewhat longer version. Islamic terrorists, led by a guy called Syed Ali, have managed to smuggle a nuclear bomb into the country and, as Islamic terrorists tend to do, have decided to detonate it in downtown Los Angeles. Jack has to stop them. Not that he's head of CTU any more. He's still out trying to put his life back together, after having his former wife offed by his former lover. And also getting his daughter Kim to talk to him again would be a good thing too. But a plea from the now President Palmer – the lucky S.O.B. who managed to divorce his evil wife, have a son on a murder charge, and *still* make it to the White House – gets him back on board. So, Jack springs immediately into action, cutting off a nonce's head in order to infiltrate his way into a terrorist group – this time an extreme right-wing one. From there, he manages to track down the author of the Islamic plot, Syed Ali. He locates the bomb, flies it out of Los Angeles, and then George Mason, the new boss of CTU, who is dying of radiation poisoning anyway, crashes it into the desert. We're still only halfway through the series and, as you might expect, there are twists and turns aplenty to come.

In addition to the Islamic plot, there is a plot by various people – including Palmer's evil ex-wife, Sherry – both inside and outside the government. The people in the government have apparently decided that Palmer is too much of a bed-wetting liberal, and, in particular, want him to take a tougher stance on the Middle East in the form of bombing it back to the Stone Age. The people outside the government are the old favourites of scriptwriters who are a bit hard up for ideas – the evil military-industrial complex. Anyway, Palmer has ordered an air strike on an unnamed Middle Eastern country – though just between you and me it looks very like Syria – and Jack has to prove that the evidence implicating Syria – sorry the undisclosed Middle Eastern country – is, in fact, a forgery. It all turns out all right in the end. Except for the fact that Jack looks to have a serious and perhaps irreversible heart condition brought on by all the torture he had to undergo at the hands of the evil military complex. Oh, and David Palmer looks like he might have been assassinated anyway, courtesy of the lovely Mandy, who we've not seen since the early episodes of series 1, where she was watching her girlfriend get blown away by a distinctly crotchety Ira Gaines.

Believe it or not, crawling diffidently out on either side of each line of this mazy plot – all 48 hours of it – is a clear and respectable philosophical theme. It's one that has had a long and distinguished philosophical history, stretching all the way back to Socrates – the ancient Greek philosopher of fifth-century BC Athens. The theme? *Justice*. Modernity, however, gives it a slightly different spin.

Justice: fundamental questions

Just about everyone agrees that justice is all about what's *right*, or, more helpfully, what's *fair*. This idea, in fact, stems all the way back to Socrates (*c.* 470–399 BC) who had this vague idea that justice involves giving people what they are owed. Treating someone justly involves giving them what they are owed, or what they deserve. Of course, working out what people deserve is the hard part, and lots of people have lots of different ideas about this.

Begin by asking yourself a question. It is, I think, the most fundamental question you can ask about justice:

Does the end justify the means?

If you answer 'yes' to this question, you are going to have one sort of view of justice; if you answer 'no', you are going to have a quite different one.

Probably the most famous 'yes' answer to the question is provided by the moral theory known as *utilitarianism*. Advocates of utilitarianism are known, not entirely unexpectedly, as *utilitarians*. The basic idea behind utilitarianism is that we should all try to increase the overall amount of happiness in the world. And an action is morally good if, and in fact only if, it increases this overall amount of happiness. So, for utilitarians, happiness is the *end* – the purpose of all action – and anything that you do to increase happiness is a *means* to that happiness. For utilitarians, just about anything can be legitimately used as a means to increasing happiness. What is crucial for them is that you increase happiness. As long as you do that everything is hunky-dory morally speaking, and how you pulled off the increase in happiness does not matter.

So, one thing that utilitarianism does seem to entail is that it is morally OK to use people as means. It is OK to trick people, deceive them, even make them desperately unhappy, as long as the overall result is an increase in the amount of happiness in the world. How could this be if you make them unhappy? Well, if their unhappiness in some way makes other people happy – lots of other people, for example – then one person's misery can result in an overall increase in happiness in the world. If so, it would be morally OK to make that person miserable. In fact, more than that – it would, for utilitarians, actually be wrong *not* to make them miserable. Their misery is a means to other people's happiness; and if the other people's happiness outweighs the first person's misery then you are, according to utilitarianism, morally obligated to make the first person miserable.

Note also that this doesn't depend on whether the person you make miserable deserves it. Whether they are innocent or guilty or whatever is irrelevant to utilitarianism. The only thing that matters is whether happiness is increased. To treat people with justice, for utilitarianism, simply involves trying to increase the overall amount of happiness in the world. And if some people have to be sacrificed in this project, sacrificing them is what justice requires us to do.

Utilitarianism is one way of interpreting the modern idea that morality is all about equality and impartiality. Utilitarianism makes people equal by treating everyone as, in effect, a means. Or, more precisely, their happiness or welfare is treated as a means, a means towards the end that is the general happiness, the happiness of society as a whole. And, as a means, everyone counts equally. My happiness is no more important and no less important than yours, and your happiness is no more important and no less important than anyone else's. In this way, utilitarianism provides a recipe for treating everyone with impartiality.

The alternative to making everybody equal by treating them as a means, of course, is to make them equal by treating them as *ends*. This is the basis of the other major modern approach to justice, an approach championed by a guy called Immanuel Kant (1724–1804). Kant, who was not exactly the clearest writer who ever lived, used to say things like:

Act so that you treat humanity, whether in your own person or
in that of another, always as an end, and never as a means only.

All he's getting at is that you shouldn't use other people as means, and you shouldn't allow yourself to be used as a means – and this applies no matter how important and pressing the end.

In more recent times, Kant's intellectual descendants have transformed his theory into a claim about human rights. The claim that people should not be used as means has become translated into the idea that people possess certain moral *rights*. Some of these rights are *inalienable* in that they cannot be overridden no matter what. No matter how much the overall amount of happiness in the world might be increased by trampling over someone's inalienable rights, you should not do this. Rights are sort of like moral *trumps* – they win out over all considerations of general happiness or welfare.

Working out a proper account of justice amounts to working out which of these two types of moral theory – utilitarianism or Kant – is correct. And *24* gives us lots of material to work with. Especially series 2, actually, although the theme is clearly evident in series 1 also. Lots of people are going to die in a nuclear explosion in Los Angeles unless the bomb is located. But locating the bomb, it seems, is going to require Jack to take off the kid gloves and ride roughshod over a whole bunch of individual rights. So, we have a situation in which individual rights have to be balanced against the general happiness. On which side of the moral divide does Jack fall? Utilitarianism or Kant? And what's the role of David Palmer?

Suppose we can sort out all these issues; work out whether Kantians or utilitarians provide the best moral theory. If we can, then we will have a theory of justice: an account that tells us what we should do if we want to treat people with justice. Even if we can get this – and I think it's fair to say that no one has yet arrived at a theory that everyone accepts – then there is still another question to be looked at.

The emphasis on justice is, itself, a feature of the modern age. A fairly standard view, for example, is to think that justice is the centrepiece of all morality. There may be other aspects to morality, but these are secondary, and subservient, to the role played by justice. Justice is thought to be so important because of the role individualism plays in shaping modern thinking. If everyone is a psychic monad, a point-centre of consciousness whose overriding moral goal is self-fulfilment, then our attachments to others are peripheral to who and what we are. Ties such as loyalty, friendship, devotion, love – these are just lifestyle choices, and can be revoked by a new choice just as they were introduced by an earlier one. And they do not reach to the core of us. The peripheral role these ideas play in modern conceptions of morality reflects the peripheral role they play in the constitution of the person. The type of morality we adopt echoes the sort of things we take ourselves to be. And what do we take ourselves to be? If we are modern, we take ourselves to be monadic selves who shape their lives through the choices they make. The primary function of morality is to inject a degree of impartiality in the ranking of these choices that will allow society to function reasonably smoothly. And so we have the emphasis on justice in modern conceptions of morality.

However, justice, when you think about it, is a cold and impersonal thing. To treat everyone with justice is to treat everyone according to the same rules and principles – no matter who they are, and no matter who they are to *you*. Sons and strangers, friends and fiends: all have to be treated according to the same rules – the rules of justice. But, on the other hand, it certainly seems as if you owe your family and (perhaps) friends more than you owe complete strangers. Or, putting the point the other way around, it seems that your family and perhaps your friends deserve more *from* you because of who they are *to* you. We could put this point in terms of the idea of *loyalty*. There are certain bonds of loyalty that exist between you and other members of your family, or between you and your friends, and these sorts of bonds cannot exist between you and strangers or mere acquaintances.

Even if we have worked out what justice is, we still have a question about where loyalty fits into the scheme of things. When justice and loyalty conflict, which comes out on top? Can loyalty outweigh justice? Or is it justice that always wins? Or does it all depend on circumstances? If so, what circumstances? And how does it depend on them?

This is, in effect, the second question of justice. The first question was 'What is justice?' The second question is 'Is justice the fundamental principle of morality?' A characteristically modern view is that justice always wins out over loyalty, and so loyalty is a secondary, less important, principle, one that has any force only after justice has had its say. If, on the other hand, justice does not always win out, then there is more to morality than simply justice, and we may have to re-evaluate the modern view.

It is the first series that provides the best materials for discussing this second question of justice. This is because the first series revolves around various kidnappings of Jack's family, particularly the inept Kim. So Jack is forced to balance the ties of loyalty he has to his family against the injustice that would be involved in killing, or helping to kill, an innocent man. Loyalty requires him to do one thing. Justice, it seems, requires him to do another. The question is not only which *does* win out over the other, but the even more important: which *should* win out?

The first question – the question of what justice actually is – is treated most fully in the second series. The basic question being examined, discussed and debated in the second series is which moral theory provides the best account of justice – utilitarianism or Kant's view. So, it is with the second series – but the first question – that we shall begin.

Utilitarianism: the greatest good for the greatest number

On the first question, 'What is justice?' it's pretty clear which side of the moral divide Jack Bauer is going to fall. He's an out and out utilitarian. No surprise there – you only have to look at his initials J.B. These are precisely the same initials as those of Jeremy Bentham (1748–1832), the English moral philosopher who founded utilitarianism.

The basic idea behind utilitarianism is simple. A good action is one that increases the overall amount of happiness in the world. A bad action is one that decreases the overall amount of happiness in the world. And if an action neither increases nor decreases the overall amount of happiness in the world then it is morally neutral. Or, as Bentham put the idea (slightly inaccurately actually, but we all know what he means): *the greatest good for the greatest number*. What we should all be trying to do, morally speaking, is produce the greatest amount of good for the greatest number of people. Utilitarians called this good or happiness that we are all supposed to increase 'utility', and that's where their name comes from.

This utilitarian principle may seem obviously true. What else could morality be about if not making the world a better place and all that sort of stuff? And how else can you make the world a better place if not by making more people happy? But there are, in fact, all sorts of problems with this utilitarian idea. The problems come in two sorts. First, there's the problem of working out exactly what happiness is. Secondly, there's the problem that all sorts of things can make people happy, and not all of these, it seems, are good.

Hopefully, by now, *Sex and the City* will have convinced you that coming up with an account of happiness is not the easiest thing in the world. But if we are supposed to try and increase the overall amount of happiness or utility in the world, then the first thing we need to know is what happiness is. And, in fact, utilitarians have been bickering about this ever since utilitarianism was up and running.

Bentham, the guy who started it all, tended to think of happiness as something like pleasure. This, as we have seen, is a characteristically modern view of happiness, and has its problems. Bentham, in fact, would have been a natural for those government-sponsored studies that ask you about how you feel when you're having sex and how you feel when you are talking to your boss, and so on. Because that's virtually what happiness amounted to for Bentham: a feeling of some sort. This feeling can accompany many different things – depending on who the person who has the feeling is, and what gets their juices flowing. Opera does it for some, mud wrestling for others. For Bentham it doesn't matter what does it for you – as long as something does. And what's important is the happiness that gets produced in you, and not what produces that happiness.

On the other hand, John Stuart Mill (1806–73), another utilitarian, disagreed. Elitist that he was, Mill thought we could distinguish higher pleasures from lower ones. 'It's better to be Socrates dissatisfied than a fool satisfied,' he claimed. And 'better to be a human dissatisfied than a pig satisfied'. And if the fool or the pig is of a different opinion, Mill claimed, this is because they are in no position to make the comparison. In other words, no human, however dissatisfied, would exchange his or her life for the life of a pig, however satisfying the pig's life may be. And Socrates, no matter how much his life sucks, would not exchange his lot for that of a fool, no matter how much sex the fool was getting. Or so Mill claimed.

I always used to think Mill was just a snob on this point. No matter how trivial the source of happiness, I thought, no matter how petty, piddling, insignificant, hackneyed, simplistic or ante-diluvian the source: happiness is happiness. But then I watched *I'm a Celebrity, Get Me Out of Here!* and realised that Mill may have been on to something. This, of course, may just be a sign of incipient middle age, or possibly intellectual fascism, on my part. But the point is that the first thing utilitarianism needs is some account of happiness that is going to satisfy everyone. And this is not an easy thing to get. We probably shouldn't be too hard on utilitarianism for this, however. Any moral theory is going to have to come up with some account of human happiness or well-being, and utilitarianism is no worse off than any other theory in this regard.

However, the problems the utilitarian has in working out the nature of happiness are just symptoms of a more serious problem. The *I'm a Celebrity* worry was that happiness could, in some people, be produced by things that are so inane, vapid and fatuous that it somehow calls into question the quality of happiness produced. This was Mill's point. But the point can be extended further, and now we are into the second type of problem. Happiness can be produced by things that are not just inane, vapid and fatuous, but also by things that are positively *wrong*.

Schadenfreude – taking delight in bad things happening to other people – is just a sad truth about the world. OK, maybe the bastards deserve it, but even so: some people are just a little too *schadenfreudic* for their own – or anyone else's – good.

Suppose, for example, the terrorists in series 2 actually succeed in detonating the nuclear bomb in Los Angeles. Then, if history is anything to go by, a lot of people are actually going to be made very happy by this. You only have to recall 9/11 and the widespread jubilation seen in the streets of many Middle Eastern countries to realise this. Does this mean that detonating the bomb was, from a utilitarian perspective, a good thing to do? Probably not. The utilitarian will reply that the amount of unhappiness felt in the US and other countries would outweigh the happiness felt in the Middle East. So, overall, the world would be an unhappier place. Therefore, detonating the bomb was a morally bad thing to do.

But the utilitarian reply here misses the point. The point is that the happiness people feel in the suffering of others is a morally illegitimate form of happiness and shouldn't be included in utilitarian calculations in the first place. We could always vary the scenario in *24* so that the amount of happiness produced by the bomb outweighs the amount of unhappiness it causes. Maybe, instead of being detonated in Los Angeles, it blew up in Bumfuk, Idaho, for example. The point is that if we were to come up with a scenario where the happiness in the Arab world actually outweighed the unhappiness in the US, it still wouldn't be right to detonate the bomb.

What we seem to need is a way of distinguishing morally legitimate from morally spurious forms of happiness. There are, it seems, certain forms of happiness that it is OK to feel and certain forms that you simply shouldn't feel because you feel them for morally illegitimate reasons. If you're sick enough to take delight in the suffering of innocent people, for example, then this sort of happiness simply should not count morally. It should not be part of utilitarian calculations used to determine the overall amount of happiness in the world.

The problem for the utilitarian is that they cannot draw this distinction between morally legitimate and morally spurious forms of happiness. What is right and what is wrong, for the utilitarian, can only emerge *after* the relevant calculations about happiness and unhappiness have been made. Something is morally right if it increases the amount of happiness in the world, and it is morally wrong if it decreases this overall amount of happiness. So, right and wrong are things that emerge only after the calculations are made. But the distinction between morally legitimate and morally spurious forms of happiness is a distinction that is supposed to operate *prior* to the calculations being made. This is because the distinction is supposed to be what decides which forms of happiness get included in the calculations in the first place. Morally legitimate forms get included, morally spurious forms do not. So, the utilitarian needs something that, by his own principles, he cannot have: a standard of moral right and wrong that exists prior to utilitarian calculations.

It is precisely at this point that the Kantian inspired alternative approach to justice is at its most persuasive. A standard of right and wrong that exists prior to utilitarian calculations, one that operates before utilitarian calculations even get going, is, so some people argue, one that is based on the idea of individual rights. The idea is that all people have rights to certain sorts of things, and certain sorts of treatment, and these rights cannot be overridden by utilitarian calculations about overall happiness. The idea is that any happiness that results from the violation of someone's rights is morally spurious or illegitimate happiness, and so should not be included in utilitarian calculations in the first place. If, for example, you have a right not to be blown up in a terrorist atrocity, then any happiness other people feel from your being blown up in such an atrocity is a morally illegitimate form of happiness. As such, it should not be included in utilitarian calculations. So what if you are an infidel, or even a bit of a bastard, and the world would be a happier place with you not in it: blowing you up still violates your moral rights, and so should not be done.

Or so the argument goes. Let's see how the dispute between utilitarians and their rights-based opponents plays out in the context of series 2 of *24*.

Jack on justice

Jack Bauer is pretty clearly a big fan of Bentham. There are very few means that are too extreme for Jack, as long as the end is important enough. The end that dominates series 2 – or, at least, the first half of series 2 – is locating the nuclear bomb that Islamic terrorists are going to detonate in Los Angeles. Admittedly – a particularly pressing and substantial end. So, what does Jack do about it? Obvious. He kills a perp he's been interrogating, and cuts his head off. Jack wants to infiltrate a terrorist group, and the perp was not very popular with the leader of this group. So Jack figures bringing him this guy's head will be a good way of ingratiating himself. The end – preventing the detonation of the bomb – is, Jack deems, important enough to justify the somewhat radical means. This is the way utilitarians think, and so to Jeremy Bentham we can add Jack Bauer to the list of illustrious utilitarians.

As a point of interest, the producers of the show are clearly not quite sure how far we, the audience, were going to side with Jack in his utilitarian predilections. So, they had to reduce our sympathies with the guy who gets his head cut off by making him a convicted nonce, indeed child killer, who was going to escape jail by way of some plea bargain, subsequent to which he would be free to hightail it back to the Internet chatrooms and prey on our children some more. So, well done Jack – you were right after all! Fuck this guy's rights to due legal process.

For utilitarianism, what is good, and ultimately the only thing that is good, is to increase the overall amount of happiness in the world. If such an increase involves riding roughshod over the rights of an individual or individuals, then that is the right thing to do. The notion of individual rights is, according to Jeremy Bentham, *nonsense*. And the idea of inalienable rights, rights that a person has no matter what, is *nonsense on stilts*! His modern-day disciple, Jack Bauer, would echo this wholeheartedly.

Strangely enough, Jack's utilitarianism is echoed in the attitudes of his terrorist adversaries. The justification for detonating the bomb in Los Angeles is not simply that America is the Great Satan, peopled by worthless infidels. At least, that's not the official justification given by Marie Warner for her involvement. Instead, the justification is that so many bad things have been happening in the Middle East for so long that a terrorist atrocity on the scale of the Los Angeles one – with a projected death toll of a couple of million or so – is the only way to change American policy permanently in the Middle East and ensure that these bad things do not continue happening. In other words, the justification is that *in the long run*, overall good, even overall happiness, will best be promoted by the detonation of the bomb. Short-term unhappiness will be great, particularly in the immediate Los Angeles vicinity, and more diffusely in the rest of the US and West. However, in the long run, more good will come of it, and this long-term good will outweigh the suffering and distress caused by the immediate aftermath of the bomb.

This reveals an interesting problem with utilitarianism. Two people, or groups of people, can be utilitarians, apply utilitarian principles in a reasonably straightforward way, and come out with completely opposite conclusions about what is the best thing to do. This, of course, has to throw into question the usefulness of utilitarianism. If utilitarians, applying utilitarian principles, can come up with completely opposite conclusions about what is the best thing to do in a given situation, then it doesn't seem as if utilitarianism can give us any real help in telling us what to do in that situation. The problem is that it's all very well being told to increase the overall amount of happiness in the world – but often, it simply isn't clear *what*, exactly, is going to increase the overall amount of happiness in the world.

Palmer's response

Despite being on the same side as him politically, David Palmer provides a nice moral counterpoint to Jack's utilitarianism. This is not to say that Palmer is never a utilitarian. Sometimes he's not averse to a little utilitarian action. When he discovers that Roger Stanton, the head of CIA, has been aiding the bombers and plotting against his presidency, he wastes no time whatsoever in sending him off for a little bit of torture. Here, the end clearly does justify overriding Stanton's individual rights, or so Mr President would have us believe.

However, a lot of the time Palmer doesn't seem to be a utilitarian at all. Take, for example, the Syed Ali torture scene. Jack has managed to capture Syed Ali, and urgently needs to extract some information from him, what with the bomb about to go off and all. The more straightforward forms of torture have yielded only mixed results, and the bomb is still unaccounted for. So Jack – good utilitarian that he is – hits on the idea of having Syed Ali's children executed in front of his eyes. If this works, then it seems exactly what we should do if we are good utilitarians. OK, Syed Ali will be none too happy about the whole thing. His wife and remaining, unexecuted, family members will be extremely unhappy too. And, of course, his children will be very unhappy indeed in the run-up to their deaths. No utilitarian will like this, of course; unhappiness is an intrinsically bad thing. But weigh this unhappiness against what would happen if the bomb actually did go off. Here the unhappiness would, in varying degrees, extend to millions. So, if we are good, and consistent, utilitarians we should be happy to endorse the execution of innocent children if this is the only way to prevent nuclear catastrophe.

Palmer, however, demurs. The execution of innocent children is, despite his flirtation with utilitarianism, apparently not his bag at all. Why should this be? Well, it seems he must think that executing innocent children is wrong – even if it has hugely beneficial consequences. Innocent children, he must think, have a moral right not to be executed, even if doing so may save millions of lives. The fact that Palmer takes this line shows, at the very least, that he is not a consistent utilitarian. The idea of moral rights plays at least some role in his moral outlook.

In the end, of course, an ideal utilitarian solution is found. But since Palmer had nothing to do with this, it can't be that he was trying to save his utilitarian principles here. It is Jack who comes up with the solution: *pretend* to execute Syed Ali's children before his eyes. The whole thing is faked, but, nevertheless, the results are just as good. Syed Ali cracks, reveals the whereabouts of the bomb, and everyone lives happily ever after. Nearly. This is an even better solution from the utilitarian perspective. Not only do the inhabitants of Los Angeles not suffer – and bring worldwide happiness levels way down – but also neither, in any long-term sense, do Syed Ali's children. Apart from the permanent psychological scarring, of course. At the very least, all parties suffer a lot less than if the children had been executed. So, well done Jack. But the question marks remain about David Palmer's moral consistency, or lack of it.

Another example of Palmer's failure to live up to utilitarian principles can be found in his determination to *do the right thing, come what may*! So, in the first series, his son may have killed a white guy who raped his sister. He swears it was an accident, but will a jury believe that? The whole thing has been covered up by his manipulative and duplicitous wife Sherry, and Karl, the Democratic Party fixer. So, the question a utilitarian would pose is this: would overall happiness best be served if the shit were allowed to hit the fan now? Who would gain from it? Palmer is going to be miserable, since his son will soon be behind bars, the bitch of a big, fat, white guy called Bubba. Sherry will be miserable, her First Lady aspirations in the garbage can of history. The son will be miserable, incarcerated and, presumably, not in any way attracted to Bubba. The sister will be miserable – feelings of responsibility weighing down on her etc. The entire Democratic Party will be miserable, since the scandal, much like Michael Dukakis in 1988, would probably destroy them as a credible threat for the foreseeable future. So, many people would be made unhappy, and few made happy, by Palmer's decision to bring things out into the open.

Does he listen to this sound utilitarian reasoning? Of course not, he's David Palmer, and he's going to do the right thing though the heavens fall! What does this show? That he has some idea of 'the right thing' that is independent of utilitarian principles. If utilitarian reasoning tells him to do one thing, but his sense of what is right tells him to do the opposite, then his sense of what is right is not a utilitarian one: it cannot be explained in terms of utilitarian principles.

David Palmer is, perhaps, a morally confused man. He is quite happy, on utilitarian grounds, to royally screw Stanton and whatever rights he has. But he doesn't think it is right to execute innocent children, even the children of terrorists about to blow up Los Angeles. This is, it seems, because he thinks they have rights – moral rights – that cannot be overridden no matter what. Moral rights are like trumps – if terrorists' children have them, then people must respect them, no matter what the utilitarian calculus says. That's what rights are: things that you are supposed to respect, though the heavens fall.

Moral confusion is not, perhaps, an ideal quality you would look for in a president. But it's not the be all and end all. On the plus side, being morally confused is a lot better than being simply confused – as Reagan arguably was through most of his two terms. And, unlike Clinton, there's no evidence that he's disposed to luring female interns into the Oval Office for a game of hide-the-cigar. And unlike Dubya, he at least tries to think things through before bombing the crap out of other countries. Say what you like about being morally confused, it's better than being morally challenged.

The pizza of life

'Life,' my momma always used to say, 'is like a pizza.' 'No,' she would add, 'not a fecking box of chocolates; a pizza.' Specifically: a *slice* of pizza. When the great pizza maker in the sky sprinkles out the toppings – the jalapeños, the pineapples, green chillies, peppers, onions, mushrooms – He's not exactly scrupulous in making sure of an even distribution. Apparently He just whacks them on and lets them fall where they may. The result is anything but fair. Some slices are lucky enough to be loaded with jalapeño and pineapples, others have to make to do with mushrooms and onions. It's just not fair. And while it doesn't really matter if you plan on eating the whole thing yourself, if you have to share it then disputes can easily break out. And sharing pizza is what life is all about.

Suppose you have the boys (or girls for that matter) around. You're all drinking beer, and the pizza has just arrived. You're watching some vicious, testosterone-fuelled contest like boxing, rugby, gridiron, or *Pop Idol*, and fights are likely to break out if everyone doesn't get a fair share of pizza. What's the best way of ensuring that everyone gets a decent slice? Basically: make sure that the person who slices the pizza doesn't know which slice he or she is going to get. Yes, I know that pizza usually comes sliced, but just suppose this pizza isn't – either because the place you bought it from is incredibly cheap, or because they like making points about the distributive character of justice. Or whatever. The best way to ensure an even – a *fair* or *just* – distribution is to make sure that the person who slices the pizza doesn't know which slice he is going to get. Make him pick last, for example. Then, he must do the slicing in what we might call a *condition of ignorance*. Then, if he is at all rational, he should make sure that the pizza is sliced as evenly as possible.

How is life like a slice of pizza? Well, just as the sprinkling of toppings on a pizza is uneven, random and often, apparently, unfair, so the sprinkling of natural talents, abilities and skills in us is often uneven, random and, apparently, unfair. Some of us look like gods or goddesses, are athletically gifted, and have IQs of 150 plus. Others of us are ugly, smelly geeks, with the IQ of a cabbage. But it's not just talents and abilities that are unevenly distributed. So too are all the features that go into making you the person you think you are. So, you're a man, rather than a woman? That's just like being a slice with onion rather than mushroom. You're black rather than white? That's just like a slice with pineapple but no green pepper. And so on. Man/woman, black/white, god/geek, athlete/dork, brain/brainless. All these sorts of features are distributed in us much as the toppings are sprinkled on a pizza.

So, what's the best way of choosing a fair society? One where someone is not penalised for having jalapeño but no pineapple? Easy – make sure that the person who chooses how society is going to be doesn't know which sprinkling of talents, abilities and features he/she is going to have. Indeed, make sure that he/she doesn't know if he/she is he or she. The person who chooses how society is going to be must choose from a *condition of ignorance*. The person who chooses doesn't know who or what he/she is going to be. Therefore, in trying to choose the best for him/her, he/she automatically chooses the best for everyone. Or so the idea goes.

The idea, in fact, comes from a political philosopher called John Rawls, an intellectual descendant of Kant. We can make sure the great pizza of life is sliced evenly if we do the slicing in a condition of ignorance. Just as we are not to know which slice of the pizza we are to get in the pizza lottery, so too we are not to know how we do in the lottery of life. To do this, imagine a situation in which you know virtually nothing about yourself. It's difficult to imagine this. But suppose you have severe, but temporary, amnesia. You're also in a dark room, and so cannot see yourself, and paralysed so you cannot feel yourself. You can fill in the details. Because of your problems, you don't, let's suppose, know whether you are a man or a woman, black or white, rich or poor, god or geek, athlete or dork, brain or brainless, and so on. Then, you have to ask yourself: how would I like society to be? Rawls calls this sort of scenario the *original position*. What you would choose in this sort of position, at least if you were rational (and we will suppose that you are) is, he thinks, a *fair* or *just* society. Since you don't know who or what you are, in choosing the best for you, you automatically choose what is best for everyone.

Of course, we can't really imagine ourselves in this sort of original position. But this doesn't really matter. The original position is just an imaginative way of making graphic a particular question: how would you feel if you were in the other guy's shoes? In effect, it's a version of the Christian golden rule: do unto others etc. So while you can't really imagine yourself not knowing whether you were a man or a woman, white or black or whatever, you can still just do the best you can. If you do, then you will be as fair as you can in your moral thinking.

One important thing you will not know in the original position is what you *value*. That is, you won't know your value system – which things you cherish, and which things you despise, and which things you don't really give a rat's arse about one way or another. It may be that you will turn out to be a Serbian fascist who cherishes ethnic cleansing and despises Jack Bauer and David Palmer. It may be that you will turn out to be someone who is ethnically cleansed. It may be that you will turn out to be Jack Bauer or David Palmer. It may be that you turn out to be a fanatical Islamic terrorist, who values the death of all infidels. It may be that you are a resident of Los Angeles who is on the business end of the fanatical terrorist's nuclear bomb. So, in the original position, you don't know what you will value, or how you will suffer because of what other people value.

The idea of the original position gives us a way of thinking what a fair or just society – even a just *global* society – would be like. If, in the original position, you would choose for society to be a certain way, then the chances are that is a fair or just way for society to be. As long as you don't screw up in your reasoning, of course. It also gives us a way of thinking about the idea of *moral rights*. When we say that someone has a right to something, what we mean, on the present suggestion, is that if someone were in the original position they would choose for that person to have that thing. Suppose someone claims they have a right to education. Then, the idea is that what this means is that someone in the original position would choose a society where this person was educated. Why would they choose this? For all they know they might turn out to be this person. Moral rights stem from the idea of justice, and justice comes down to how you would choose society to be if you had to make the choice from the perspective of the original position. People have moral rights because that is what is *fair*, and so that is what is *just*.

So, the original position provides us with a way of providing what seemed to be lacking in utilitarianism: a notion of moral rights. What it doesn't seem to provide, however, is any useful way of making moral decisions. Not generally anyway. I mean some cases are pretty clear. Presumably, if you had any sense, you wouldn't choose a society in which people routinely detonated nuclear devices in large cities. That would be way too risky. You don't know who you are, and the chances are that you could be living in that city. If, say, two people were involved in detonating it, and two million people died as a result, then there is a far greater likelihood that you will be one of the two million rather than one of the two. So, you could say that you have a moral right to not have nuclear devices detonated in your vicinity. And since, in the original position, you don't know where your vicinity is, this is the same as saying that people, in general, have a moral right not to have nuclear devices detonated in their vicinity.

How about some more difficult cases? Would you, in the original position, choose a society that permitted torture? No, you might think, because I could be one of the people tortured. But what if the torture was, as in the case of Roger Stanton, aimed at uncovering information that could save millions of lives? If you were rational, it seems that you should choose a world where this was allowed. If two million people were to die in the nuclear explosion, then you are two million times more likely to die in the nuclear explosion than be the torture victim. So, it would be rational to choose a society that permitted torture under these circumstances. So, Palmer got it right? Maybe. But then the problem becomes how you decide what circumstances are important enough to justify torture. How many people have to die? What is the probability that the event in question will happen? How many people can be tortured in order to prevent this? And so on.

In the end, the chances are that this approach will be just as vague as utilitarianism when it comes to handing out any sort of decent moral advice. And, I think, that's what morality comes down to in the end – all these grey areas that we really have no idea how to adjudicate, and where no moral theory gives us any concrete or useful advice on what to do. There's a lesson in this for all of us. If you want to know what to do in any concrete situation, don't ask a moral philosopher. We're crap at that sort of thing. The logical foundations of things – that's what we're good at. And at least we now have a general way of thinking about what's fair or just and what isn't. And we can make at least some sense of the idea of a moral right. That's what philosophy's good at – making sense of things – not telling people what to do.

Loyalty versus justice

So, we have two differing and competing conceptions of justice. On the one hand, we have the utilitarian version, based on the idea of justice as maximisation of happiness or utility. On the other, there is the rights-based conception, based on the idea of justice as fairness and the respect for individual rights. Which one is right? Who knows? Both versions have their defenders and their detractors, and the dispute between them rages on.

Suppose we could pick one; come down on one side or the other. Then would we know everything there is to know about morality? In other words, is justice all there is to morality? The answer modernity gives is, predominantly, 'yes'. And the two accounts we have just looked at – utilitarianism and the rights-based alternative – are both versions of moral theories inspired by modernity. But this, I think, is to adopt a very cold and austere form of morality. It's a simple fact about life that we love some people, hate others, and know nothing about almost everybody else. Justice is supposedly an impartial principle that applies equally to everybody. So, in terms of justice alone, you owe as much to a complete stranger as you do to your partner, as much to the boss you hate as to your son or daughter. The big thing about justice is that everybody is to be treated with the same consideration, given the same moral weight, no matter who they are, and no matter who they are *to you*.

So, to think of morality solely in terms of the idea of justice seems to miss something out. It seems to miss out the feelings of love, affection, fondness, warmth and care that we have to our family and friends. I'll refer to these with the catch-all 'loyalty' which isn't really inclusive enough but will allow us to frame the question we're interested in. In morality, what is the relation between justice and loyalty? If you think that justice is all there is to morality, then you are going to have to say that loyalty is morally irrelevant. And, to many people, this just doesn't seem right.

Series 1 provides lots of good material for thinking about the relation between justice and loyalty. Much of the series revolves around the kidnapping of Jack's wife Teri, and his daughter Kim. Ira Gaines, who kidnaps them both the first time, has a plan to use Jack to help him kill David Palmer. So, he uses Jack to do most of the hard work in setting up the hit – smuggling the gun into the press conference, and receiving the gun from the hitter after the hit is completed. If Jack doesn't comply, his wife and daughter are history.

Of course, Jack manages to foil him in the end. He doesn't really have much choice – he knows that Ira is going to kill his wife and daughter after the hit anyway, no matter what he does. So, foiling the hit in a way that suggests he wasn't the person to foil it is his only real option anyway. But suppose things were slightly different. Suppose Jack knew – or had strong reasons for thinking – that if he did comply and allow Palmer to be killed, his wife and daughter would be released safe and sound. And suppose he also knew that if Palmer were not to be killed for any reason – even if that reason had nothing whatsoever to do with Jack – then Gaines would immediately kill his wife and daughter. Then what should he do?

Jack, you remember, is a utilitarian of the frothing at the mouth Benthamesque variety. And, unfortunately for Teri and Kim, this probably means it's curtains for them. As people keep telling us throughout the series, if David 'the first African-American with a realistic shot at the White House' Palmer gets whacked, it will 'tear the country apart'. Civil unrest would ensue on a scale that would make the Rodney King riots look a Sunday school picnic. Add to this the extreme unhappiness of his wife Sherry, who has been gagging to get to the White House for years. And then, of course, Palmer has two children to be unhappy at his death. If Teri and Kim got whacked, there would only be Jack. So the numbers are all coming down in favour of Palmer, and, for utilitarianism, numbers are what it's all about.

In fact, even if Jack has a sudden conversion to the idea of justice as fairness, and starts banging on about the rights of his wife and daughter, it's far from clear that this is going to help Teri and Kim. In the original position, would you choose a society in which people routinely aid in the execution of other people? Even if they did so only to save members of their family? It would be very risky to choose this. Think of all the people out there who could, at this very moment, be aiding in your execution. If you chose for society to be this way, you could benefit only a very small number of people – the members of your family – but you could be harmed by any one of several billion people. So, simple risk assessment suggests that it would be irrational to choose a society where people are permitted to aid in the execution of others. But if it is irrational in the original position, then it is unjust in the real world. Or so the idea goes. Considerations of justice, then, again seem to come down on the side of David Palmer.

On the other hand, there certainly seems to be something to the idea that Jack has *extra* obligations to his wife and daughter, simply because of who they are. These extra obligations cannot be obligations of justice, but they seem to be real nonetheless. They are obligations grounded in loyalty rather than justice. The question, then, is: how do we weigh up, measure against one another, loyalty versus justice? Which is the more important? When loyalty and justice conflict, which wins out?

This is one of *those* questions: not only is it difficult to work out the answer, it's difficult even to work out what an answer would look like. The first problem is whether we can even compare loyalty and justice in the way that would be necessary if we are to weigh them against each other. Justice and loyalty may turn out to be like apples and oranges; we simply cannot measure them against each other in any sort of meaningful way.

But there's more of a problem than that. If you were trying to work out which is the most important, justice or loyalty, from what perspective would you decide this question? In other words, what principles would you use to decide the issue? You cannot use principles of justice, because that, as philosophers tend to put it, would *beg the question*. That is, it would presuppose that justice is more important.[17] You cannot use principles of justice to show that justice is more important than anything else. Nor, for the same reason, can you answer the question by using values deriving from loyalty. That would presuppose that loyalty is more important.

The problem is that when we look at the history of philosophy we find, in broad outline, that morality comes in two basic forms. There is a tradition, most fully developed in the modern theories of utilitarianism and Kant, which sees justice as the primary moral virtue. So, morality gains its point and legitimacy from its adherence to the idea of justice. There is also a tradition, associated with David Hume, whom we met in the *Buffy* chapter, that sees loyalty – broadly construed to include feelings of kindness, warmth, affection, sympathy and so on – as the driving force behind morality. So, morality gains its point and legitimacy from its being an expression of the general idea of loyalty. The result is that we have systems of morality based on justice, and we have systems based on loyalty. The problem is that we have no way of choosing between them. You cannot object to a system of morality based on justice by assuming a system based on loyalty, and you can't object to a system based on loyalty by assuming a system based on justice. At least, you can't do it without begging the question. So, it seems, when justice and loyalty conflict, as they do in series 1 of *24*, we have no legitimate way of deciding which should win out.

In the end, all we can do is point out the consequences of what we choose for the type of person we will thereby become. What

---

17. If there's one thing that pisses philosophers off more than anything else, it's the current misuse of the phrase by the general public. People nowadays tend to use it to mean something like 'raises the question'. But it doesn't mean this, it means: implicitly assumes an answer to the question you are asking. So, to beg the question is not to provide an answer to a question, it is to assume or presuppose an answer to the question in the way you framed it. The Latin form was *petitio principii*, and was employed by medieval logicians.

would it be like to be a person whose life revolved around justice? What sort of person would you be if you were like that? If justice really is your only guiding principle, then there would perhaps be something strangely mechanical, or robotic, about you. What would happen to the ties of loyalty, warmth and affection that you have towards others? Any such ties you might form would be disturbingly superficial: you know that you might have to jettison them at any time, whenever the impersonal demands of justice come knocking at your door. Loyalty would be something that you could put on and take off like a jacket, and it is always justice that decides if you are appropriately dressed.

The question is: how could you be like this without somehow pulling away from your closest family and friends? David Palmer asked this question of his wife Sherry around about 8.50 p.m. in series 1. He was asking it in a somewhat different context. She had concealed from him, for the last seven years or so, the truth about his son's involvement in the death of the guy who raped his sister. Palmer's claim was that she could not do this without in some way 'pulling away', emotionally distancing herself, from him. We can ask the same sort of question about someone who values justice so highly that they always, invariably, allow considerations of justice to override those of loyalty. How could they do this without pulling away from the people they supposedly love? The answer, I think, is that they could not. To make justice your overriding authority is to live somewhere where real love, real affection and real friendship are not possible. It is to live a life that is less, far less, than fully human. In fact, it's not even to live the life of an animal – for whom feelings of loyalty and affection are real and important, and far more important than any notion of justice. To base your life on justice alone is to be a machine rather than a mammal.

On the other hand, the pitfalls of allowing loyalty to automatically and invariably override justice are equally clear. A society where, come what may, everyone automatically and invariably favours their own over others would soon cease to be a society at all. No society could function along those lines. It would be a gangster society, of the sort we encountered in *The Sopranos*, writ large: society would be divided into warring factions, each faction consisting of a small, and probably unstable, coalition of loyal friends and family. Society, in any more real sense, requires that everyone is treated fairly – whether this means making some sort of provision for the public good, or respecting the rights of individuals. And a widespread breakdown of justice heralds a widespread breakdown of society. This is fairly obvious. But humans, in addition to being loving and loyal animals, are also social animals. So to live a life where loyalty is your sole and overriding authority will again, ultimately, involve living a life that is less than fully human. Every moral decision we make must therefore be a balancing of justice and loyalty, where we really have no guidance on how to pull off this balancing act. One foot wrong on either side of the rope and your humanity is, in one way or another, thereby diminished. That's what being human is, it seems, all about.

six
SEINFELD

WHAT IS SELFISHNESS?
AND IS THERE ANYTHING WRONG WITH IT?

Individualism and selfishness

As we have seen, modernity is built on the idea of *individualism*: the whole point of living is self-development. If there is such a thing as the meaning of life, then this meaning consists in self-fulfilment. So, your overriding moral goal is to realise, develop or fulfil yourself to the best of your abilities, to become the best you can be and all that sort of stuff. And this tells you something important about the sort of being you are. Your attachments to things outside of you, and people outside of you, are never identity-constituting ones; they are at most identity-reflecting. Such attachments do not *make* you the person you are. They merely reflect the person you are – and this person you have become by other means and through other factors. The only self-constituting attachment you have is an attachment to yourself.

I have been banging on about individualism and its associated tribulations for around 200 pages now. And in all this time, I may well have given the impression that individualism is a form of selfishness. If so, it's time to correct that impression. There is nothing necessarily selfish about the modern age. I don't think, in fact, people are noticeably more selfish now than in previous times. Of course, there's not exactly a dearth of selfish bastards in the world today, but thus, presumably, has it always been. Individualism, in fact, is not in itself a form of selfishness, but it can be interpreted in a selfish way. Indeed, we might regard selfishness as a corrupt or debased form of individualism. But that way of putting it is, of course, tendentious. It presupposes that there is something wrong with being selfish – and while many people believe that, many people deny it too.

So this chapter has two purposes. The first is to chart the relationship between individualism and selfishness and so answer the question: *to what extent is the modern age a selfish one?* And, in keeping with the age, the second question is focused at the level of the individual. In our lives, we have many opportunities, and many temptations, to act selfishly. The question is: is there anything wrong with that? *Is there anything wrong with being selfish?*

These issues can be explored by way of the king of the sitcoms, *Seinfeld* (1990–98). To the extent that this series was about anything at all (and it was officially, of course, always about nothing), it was about selfishness, self-absorption and their potential pitfalls.

Good Samaritans

What a way to go out! The ignominy. Jailed for a flagrant failure to be thy brother's keeper. Jailed, in effect, for being callous, indifferent and self-absorbed – surely the greatest end to any TV sitcom ever. In the previous 168 episodes, we have been making the acquaintance of Jerry Seinfeld – a New York comedian playing himself – and his friends, George Costanza, Cosmo Kramer and Elaine Benes: a quartet who have, with one or two occasional slips into benevolence, managed to raise moral apathy into an art form. Finally, in episode 169 their luck – such as it has been – runs out. They manage to find themselves in a place where selfishness and indifference are not only immoral, they're also illegal. That place is the (fictional) town of Latham, Massachusetts.

Jerry is about to make the big time. NBC have been sitting on the pilot of his TV show for five years, but have finally decided to go ahead with the series. As a sweetener, and an apology for keeping the pilot on the shelf for so long, they give him use of a company jet. So, Jerry, George, Kramer and Elaine are on their way to Paris when Kramer starts jumping around the plane trying to get some water out of his ears, crashes into the cockpit, and causes the plane to crash near the town of Latham. Here they witness a fat man getting carjacked at gunpoint. Their reaction exhibits the sort of 'selfishness, self-absorption, immaturity, and greed' (as the judge, Art Vandelay, eventually put it) and, more generally, the sort of callous disregard for other human beings that we had come to know and love over the past nine years. So what do they do? Kramer? He videotapes the whole event. George and Elaine crack jokes:

> *Elaine*: You see, the great thing about robbing a fat guy is the easy getaway. They can't really chase you.
> *George*: They're actually doing him a favour. There's less money for him to buy food.

And Jerry? He was talking on a cell phone, or trying to. The best he could muster: 'Ah, that's a shame.'

This sort of behaviour is by no means an aberration. It would be unfair to accuse Jerry and the gang of *always* being selfish, callous or indifferent. Nevertheless – you've got to say – there is a definite pattern here. To a considerable extent, self-absorption, shallowness and, on more than one occasion, callous insensitivity have been the hallmark of these characters through the past 168 episodes. George is the most obvious example. George was the cheapskate who insisted on bargain basement wedding invitations for his upcoming nuptials to Susan. So cheap are they, in fact, that Susan, who George makes do all the work anyway, is fatally poisoned from licking too many envelopes. So what does George do? How does he feel? Well, first of all he has a suitable period of 'mourning'. However, this, for George, largely involves lying around the house in his boxers, eating pizza, and generally doing the sorts of slobby things he always wanted to do but Susan wouldn't let him get away with when she was alive. Then after an appropriate time has elapsed, George decides it's time to 'live again' and uses a photograph of Susan to pick up other women.

But if George is the least subtle in his pursuit of unbridled self-interest, the others are not far behind. Jerry once kindly swapped apartments with Kramer because Kramer was becoming steadily more and more disoriented by the garish red light streaming in from the Kenny Rogers fried chicken place that had opened across the street. This, in fact, is largely motivated by Jerry's desire to assuage his guilt about his part in getting his friend fired from his former job. His friend is now manager of the fried chicken place, and Kramer's protests – displaying large banners and yelling out 'bad meat!' to people as they were about to go in – were threatening to put it out of business. Nonetheless, despite his motivation, this was clearly a good deed on the part of Jerry. And how does Kramer repay him? By developing a secret liking for Kenny's chicken, thus helping it to thrive, leading Jerry's friend to not look for other jobs, and so prolonging Jerry's exile from his apartment. There are many other examples of Kramer's selfishness, but this is particularly good one – it emphasises just how much Kramer is unable to control his inclinations or appetites, even when this inability has unfortunate consequences for his friends.

Elaine is scarcely any better – although her self-absorption is, perhaps, more likely to manifest itself in terms of feelings of seething resentment rather than overt actions. When George announces his engagement to Susan, Elaine is secretly furious. The whole thing, she tells her rabbi, makes her feel sick. She feels no happiness for George, just a feeling that she should be the one getting married: 'It should have been *me*. *I'm* smart, *I'm* attractive.' Of course, she has plenty of men to date, but doesn't want to get serious with any of them. Again, this is a manifestation of the sort of self-absorption that runs through all of the characters – the obsessive regard for, or focus on, one's own situation makes it impossible to feel genuine happiness for others when good things happen to them, or genuine sorrow when bad things happen to them. Everything reflects back on Elaine. When good things happen to other people, this reflects negatively back on her – precisely because the good things are not happening to *her*. When bad things happen, she finds it impossible to feel genuine sorrow. Instead, these events are usually interpreted in terms of what they say about her. She is more likely to feel relief than have genuine sympathy. That's the thing about self-absorption – undue focusing on yourself does tend to turn into callous insensitivity towards others, both in terms of how you act and how you feel towards them.

Or, if more evidence is needed, consider an episode that nicely implicates all four of them. In 'The Junior Mint', Jerry and Kramer have been invited to watch surgery being performed on Elaine's former artist boyfriend. Elaine dumped him because he was too fat, but the break-up and illness has made him lose lots of weight, and she is attracted to him again. During the surgery, Kramer tries to force Jerry to eat a Junior Mint, and in the ensuing struggle the mint is knocked out of Kramer's hand into the open abdominal cavity of the artist. After the surgery, he takes a turn for the worse and is expected to die. Consider the reactions of each of the gang. Elaine is disgusted that he is going to die just when he has become thin and attractive again – and considers the whole thing to be an example of *her* bad luck. Jerry feels guilty, and wants to tell someone what happened in the hope that this might save his life. But he doesn't, apparently, feel guilty enough to actually follow through on this – not when there is the prospect of him getting into trouble. In this, Jerry is facilitated by Kramer's staunch refusal to own up or even allow Jerry to do so – and the fear of getting into trouble is also what motivates Kramer. And George? George has invested in some of the artist's work, and is greedily anticipating a marked increase in its value if he dies. At one point, when Jerry looks like he's going to own up, George shouts at him in exasperation: 'Who are you to play God!' None of this is, of course, pretty.

However, as I said, it would be unfair to say that Jerry, George, Kramer and Elaine have been nothing but callous and self-absorbed. There was Jerry's visit to the bubble boy, for example, or attempting to help his friend working in Kenny Rogers Roasters. And George once actually helped a busboy. Of course, the motivations for these apparently selfless acts are not entirely praiseworthy. It is Jerry's desire to avoid further hassle from the boy's nagging father that largely seems to underlie his visit to the bubble boy. And it is guilt that underlies his attempt to help his friend. But the fact that he can feel guilt in a situation like this, and the fact that the father's nagging can get to him in the way it did, suggests the existence of a genuine moral sensitivity and regard for others. Even Kramer's encouraging a woman to have cosmetic surgery because 'someone needed to tell her', while being massively and naively insensitive in a way only Kramer can be, seems motivated by the desire to help someone else.

We also shouldn't forget that Jerry, George, Kramer and Elaine are very good friends to each other. And, as Aristotle pointed out in connection with *Friends*, bad people just do not have good friends. Sure, their friendship does involves continual sparring, even bickering, and this can often escalate into wounding sarcasm. But it is pretty obvious that the characters both depend on and care about each other. And they are usually willing to help each other out in whatever way they can. So, we find, for example, George trying to help Jerry with the 'impossible' roommate switch, and Kramer posing as Elaine's lover. Their friendship is based, as all friendships are, on at least a certain amount of sympathy, empathy, fellow-feeling and good will. So Jerry and the gang are certainly capable of feeling these emotions.

Jerry, George, Kramer and Elaine would not, in fact, be interesting if they were totally selfish and self-absorbed. Jerry and the gang are, in fact, pretty much like most of us. We find them interesting largely because we see something in them that we recognise, all too clearly, is in us too. Each one of us has his or her kindly, sympathetic, even benevolent side. And each one of us also has his or her indifferent, navel-gazing and even selfish side. The problem for Jerry and the gang is that, at least in the final episode, their selfish and indifferent tendencies have got a little away from them. And they've found themselves in a place where allowing this to happen is illegal as well as immoral.

Latham has a *good Samaritan law* that 'requires you to help or assist anyone in danger as long as it is reasonable to do so'. George, predictably, is incredulous: 'Why would we want to help someone? That's what nuns and Red Cross workers are for.' This incredulity is also shared by their lawyer, Jackie Chiles: 'You don't have to help anybody – that's what this country is all about.' Nevertheless, the New York Four, as they become known, are jailed pending trial.

And at the trial, they are found guilty of violating Latham's good Samaritan law, exhibiting, in the words of Judge Art Vandelay, a 'callous indifference and utter disregard for everything that is good and decent'. The sentence is one year in jail.

George and Bizarro George

Individualism is not the same thing as selfishness. Individualism tells us that the point of living, and your overriding goal, is to fulfil yourself. But it says nothing at all about *how* you go about doing this. It virtually leaves all your options open. Individualism leaves it entirely open whether you are to be a George Costanza or a *Bizarro* George. The term Bizarro George refers to the episode 'The Bizarro Jerry'. Elaine has been seeing new friends. In fact, they are strikingly similar to Jerry, George and Kramer in some respects, and almost the exact opposites of them in every other. The similarities are predominantly physical and, to a lesser extent, social. Bizarro Jerry, George and Kramer look strikingly like their non-Bizarro counterparts, and dress like them too. And they have, in some ways, a similar type of group dynamic going on. Bizarro Jerry lives in an apartment similar to Jerry. Feldman – Bizarro Kramer – pops in and out much like Kramer. Bizarro George is often around too. But there the similarities end. Kramer is, of course, famous for bursting into Jerry's apartment, and without knocking (at least once an episode – it's his trademark). Once he's there, he also famously helps himself, without asking, to the contents of Jerry's refrigerator. Bizarro Kramer always knocks before coming in (Bizarro's Jerry's apartment, unlike Jerry's apartment, is always carefully locked anyway). And if he does take something from the refrigerator – which he would never do without asking – he always replaces it later.

You get the basic idea. Bizarro Jerry, George and Kramer are intended to be psychological mirror images of Jerry, George and Kramer. They might be physically similar, but psychologically they are doppelgangers: mirror-reversals. So, to the extent that Jerry, George and Kramer are characterised by insensitivity to the plight of others, their Bizarro counterparts will be characterised by sensitivity. To the extent that Jerry, George and Kramer are unduly self-absorbed, their Bizarro counterparts won't be. To the extent that Jerry, George and Kramer are selfish, to that extent their Bizarro counterparts will be altruistic.

You might suppose that George, being often insensitive, self-absorbed and selfish, fits the individualist strand of modernity much better than his Bizarro equivalent. But you would be mistaken. Individualism only says that you should develop or fulfil yourself to the best of your abilities but it doesn't, crucially, say *how* you should do that. You can, compatible with individualism, develop or fulfil yourself in a variety of ways – it all depends on what gets your pulse going. Perhaps advancing your interests at the expense of everyone else is what does it for you – in many ways, and at many times, this seems to be what does it for George. But it doesn't have to be that way. Perhaps a life of selfless devotion is what gets your juices flowing, and you decide you want to explore that particular avenue as the way of fulfilling yourself. Perhaps this is the way it is with Bizarro George? Who knows? But the point is that both George and Bizarro George can be equally individualistic. To say that self-fulfilment is your overriding goal is not to say *how* you find that fulfilment; and it is not to say *what* you should find fulfilment *in*.

This is why individualism is not the same thing as selfishness. Selfishness says more than individualism. Being selfish is more than simply putting your own self-fulfilment first. It is also a claim about how you will find that fulfilment. It says you will find fulfilment in, and only in, advancing your own interests. And where your interests clash with someone else's, it says that you should pursue your own interests at the expense of the other person's – no matter who they are, and no matter what their interests are. The difference is this. Individualism tells us that self-fulfilment is the ultimate good, but leaves it entirely open where or in what you will find self-fulfilment. Selfishness, on the other hand, tells us what self-fulfilment consists in. The two concepts are quite different.

This point often tends to get confused. Often, for example, you will hear this tired little argument. 'Everyone is selfish because everyone, ultimately, does only what they want to do. The fact that they did it shows that they really wanted to do it all along.' So, you are faced with a choice of helping a fat guy who is getting car-jacked or simply telling jokes at his expense. Quite frankly, the joke angle really appeals to you – it's a lot safer for one thing. But, instead, you do the Boy Scout thing and go to his aid. If so, you may hear someone telling you this: 'In fact, you were being selfish because you were just doing what you wanted to do. OK, you may have wanted to do it because you thought it was the right thing to do. But then you acted the way you did because you wanted to do the right thing. So, you did what you wanted to do, and so were acting selfishly.'

This is not a good argument. It is based on a confusion about what selfishness actually is. Selfishness is not the idea that you always do what you want. Maybe we always do what we want; maybe not. But, either way, it's not a very interesting claim, turning, I think, largely on what we mean by 'want'. Rather, selfishness is a claim about what it is you want – it claims that all we want to do is to advance our own interests at the expense of everyone else's. For example: Mother Teresa – that selfish bitch! All she ever wanted to do was help other people, and she arranged her life so she could spend all of it gratifying her desires. What's gone wrong? Whether or not Mother Teresa counts as selfish does not in any way depend on whether she always did what she wanted. It depends only on *what* it is she wanted, and not whether she did what she wanted. The fact that she wanted to help other people is, in fact, an indication of her extreme *unselfishness*. Whether you are selfish or not depends on what it is you want and not on whether you do whatever it is you want.

So there is a clear difference between individualism and selfishness. The two words express different ideas. However, you can see why people tend to confuse them. After all, if it is your fulfilment that is your overriding goal, the whole point of your being here, then why shouldn't your own interests, as well as your own fulfilment, come first too? In fact, we might think of selfishness as a sort of base or corrupt form of individualism. Selfishness is what individualism can mutate into, especially if our thinking becomes sloppy. And of course it often does. And so individualism, which initially started out as a moral ideal about how the best sort of life is to be lived – has now largely degenerated into the obsessed self-absorption and insistent demand for self-gratification exemplified by the *me generation*. And, at his worst, there is no one who exemplifies this generation better than George Costanza.

Self-absorbed, selfish, corrupt? You can imagine what George's response might, perhaps, be: *not that there is anything wrong with that*! And this is what we are going to look at now. Is there anything wrong with being self-absorbed or selfish? Is there anything wrong with displaying – whether in one's feelings or one's actions – a callous insensitivity towards other people? In fact, I think there is. But working out exactly what is not easy at all.

The virtue of selfishness?

In the history of thought, very few people can actually bring themselves to defend selfishness for what it is in itself. Most people who
defend selfishness do so by pretending it is really something else. Or,
more typically, by claiming that it is useful for producing something
else: the public good. Implicit in this type of defence, I suppose, is the
idea that there really is something wrong with being selfish – that in
itself it is not a very nice way to be at all, but should be tolerated, or
even encouraged, solely because it is useful in producing something
else that is very useful, and that outweighs the selfishness that has gone
into producing it. It is this sort of idea that underpins the classic
defence of selfishness associated with the economist Adam Smith.

Smith argued that little good is done in the world by those who
try to do what is best for everyone. Try it. You are given *carte
blanche* to devise a society of your own making – you are to be that
society's architect – and the only constraint on you is that the society must be designed to ensure the maximum benefits for each of
its members. This is like the utilitarian idea defended by Jeremy
Bentham and Jack Bauer in the previous chapter. What you have to
try and do is ensure the greatest good for the greatest number, at
least roughly. So, what you have to do, it seems, is to ensure an
equitable distribution of what we might call *goods* – good things to
have – where these would, at the very least, include:

> *commodities* (material possessions – e.g. food, water, shelter);
> *freedoms* (abilities to do certain things, or pursue certain
> ways of living your life – e.g. the pursuit of wealth, happi-
> ness, and stuff like that);
> *entitlements* (rights to be treated in certain ways, or not to
> be treated in certain other ways – e.g. the right to be
> educated, the right not to be tortured, etc.).

These are the sorts of things you have to juggle with; they may not be the only things, but they'll do for the sake of argument. What you have to do is try and ensure the maximum number of these sorts of things for the maximum number of people.

Smith's basic argument was simply that you won't be able to do this. Economic and social systems are just too complex. There are just too many factors to take into account, too many variables to get your head around. So, while you may try to do your best to produce the greatest good for the greatest number, you will inevitably mess things up. In fact, according to Smith, the best way of ensuring the optimal distribution of goods – commodities, freedoms and entitlements – is to forget about trying to do the best for everyone, and simply focus on trying to do the best for yourself.

All of us today, probably, know what Smith is talking about. His idea is the foundation of modernity's dominant economic system: *capitalism*. Take the idea of *trickle-down economics*, for example – an important recent expression of the capitalist idea. Good capitalist that you are, you go and make yourself rich as possible, and screw everyone else. What happens then? Well, there's no point in having all this money sitting in your bank doing nothing. You might as well go and spend some of it. So you buy your house, and your Ferrari, and your cocaine – and in doing so, you spread some of your wealth around. This, in all essentials, is the capitalist answer to the problem of redistribution of wealth: spending. And this, according to capitalists, is the best way of distributing the sorts of commodities you were supposed to distribute if you were society's architect.

In this we find the essence of the capitalist justification for unbridled selfishness. By being a selfish and acquisitive little prick you acquire wealth that, eventually, will inevitably be redistributed back to other people. Thus, society's most ruthless and selfish tossers are, at the same time, their most beneficent philanthropists – albeit, unintentionally, unknowingly, and, in the case of many of them, probably unwillingly.

As I said earlier, what's noticeable about this defence of selfishness is that it doesn't try to defend it for what it is in itself. Very few people think that being a selfish, acquisitive little prick is a good thing in itself. That's going to be a very hard claim to swing. The basis of this defence, however, is that being a selfish, acquisitive prick (henceforth, I shall use the acronym SAP) is good as a *means* to something else – namely the good of society as a whole. We came across this means–end distinction earlier when we were talking about utilitarianism and Kant. SAPs are, basically, necessary evils – they are a bad means to a good end.

This sort of Smithian econo-ethical capitalism is, in many ways, an extremely elegant theory. And certainly no other econo-ethical theory is anywhere near as convincing. The problem with the old socialist versions of econo-ethics, for example, was basically that there was no realistic way of fixing the value of commodities, freedoms and entitlements. The problem is most obvious in the case of commodities. How do you fix the price of a commodity – a house, or car, or line of cocaine? The capitalist free-market answer is, a few subtleties aside, that its price is fixed by whatever people are willing to pay for it – and this is a function of need, scarcity and things like that. The traditional socialist answer, on the other hand, was based on a *labour theory of value*: the value of a commodity is a function of the amount of labour that had to be put into producing it. The problem with the labour theory of value, however, was that people just wouldn't play ball and kept insisting on paying amounts of money for things that were totally unrelated to the labour that had gone into producing them. And, it seems, the only realistic way of fixing prices is in terms of what people actually *do* pay for something, not what they *should* pay for something, if the favourite theory of value is true.[18]

On the other hand, econo-ethical capitalism has its problems too. Basically, it seems to entail that we're all screwed! The basic problem capitalism faces is what's sometimes called a *tragedy of the commons* scenario. There are certain commodities that are *common* to all of us – indeed, to all life on this planet. These are common to us in that they are necessary prerequisites of our survival, and cannot be separated off into little parcels that can be given to each one of us individually. Air is the most obvious example. You can't separate off a little bit of air and say, 'Right, this is your air – use it well!' Air just isn't like that. Neither is water. Neither, in this era of urbanisation and overpopulation, is food. In fact, most of the basic commodities seem to be common in this sense.

Suppose now, however, you are a SAP and are trying to maximise your own wealth. So you build yourself a little factory producing whatever it is you think will make you the most money. The problem is that a by-product of your little venture is pollution of one or more of the commons. You run a little effluent off into the adjacent river, for example. Or puff a little smoke up into the surrounding air. Initially, no one bothers about this – the effects are unnoticed. It's only when glow-in-the-dark babies start getting born in the neighbouring villages that people start to take umbrage. Of course, any definite connection between your factory and glowing babies is difficult to prove – especially if you have a good lawyer. So, you'll probably avoid (successful) lawsuits. But maybe you'll start getting hit with a 'polluter pays' tax. Will this stop you? Only if the tax is greater than the profit you are already

---

18. I would like to claim credit for this critique of socialism but, in fact, Ludwig von Mises got there before me – by about 80 years or so. See his classic, *Socialism: An Economic and Sociological Analysis* (Jonathan Cape: New York, 1951).

making – which, if history is anything to go by, is unlikely. And even if it is, you can just relocate your production operation to some country where the people are starving and willing to put up with just about anything for the sake of a little inward investment. So off you go to BFE, or wherever, and continue spewing out the same toxic cocktail into the air. Will this make your original country any better off? Only temporarily. Air, the problem is, doesn't respect national boundaries, and your toxic cocktail will work its way into the atmosphere and weather system, and, eventually, produce deleterious consequences for everyone.

The reasons for pessimism about the commons stem from the fact that the associated problems all have a common structure. They always involve an opposition between individual wealth acquisition and a common problem. It is only you who stands to amass the wealth, but the problem is going to be one faced by everyone. But a problem shared is a problem halved as the old, and in this context rather depressing, adage goes. And a problem divided by six and a half billion people is, you might think, one six-and-a-half-billionth of a problem. So, you've got lots of money and only one-six-and-a-half-billionth of a problem. So, SAP that you are, it always makes sense to screw everyone else's commons if you can get away with it.

There is another old saying: you don't shit on your own doorstep. And that, as old sayings go, is pretty good advice. But if you have absolutely positively to go somewhere, and someone else's doorstep is handy, then why not? If you can get away with it, of course. Continuing in the same vein, consider an example of the commons we are all too familiar with: the train toilet seat. Covered in pee. At the very least. If you're a woman, you'll already be reaching for the toilet paper to wipe it, so let's just hope there's still some left in the dispenser. But males are the great polluters here, so for the purpose of this example, we'll assume you're a man – and you know you really should lift that seat – you really should. But it's pretty nasty, and you don't know who's been there. Sure, you could try lifting it with your foot. But the floor, as usual, is awash – with what you don't really want to dwell on – and the last thing you want is to go slipping on that. So, you just pee, and, of course, the movement of the train makes it inevitable that you do it all over the seat.

The toilet seat, in this case, is a *common*. And the state of the seat is, thus, a common problem. So, it's not specifically your problem. So, why should you make the sort of sacrifice involved in lifting it, or even, God forbid, wiping it with some paper? And this is why there is a problem with the commons. A common problem is not your problem. At most only a fraction of it is your problem. So why should you take a hit – make some sacrifice like touching a nasty toilet seat, or forgoing some wealth amassing possibilities – for a problem that is hardly yours at all. I'm not, of course, endorsing this line of argument, but I am trying to point out why unbridled capitalism is going to have a problem with the commons – a problem in solving common problems. You are, we are supposing, a SAP – a selfish, acquisitive prick. Therefore, why should you take a hit to solve what is, in essence, hardly your problem at all?

So we face, in this modern time of economic approaches to ethics, something of a dilemma. Socialism isn't going to work – the labour theory of value is a non-starter. And capitalism is going to have precisely the sorts of problems with commons such as the environment that we all know it does have. One of the problems of modernity is, therefore, working out just what sort of economic system is, in the long run, going to work. Personally I don't have a clue, and suspect we're all screwed. So let's focus on the narrower question: apart from entailing the destruction of the human race and the end of life on this planet as we know it, does the capitalist defence of selfishness have any serious problems?

Can't be bothered?

The car-jacking incident in Latham does, I think, highlight a serious problem for the Adam Smith capitalist defence of selfishness. The capitalist defence of selfishness is based on the idea that selfishness is necessary for the acquisition of wealth and other commodities that can then be redistributed in the form of spending. What the final episode of *Seinfeld* highlights very well is that selfishness often has absolutely nothing to do with the acquisition of wealth or other commodities, ones that may then trickle down to everyone else. George and Elaine are cracking jokes. Kramer is videotaping the incident for posterity – not so that he can provide evidence for the police, but for his later entertainment and that of his friends. Jerry is more concerned with his phone conversation. Since that was for the purpose of getting them out of Latham, one might argue that this was for the purposes of amassing wealth – since he couldn't do that in Latham. But that would, to say the least, be *reaching*. So, the first thing that the final episode of Seinfeld shows, I think, is that the capitalist defence of selfishness is very limited. It might apply to some of the actions we regard as selfish, but a lot – probably most – of the things we regard as selfish cannot be defended in this way. Usually, I think, selfishness has nothing whatsoever to do with the amassing of wealth and commodities that can then be redistributed in the form of spending. Most of the time selfishness is simply the result of the fact that we can't be bothered.

More subtly, it could be argued that to suppose selfishness is OK in some contexts – wealth amassing ones – is, in part, what is responsible for the sort of callous insensitivity to others that is exhibited by Jerry and co. Suppose, for example, you witnessed the same car-jacking. At the time you were on the phone, closing out some great business deal that is going to help you amass some serious wealth. The best you can muster, in response to the scene, is, like Jerry, 'Ah, that's a shame.' But this is OK. Good capitalist that you are, you are willing to allow that selfishness – and any callous insensitivity that happens to go with it – is perfectly OK in wealth amassing contexts. The question is: could you exhibit this sort of insensitivity to the plight of others in some contexts without it spilling over into other contexts also?

After all, what seems to be common to both contexts is a sort of *can't be bothered* attitude. In effect, you can't be bothered to help the portly car-jackee because you are in the business of amassing wealth. Jerry and co. can't be bothered to help the jackee simply because they can't be bothered. You, SAP that you are, think that you have a justification. But in both cases we have the sort of callous insensitivity to the plight of others that underlies your can't-be-bothered attitude. And callous insensitivity is callous insensitivity. It seems the sort of psychological attitude that couldn't care less about issues of justification. If you have it in one context, then it seems precisely the sort of thing you will have in other contexts too. So, the capitalist defence of selfishness, perhaps, is the sort of thing that could instil in us *bad habits* – in this case bad psychological habits: of feeling the sorts of things we shouldn't feel and not feeling the sorts of things we should. The sort of callous insensitivity to the plight of others, that can be justified by the capitalist in certain contexts, threatens to spill over to contexts where it can't be justified, and infect the rest of our lives, and our dealings with others, too.

Not that there's anything wrong with that

Is there any reason not to be a SAP? Apologists like Adam Smith try to defend being a SAP by arguing that it is a useful means to a valuable end: the general public good or welfare. But this doesn't work: many, perhaps most, forms of selfishness do not contribute to the public good. So maybe we should just bite the bullet and say: *not that there's anything wrong with that*! That is, maybe we can argue that there is absolutely nothing wrong with being a SAP, irrespective of the question of the public good.

In the history of philosophy, in fact, we don't really find any good arguments against being a SAP. To be sure, many have tried – from Plato onwards – but their arguments never really worked. In my view, there is a very good reason for this. It's simply not the sort of thing that can be argued against. Not because it's right, but because it's not the sort of thing that can be right or wrong.

To see this, first consider that we might have at least two reasons for doing something. The first sort of reason is that the thing we are going to do is in our interests. You should give up smoking because you have a pair of lungs that look like fractured tarmac. I should give up drinking because my liver is the size of a football, and so on. These sorts of reasons are what we might call *pruden-tial* reasons – reasons of prudence. The sense in which giving up smoking and drinking are good things for us to do is what we might call a *prudential* sense of good.

But there is another sense of good, hence another sort of reason for doing something: a *moral* sense. When you do something because you think it is the right thing to do, irrespective of whether you want to do it, and irrespective of whether it is in your (pruden-tial) interests to do it, you are acting from what we might call a *moral* reason. If what you do is good in this sense, then this is a moral sense of good rather than a prudential one.

And in terms of the reasons we might have for doing something, that, I think, is more or less it.[19] SAPs are basically selfish and acquisitive because they always let prudential reasons override moral reasons. They always do what is in their prudential interests, irrespective of whether it is the right thing to do. That's what being a SAP is all about. So, how could you convince a SAP to reconsider their position? To do this would be to provide them with reasons for doing something – for changing their stance on how to act. So what sorts of reasons could you provide? It seems you have two options. You could provide them with moral reasons or prudential reasons.

Giving them moral reasons isn't going to cut any ice with a SAP. I mean, for them, the whole issue is whether moral reasons should win out over prudential ones or prudential reasons win out over moral ones. Their stance is that prudential should always win out over moral. So, giving them a list of moral reasons isn't going to work – for that would implicitly presuppose that moral reasons can win out over prudential reasons, and that is precisely what the SAP is going to deny. To argue like this against the SAP, then, is to commit what's known as the fallacy of *begging the question*. You've basically presupposed what you are trying to show: that SAPs shouldn't be SAPs.

So you might try giving them prudential reasons. For example, you might want to point out that people generally don't like SAPs. More to the point, people often don't like and/or trust them to such an extent that they won't cooperate with their wealth amassing projects, thus seriously cutting down on how much amassing

---

19. Actually, there is another sense, largely associated with Kant, according to which you have a reason for doing something because not to do it would be, in some way, inconsistent. This is not relevant to our present concerns, so I'll leave it out here. See my *The Philosopher at the End of the Universe*, chapter 6, for further discussion.

they can do. But this isn't any sort of reason for *not* being a SAP. All you have done is provide them with reasons for being a cleverer or subtler SAP. You've taught them that if they're going to screw anyone over, they'd better be sneaky about it – a stab in the back rather than a thumb in the eye. As long as the face they present to the world is charming, affable, kind and sensitive, all will be well in their dealings, no matter how much they destroy others in private. So once again, you have not given them any reasons for not being a SAP.

This means that there are no reasons you can provide a SAP with for not being a SAP. So, there are no good arguments for not being a SAP. But neither, for the same sorts of reasons, are there any good arguments for being a SAP! Take the opposite of a SAP – let's call them a SAINT for the sake of argument, this time not an acronym but a (sarcastic) description. A SAINT is someone who always lets moral reasons win out over prudential reasons – they always do the (morally) right thing, no matter what the cost to their own interests. If you were a SAP, how would you convince them to change this policy? What sorts of reasons could you use to convince them that they should not be a SAINT?

Again, you have two options. You can give them moral reasons or prudential reasons. But giving them moral reasons isn't going to work because the whole point of being a SAINT is that moral reasons always win out anyway. So their accepting the moral reasons would just be another instance of moral reasons winning out – which puts us right back where we started. But neither will prudential reasons work. What the SAINT requires is a reason why prudential reasons should, at least sometimes, win out over moral reasons. But to give them prudential reasons in favour of this is not to argue that prudential reasons should win out over moral ones; it is to presuppose that prudential reasons should win out. Once again, as in the parallel case for the SAP, we would be simply begging the question: presupposing the answer we want rather than arguing for it.

The upshot is that you can't give any reasons for not being a SAP, but neither can you give any reasons for *not* not being a SAP – which is equivalent to saying you can't give any reasons either for or against being a SAP. So being a SAP is not the sort of thing you can argue either for or against, which means it is also simply not the sort of thing that can be proven right or wrong. Not that there is anything wrong with being a SAP, but nor is there anything right with it either.

The hardest thing I've ever had to do

Being a SAP or a SAINT is not something you can argue for or defend by way of the usual forms of argument. But there's more than one way of convincing someone of something, a way not based on argument – although philosophers tend to forget this because arguments are what they do. The other way of convincing someone is by drawing them a picture. This is one of the things *Seinfeld* was very good at.

There is a certain view of religious language, associated with the twentieth-century Austrian philosopher Wittgenstein, which sees it as a kind of metaphor. When you say religious things like 'When I die I'll go to heaven', you are not really saying what you think you are saying. Instead of expressing a belief in an afterlife in general, and the quality of the afterlife you can expect in particular, you are really saying something about your attitude to your life and how you think you have lived it. You are saying something like, 'I've lived a pretty good life, and I've got nothing to really be ashamed of', or something along those lines. Religious language is like this, according to Wittgenstein. It is a sort of metaphor that we have forgotten is a metaphor.

And, a metaphor is probably the best way of looking at the final episode of *Seinfeld*. The plane crash, followed by the trial with its long line of character witnesses, these are all metaphors for the judgment of the soul on Judgment Day. Particularly, since the character witnesses are almost invariably people that Jerry, George, Kramer or Elaine have screwed over in one way or another during the previous 168 episodes – like, for example, the old lady whom Jerry mugged for a marble rye. Add to this the fact that the name of the judge, Art Vandelay, is a pseudonym occasionally employed by George. The implication that some might want to draw is that Jerry, George, Kramer and Elaine really died in the plane crash, and the courthouse in Latham is the representation of the place of judgment. Of course, we don't have to say they really died, especially if we believe Wittgenstein, because then the idea of the judgment of the soul is itself a metaphor. So the final episode is, maybe, a metaphor of a metaphor: and once we get to metaphors of metaphors, we have to admit, I think, that we have no idea what *really* happened – even if we could talk meaningfully about what *really* happened in a fictional TV series.

So let's set aside the question of whether Jerry, George, Kramer and Elaine are *really* dead, and, instead, look at the content of the metaphor. What is the point of the metaphor? The point is to paint a picture of the sort of person you will become if you lead a life of unbridled self-absorption and self-interest.

Possibly the most striking feature of Jerry, George, Kramer and Elaine is that none of them is happy. And throughout the preceding 168 episodes any happiness they have felt has been fleeting in the extreme. George provides a perfect illustration of what is wrong. George has what we might regard as *temporary brushes* with happiness. Happiness, for George, consists in a sort of momentary elation that almost always results from his feeling that he has achieved some victory over others. And the idea of victory is so important in George's life because of his underlying worldview that sees things always in a context of scarcity. There is never enough to go around, and there must always be a loser. Usually this is him but when it isn't, momentary elation is the result. We all know, of course, that this will soon be replaced by some paroxysm of rage, frustration and/or insecurity that will result from his perceived defeat concerning some equally insignificant matter.

The episode 'The parking spot' provides a very good example of this. Here is George explaining the issue to Jerry:

> *George*: My father didn't pay for parking, my mother, my brother, nobody. It's like going to a prostitute. Why should I pay for it? If I apply myself, maybe I can get it for free.

If George were successful in this, which he wasn't, then there would no doubt have been his customary explosion of joy: a victory to be savoured until the next inevitable defeat comes along.

George is, of course, a caricature. But there are probably very few of us for whom this doesn't ring at least some bells. How easy it is to see life as a succession of victories and defeats. Typically these are minor victories and defeats, because our lives are largely occupied by minor affairs. But we care about these little things passionately. Why? Because, like George, it is in terms of these little victories and defeats that we measure ourselves against others. That's easy, but the real question is: why would this be? Why would we measure ourselves in this way?

You are a citizen of modernity, a separate, isolated ego whose essential identity does not depend on anyone or anything else. The world around you – being inherently alien or other to you – is thereby something that can have only *instrumental* value for you. The world, in effect, is something to which you can stake a *claim*. The world is something you can have, but so is it too something all the other isolated egos can have. Accordingly, you can have more of this world than other egos, or you can have less of it. If you accept all this, then how easy it would be to think of your own significance in terms of the amount of the world to which you can stake claim, the amount of world you can possess. You possess more of it than another ego? Then you are stronger, more power-ful, *better* than that ego.

These little victories and defeats, these points we score against all the other isolated egos out there, become ways of measuring ourselves, of judging our quality, of working out if there is any point to our existence. But they are all, of necessity, *small* victories. The relations we bear to things outside of us – the world and the other egos in it – are all identity-reflecting, rather than identity-constituting, relations. They reflect an identity that has been fixed prior to them. They do not, and cannot, constitute or define that identity. So whatever points we score, whatever victories we win, these cannot be, because of the sort of thing we take ourselves to be, self-defining victories.

A boxer, for example, might, legitimately, talk of a *career-defining* fight. He can legitimately talk this way because his career is a relational entity: the significance of his career is to be found in the relations between his fights, the relations to the people he fought, and the relations to the people they fought. Victories are relational – a victory is always a victory of one thing over another – but selves are not. But the modern self is non-relational: it cannot similarly be defined by the relations it bears to things outside it. In the modern age, there can be no self-defining victories.

The consequence is that all our victories are small ones. So too are all of our defeats. They just don't matter enough. They just don't really matter any more. We've come across this idea before – several times in fact. There's nothing *big* in our lives any more. Modernity makes our lives small – and this is true no matter how big they may seem to us. Selfishness is just one manifestation of this deeper phenomenon.

The result we might regard as a kind of purgatory. But it's a purgatory not of terrible things, but only mediocre ones. Or, more accurately, it's a purgatory of things that are terrible only in their insignificance. Our purgatory is that of Jerry who, while in prison, is forced to eat cereal with only half of his usual serving of milk. 'This,' he confessed, 'is the hardest thing I have ever had to do.' And what's terrible about this purgatory is precisely that it *is* the hardest thing he has ever had to do.

seven
THE SIMPSONS

WHAT IS THE BEST WAY TO LIVE?

Life and linguistic analysis

Can't talk, eating.

1. Homer ate the doughnut in the bathroom at midnight.

It follows logically from this sentence that:

2. Homer ate the doughnut in the bathroom.

And:

3. Homer ate the doughnut.

And indeed:

4. Homer ate something.

The late, great Donald Davidson showed that the only way of explaining this set of entailments, from sentence (1) to sentences (2), (3) and (4) is by understanding (1) as saying:

$(\exists x)$(Homer, x & in the bathroom, x & at midnight, x)

(∃x) is what's known as an *existential quantifier*, a claim of exis-tence. (∃x) says: 'there exists something, call it x'. So what the above says is, basically:

> There is something, let's call it x, and x was by Homer and x was in the bathroom, and x was at midnight.

What is x? An *event*: the event that was the eating of the doughnut by Homer. This means that we have to do what is known as *quan-tify* over an event. But, according to another philosopher, Willard Quine, if you have to quantify over something of a certain kind, you are committed to believing in the existence of things of that kind. So, Davidson concludes, we are committed to believing in the existence of events. Reality, as well as being made up of objects is also made up of events – understood as an irreducible category of existing things. Pretty exciting stuff, huh?

Now, there is no way I am going to diss *The Don*. Donald Davidson was a really good philosopher, perhaps a great one, certainly one of the best of the twentieth century. But, respect him though I do, there was no way I would have ever asked The Don for advice on life or how to live life; nor would he have wanted me to. He just didn't do that stuff. Neither, really, do the rest of us academic philosophers either. It's just not our bag at all, baby.

Instead, if we want to find out about life, what makes it worth living, and how we should live it, we have to look to a dysfunctional family of little yellow people – *The Simpsons* (1989–). In Homer, Marge, Lisa and Bart, and in the good people of Springfield more generally, we find all the great theories about how to live life and what makes it worth living. Unfortunately, the theories are all kind of jumbled up in various ways. This is inevitable, really, given that Springfield comprises a collection of fuckwits and losers. Most of them provide failed examples of the great theories about how to live life and what makes life worth living. What did you expect? Did you really think Homer would actually *succeed* in exemplifying a great philosophical theory when he has, arguably, failed at just about everything else he has ever attempted? But putting aside the limitations of the good people of Springfield, exemplifying great philosophical theories about how life should be lived isn't easy at the best of times. Most of us fail. I know I do. In most of us, we find a variety of theories, all jostling for supremacy. We are all failed examples of something or other. It's working out what we are failed examples of that is the difficult part.

Modernity and the good life

Ultimately, at the end of the day, when all's said and done, when all stones have been turned, avenues have been explored, and the fat lady has sung, there are just two types of theory about how to live your life. First, there are those theories that tell you to be happy with what you've got. Secondly, there are those theories that tell you to *not* be happy with what you've got. And that's it, ultimately, and at the end of the day. But you end up with very different views of life, and the point of living it, depending on which option you take.

This distinction between theories about how to live your life maps on, fairly neatly, to the distinction between modernity and pre-modernity. With a few complications here and there, modern theories are based on the idea of not being happy with what you've got. Pre-modern theories, on the other hand, especially the theories of the ancient Greeks and people like that, are all based on the idea of finding ways of being happy with what you've got.

We'll start our exploration of the good life with Homer, in whose blood, believe it or not, the wisdom of the ancients still

runs strong. And you thought it was just Duff beer that ran strong
in Homer.

Not exactly the Hefner mansion

The first thing that stands out about Homer is that he is what's
known as a hedonist. Hedonism is an ancient school of philosophy
associated with a guy called Epicurus (*c.* 342–270 BC). According
to Epicurus, the only thing that, ultimately, makes life worth living
is pleasure: pleasure, and the absence of pain. And this is what
hedonism is: the idea that pleasure is the highest good, the whole
point of living. Ask yourself two things: *what do you want?* And,
why do you want it? There are lots of possible answers to the first
question: money, power, fame, sex, drugs, rock 'n' roll, health,
friends, family, children, or whatever. But the answer to the second
question, hedonists claim, is always the same: *pleasure.* To the
extent you want the things on the list, you want them because they
will give you pleasure, or you think they will.

You may doubt this. You slogged your way through the tedium
of school, so you could go and do something boring at university,
so you could go on and get a boring job, marry a spiteful and
venomous spouse and raise ugly and ungrateful children who you
are grooming to start the same process all over again. Where's the
pleasure in that? Well, we all tend to lose the mission eventually –
but that's our fault. Yet, the only reason we did all these things,
according to the hedonist, is the pleasure they brought us, at least
at the time. There was the pleasurable thrill of doing well in your
exams, of rising above your colleagues in the job you eventually
got, of using your success to get so-and-so into bed, and so on.
That was fun, even if it all eventually went belly up.

Pleasure, it seems, often gives rise to pain. I write this page with a savage hangover, so I know exactly what I'm talking about. The question is, what do you do about this? This question divides hedonists into two sorts.

The first sort is exemplified by a guy called Aristippus (435–350 BC) who said, basically, that you should go for it anyway. Life should be dedicated to the pursuit of as many intense pleasures as possible, and screw the consequences. Even when they lead to subsequent intense pain, you should still go for it – for a life without pleasure or pain, Aristippus argued, would be unremittingly boring. Aristippus was from a place called Cyrene, and his view became known as Cyrenaicism.

The second sort of hedonist was Epicurus, who came up with a different strategy. Most people, he said, are simply not equipped to pursue pleasure with the same dogged determination as Aristippus. The key to life, according to Epicurus, is learning how to balance pleasure and pain. Not just any pleasure will do – not if it is followed by years of pain that more than cancel it out. And this is the really hard part about working out how to live – understanding which things are going to bring long-term pleasure. This view, understandably enough, became known as Epicureanism.

Epicurus's actual lifestyle always comes as a bit of a disappointment when you discover what it was. Sure, the initial press reports were promising. According to Timocrates, one disgruntled former member of his group, Epicurus was the first notable bulimic – having to throw up twice a day because he stuffed himself so much. And a guy called Diotimus took it on himself to publish fifty filthy letters allegedly written by Epicurus when he was drunk and gagging for it. Allegedly. Thus has it always been. If you're having a good time, then other people are going to hate you for it. In fact, you don't even need to be actually having a good time. If other people even think, or merely suspect, that you're having a better time than them, they're going to be slagging you off left, right and centre. It's apparently a basic human impulse to hate anyone happier than you are. That's why the tabloids still do such great business today.

The reality of Epicurus's life was, in fact, quite different. He lived with a group of friends. They spent most of their time in the garden, and ate rather crappy vegetarian food – and I'm sure it didn't taste any better then than it does today. And Epicurus was sad enough to drink water rather than wine. In fact, such a sad case was he that he even begged a friend to send him some cheese 'that I may have a feast whenever I like'.

Not exactly the Hefner mansion is it? For those of you expecting Epicurus to be a leader of a sort of free love posse, who when he wasn't shagging someone was Jonesing his food and drinking like Oliver Reed, will be somewhat disappointed with this. How could the father of the 'pleasure is everything' movement be such a sad bastard?

The answer, of course, will strike a chord with anyone who has racked up the pounds like Oprah Winfrey, or whose liver looks like it was donated by Richard Harris: short-term pleasure does not always translate into long-term pleasure. In fact, short-term pleasure often translates into long-term *displeasure*. But if you think pleasure is everything, then you should be concerned with long-term pleasure rather than its short-term counterpart. How do we guard against this sort of problem? The answer is: we have to be careful what we take pleasure in. This was Epicurus's major insight – let's hope that he at least had a lot of fun working it out.

The thing about pleasure is this: it derives from the satisfaction of desires. If you have a desire – to do something or have something – then if you satisfy this desire, pleasure is the typical result. Not always, but usually. On the other hand, *not* satisfying your desires usually leads to the opposite of pleasure: pain, frustration, and disappointment. But if pleasure is everything, and long-term pleasure is more important than short-term pleasure, then it seems you have to set up a sort of score sheet, one which sets out the short-term pleasures you have experienced versus the short-term pains you have experienced. The long-term pleasure you experience depends on how the short-term pleasures measure up against the short-term pains.

In this battle of pleasure against pain, there are two things that will determine the outcome. The key to the battle is learning how to satisfy the maximum number of pleasures while, at the same time, learning how to minimise the amount of desires that go unsatisfied. What is the best way to do this? The strategy Epicurus hit upon is simple and obvious: you try and restrict your desires to the ones that you *must* satisfy or that it is *easy* for you to satisfy.

Take the *must* part of the equation first. There are, Epicurus argued, three types of desire:

1. those that are *natural* and *must* be satisfied if you are to have any sort of life worth living (desires for food, water, and shelter, for example);
2. those that are *natural* but *need not* necessarily be satisfied if you are to have any sort of pleasant life (Epicurus, questionably in my view, listed the desire for sex as one of these);
3. desires that are *neither* natural *nor* must be satisfied if you are to have a pleasant life (desires for wealth or fame, for example).

So, the basic idea so far is that some desires you absolutely positively have to satisfy in order to have a pleasant life, but some desires you don't. So, it's best to focus your efforts on the ones that you have to satisfy rather than the ones you don't.

This point is then reinforced for Epicurus by the thought that it is *easier* to satisfy some desires than others. And, crucially, the desires that you've absolutely, positively got to satisfy are, typically, easier to satisfy than the ones you don't. A desire for basic food – bread and cheese, for example – is a lot easier to satisfy than a desire for lobster thermador. A desire for water is a lot easier to satisfy than one for Hermitage La Chapelle. A crappy little hut is a lot easier to get hold of than a mansion. So, by some happy coincidence or what, the desires that it is essential to satisfy are the ones that are easiest to satisfy. This idea provides the cornerstone of Epicurus's philosophy.

There are any number of desires you may have. But some are far more essential and easier to satisfy than others. If you have lots of desires that are inessential and difficult to satisfy, then your life will contain a lot less pleasure than if you have lots of desires that are essential and easy to satisfy. Or, more precisely, the pleasure-to-pain ratio of your life will be a lot better if you have relatively few desires – you've restricted yourself to the essential ones – all of which are easy to satisfy. The key to the good life – the key to happiness – is learning to moderate your desires so that you only have the ones that you have to have and that are easy to satisfy. And so Epicurus emphasised the simple life. The cultivation of easy to attain pleasures and the avoidance of difficult to obtain pleasures: this is the key to living well.

We can put what Epicurus was getting at in slightly different terms. We've got to distinguish between what we *want* and what we *need*. We can want any number of things, and some of these will be easier to get than others. And it's a sad fact about human nature that, often, the more we have the more we want. So, wants have a habit of multiplying, depending on how successful we are at getting what we want. But we need relatively few things, and these are usually easier to get than what we want. So, the key to the good life, for Epicurus, is making sure that our needs are taken care of, and restricting our wants as much as we can. Homer, as we shall now see, gets pretty close to pulling off this Epicurean strategy.

Homer's Epicurean lifestyle

I think it's pretty clear that Homer accepts the basic Epicurean premise that pleasure is what it's all about. Obviously Duff beer and doughnuts are going to be centrally involved in whatever pleasure he is able to enjoy. So too are pizza, hot dogs, and foot-long subs. But what we are interested in is the way in which Homer cleverly follows the basic Epicurean recipe for the good life.

When will a desire be difficult to satisfy? The most obvious case is when the satisfaction of your desire is outside your control – when, for example, it depends on someone else. If you have a job and someone else is your boss, then many of your work-related desires are going to be outside your control. If you are doing what *The Man* tells you to do, then whether you get what you want will depend on the will of *The Man*, and since you have no control over this, you have no control over whether your desires get satisfied. So, according to Epicurus, freedom, the self-determination of your desires, is necessary for the good life. That is, it's wise to have desires whose satisfaction depends on you and not anyone else. This isn't always possible, but it's a good rule of thumb to follow as far as possible.

So, one thing Epicurus advocated is giving up your job. In fact, he didn't just advocate this – he practised it too. He set up a sort of hippie commune, where he couldn't be jerked around by *The*

Man. This is, of course, sounding worse and worse for the whole pleasure-is-everything idea – because, as everyone knows, hippie communes are the epitome of hell on earth, what with all the lentils and patchouli oil and stuff.

Homer doesn't join a hippie commune. The closest he came to it, I suppose, was in the Lollapaloosa episode, where Homer runs away to join a travelling rock concert/freak show. His act involved being shot at in the gut by a cannon, and his life on the road did represent an escape from the oppressive authority of Mr Montgomery Burns – *The Simpsons* version of *The Man*. Homer has, in fact, had many jobs – astronaut, pin monkey, country music manager, boxer, pizza deliverer, travelling freak, snake oil salesman, chauffeur, car designer, barbershop singer, the list goes on – but, by and large, he has always kept up his job at the nuclear plant. Having three kids to feed, he basically has no option, or so it seems to him. So, for most of his life at least, Homer has always been in tow to Mr Burns.

However, to negate the baleful influence of Mr Burns, Homer has another, quite ingenious – and surprising given his well-documented intellectual shortcomings – strategy. *He has no work-related ambitions whatsoever!* Homer's reasoning is, presumably, something like this. If someone else has something you want, then your happiness depends on whether they give it to you. So, the more you have work-related ambitions – for promotion and stuff like that – then the more the satisfaction of your desires is outside your control. That depends on Mr Burns as much as you. Homer knows the trouble this can bring. Once, when he let his principles slip, he harboured the ambition to be named employee of the month. Admittedly, he only harboured this ambition because everybody else in the entire nuclear plant had already won it, and he figured he was a shoe in. The result? The award was given to an inanimate carbon rod, and Homer had to suffer the frustration of a thwarted work-related desire. Better by far not to have any such desires.

So, one basic Epicurean principle that Homer adopts is based on the idea that the less control you have over whether your desires get satisfied, the greater will be your frustration and dissatisfaction with life. So, one rule for life is to try not to have desires whose satisfaction is outside your control. And career ambitions are a prime example of this. Homer, of course, handles this problem like the Epicurean genius that he is. But when else are desires difficult to satisfy? Another obvious situation is when satisfying them is expensive. This second situation, of course, becomes particularly pressing if, like Homer, you have adopted the first Epicurean lesson and renounced all career-related ambitions. How does Homer get around this problem?

Desires, of course, differ in the amount of money it takes to satisfy them. The key is to moderate your desires so that you only have the ones that don't require much money. Homer is a master of this sort of strategy. Consider, for example, the role Duff beer plays in his life. Homer is, of course, not averse to getting drunk. But there are various ways of doing this. When Homer heads over to Moe's Tavern, does he insist on Bollinger? No, and not for the simple reason that Moe isn't going to have any. No, it's not just that Homer doesn't order Bollinger; he's made sure that he doesn't *want* it. Homer has carefully cultivated his alcohol-related desires so that – the plentiful and cheap – Duff beer is his favourite.

Likewise with his food. Is lobster quadrille his favourite meal? Not at all – usually it's a toss up between pizza and hot dogs. And even when he is in the mood for something exotic, it's down to the Captain's all-you-can-eat fish buffet for him and the family, where he renders somewhat uncertain the future of the diner's all-you-can-eat buffet. And just think about his clothes. He's been wearing the same shirt and pants for well over a decade. And they're not exactly Versace or D&G to begin with.[20] By taking pleasure in cheap, and therefore easier to obtain, things, Homer embodies another Epicurean rule for life.

Another of the Epicurean pleasures is friendship. This is a bit of a departure from the 'try not to have any desires whose satisfaction depends on other people' line of thought, because whether or not you have friends does, to some extent, depend on other people. But this is not a big problem for Epicurus. He saw friendship as a basic human need, alongside the need for food, shelter and so on. And Epicurus only says *in so far as it is possible*, try not to have desires whose satisfaction depends on other people. Sometimes it simply is not possible, and friendship is a case in point. Besides, a desire for friendship is cheap and easy to satisfy, precisely because it is a basic human need. If everyone wants to have friends, there are going to be a plentiful supply of desperate people around ready to be someone's friend. Homer does seem to have lots of friends. There's Moe, Barney, Karl. Even Flanders could be counted among Homer's friends, if only for one episode. Nevertheless, his friends always seem to be somewhat peripheral to Homer's life. He hangs out with them when he wants to go drinking, for example, but that seems to be about it. None of them is what you could call a bosom buddy. This, I think, is because Homer has another friend – a life-long companion, soulmate even. Not Marge, but ... TV. The hours of uncomplicated, no strings attached entertainment adds up to years of Homer's life, and makes TV his most constant and unswerving companion. ('Marge,' he says, 'TV gives so much and asks so little. It's a boy's best friend.')

---

20. Or are they? He once mentioned to Moe that his trousers cost $600 – which precipitated Moe's mugging of him at gunpoint.

There is one Epicurean ingredient for the good life that Homer probably falls down on quite badly. It's not surprising, really, given his proclivity for Duff beer and TV: *thought*. In particular, thinking about life. Epicurus thought that analysing or understanding yourself was essential to the best sort of life. If you think about your typical anxieties – money worries, illness, death – and stuff life that, then you will eventually realise, Epicurus claimed, that there is nothing to worry about. Take death, for example. Remember the episode when Homer was going to die from eating a puffer fish in the Japanese restaurant? Not entirely happy about the whole thing was Homer. If he had taken Epicurus's advice, he would have realised that there is nothing to worry about. Death can't hurt you. When you're alive, death can't hurt you because it hasn't happened yet. When you're dead, you're no longer around for it to hurt. So, either way, death can't hurt you.

Admittedly, Homer did at least once talk about devoting more time to thinking, perhaps because of a tacit Epicurean realisation that his life was lacking in this respect. He once imagined living alone in the woods and keeping a journal of his thoughts. Unfortunately his thoughts seemed to amount to this: I wish I had brought my TV, I miss my TV so much … Oh God, why didn't I bring my TV! The problem, Homer realised, was simply that he didn't have enough thoughts to make thinking a viable proposition.

Nevertheless, Homer doesn't do a bad job of being an Epicurean. He's got the freedom thing down, liberating himself from the domination of career-related ambitions. He's got the restriction of desires thing down, liberating himself from the domination of expensive tastes. TV takes care of the friendship thing. It's just the thinking aspect of the deal that's the problem. But three out of four isn't bad. Homer is, we might say, 75 per cent Epicurean.

Strangely enough, Homer might actually be surpassed by Barney in the Epicurean lifestyle stakes. Barney has no career-related ambitions whatsoever. He has reduced his desires all the way down to one: Duff beer – a desire that's cheaply and easily satisfied. He has plenty of friends – mostly barflies, admittedly, but a friend's a friend. How about thinking? Does Barney show any sign of being able to think cogently about the human predicament? Well, remember the episode where Springfield had a film festival.[21] Barney wins first prize for creating a touching and perceptive film about his alcoholism ('Don't cry for me, I'm already dead' etc.), and this suggests that he does engage in the sort of complex and sophisticated thought about himself that would win brownie points from Epicurus. In his acceptance speech, Barney swears off alcohol, but, unfortunately for him, the first prize is a lorryload of Duff beer, and we all know how that turned out ('Just hook it straight up to my veins!').

So Barney seems pretty close to being the perfect Epicurean. Which, when you come to think of it, is a pretty damning refutation of Epicurus and his so-called good life. In fact, so serious is this objection I think that we might give it a name: the *Gumble Objection* to Epicureanism. If you come up with a theory of what life is all about, or about what makes life worth living, and Barney Gumble comes out as your ideal person, you've just got to think your theory is pretty screwed.[22] Time to move on, it seems.

---

21. To jog your memory, think of George C. Scott playing a man who gets hit in the nuts by an American football.

22. Philosophical translation of 'pretty screwed': 'refuted *modus tollens*'. Theory T (Epicurean account of the good life) entails claim C (Barney Gumble is ideal person). C is false. It follows, *modus tollens*, that T is false. The logical form of the argument is: T ? C, ¬C ? ¬T. The argument form is known as *modus tollens*. If your theory gets refuted *modus tollens* then you are, philosophically speaking, pretty screwed.

Marge and stoicism

Earlier I said that philosophical theories about the good life could be divided into two sorts – pre-modern ones that tell you to be happy with what you've got, and modern ones that tell you to not be happy with what you've got. Epicureanism was one version of the first type of theory. Another version is what's known as *stoicism*, a philosophical movement founded by a guy called Zeno. This is Zeno of Citium (*c.* 336–264 BC) we're talking about here, not Zeno of Elea (born *c.* 490 BC – no one knew when he died), who made his name, if not his fortune, trying to work out who would win a foot race between Achilles and a tortoise. The name stoicism comes from the fact that Zeno (of Citium) used to meet his gang at the *Stoa Poikile* – a hall in Athens (and not, as legend has it, on the *stoa* or front porch of his house).

It's not so much that stoicism says you should be happy with what you've got. It's more that you've simply got to put up with what you've got – because there isn't a thing you can do about it. The central idea behind stoicism is that you have to learn to become indifferent to whatever happens to you. So you married a big fat slob with few, if any, redeeming features. Your son has some fairly significant behavioural problems and will almost certainly never amount to anything (in some of your darker moments you think he will become a male stripper – and not a very good one at that). Your eldest daughter, while intelligent, is extremely anal. Your younger daughter is probably too young to have become seriously messed up yet, but give her time. Your life is one of drudgery – you make their breakfast, do the shopping, change the diapers, make the dinner and go to bed where you will probably not get to have sex, and if you do it will be brief and unsatisfying. Once, you almost had an affair with a French bowler you met at the bowling alley after your clod of a husband got you a bowling ball for your birthday, but that's the most exciting your life has been in recent years. You even had a better time when you went to jail. Or when you joined the police.

Pretty grim? Not according to the stoics. First of all, you have got to understand that this was all inevitable. The universe is governed by iron necessity. Things that happen are destined to happen – they couldn't possibly have happened any other way. If you married Homer, this is because it was your destiny to marry the loser. Your sisters, Pattie and Selma, thought you should have married Archie, but he was a bit of a jerk anyway. In fact, you had no choice in the matter. Whatever happens does so through necessity: everything is *predestined*. So this should take care of any tendency you have to blame yourself. It's not your fault – nothing is ever anybody's fault.

So far so good, at least on the blame front. But there is still the little matter of the tedium of your life. So what if you can't blame yourself for it – it's still a crap life. According to stoicism, this is not necessarily true. It's as bad as you let it be. The crapulence, or otherwise, of your life depends entirely on you, and the attitude you bring to it. To the extent you let events bother you, your life is a bad one. The key is to cultivate an attitude of indifference to everything that happens. To the extent you can do that, what happens will have no power over you. And nor will other people.

There is, as you might have spotted, a fundamental paradox at the core of this theory. If everything is inevitable or predestined, then whether or not you succeed in cultivating an attitude of indifference to what happens to you is something that is entirely beyond your control. If you do succeed, that was inevitable; if you don't, that was inevitable too. But I suppose this doesn't really matter. You can think of stoicism as telling you the best way to be – the best way to approach life – even if that way is impossible for you to achieve.

Marge does her best to be stoical. She's basically accepted that there's nothing she can do to change Homer or the kids. It's inevitable that Homer will drink too much Duff and eat too many hot dogs and doughnuts. It's inevitable that he will remain fat, go bald, never amount to anything, and generally be rather slow. She can do nothing to change this, so she does the best she can to cultivate an attitude of indifference. To the extent that she doesn't let these things bother her, they are really not bad things at all. Of course, maintaining her indifference through all the atrocities inflicted on her by Homer is not always easy. Sometimes she just snaps – as when she kicked Homer out for revealing their bedroom secrets to his adult education class. Most of the time, however, her reaction is not so extreme. She quietly bridles at the injustice of it all – her tell-tale growl, or whatever the word is for that sound she makes, being the only outward sign of the battle going on within. Marge may not completely succeed in being a stoic, but neither, for that matter, do most stoics. She does the best she can. And if you're a stoic, that's all you can ask for.

Ned Flanders and Christianity

Although Christianity has been around a long time, it qualifies as a modern theory. Christianity is an example of the second type of theory about how to live – it very definitely emphasises not being happy with what you've got. You can't be happy with this life; it's just a precursor of the life to come. In fact, the whole point of this life is to get you in the right place – upstairs rather than downstairs – in the life to come. So, being happy with this life – in the sense of not wanting anything more – would constitute a dangerous form of blasphemy.

Springfield's most famous Christian – outshining even the Reverend Lovejoy – is Ned 'hi-diddly-ho' Flanders. Like the good

Christian that he is, the first thing Ned is not happy about in his life is any sort of inappropriate desire – where 'inappropriate' covers just about anything fun: desires for sex (if not for the purposes of reproduction), drink, drugs, you name it. Even laughing at a joke on Fox TV's *Married with Children* is a distinct no-no.[23] To counteract these inappropriate desires, Flanders's strategy involves the tried and trusted Christian method of stamping them out: 'If thy hand offend thee, cut it off; if they eye offend thee, pluck it out', and all that sort of Old Testament stuff.

Actually, there is a good reason for Ned's distrust of desires and emotions – and it's not simply because he's a God-boy. Flanders's parents were, in fact, beatniks, who didn't believe in discipline – part of their general ideological objection to rules of any sort. As a result, the young Flanders was an out of control bully. The treatment eventually devised by his child psychologist was the University of Minnesota 'spankological protocol': he was spanked non-stop for eight months. The end result was a young Ned who was completely unable to express his feelings in any way. Any attempt to do so resulted in a meaningless string of dang-diddly, dang-diddly, verbal nonsense. Since his whole adult personality has been constructed around the inability to express feelings, Christianity may, in fact, be the perfect religion for Ned.

The other pillar around which Ned's approach to life is built is *turning the other cheek*. And as Homer once put it, Flanders has turned every cheek on his body at one time or another.[24] No matter what people do to you – and by 'people' I largely mean Homer – don't react. If they borrow your garden tools and never bring them

---

23. The joke: *Al*: Peg, this plant's all limp and lifeless. *Peg*: Gee, Al, maybe it would be more at home in the bedroom.
24. The episode where Homer was Flanders's friend, after he got him the game ball from the Springfield Atoms/Shelbyville Sharks football game.

back, don't react. If they blatantly steal your air conditioner, just ask for it back – but ask politely. Whenever they insult you, tell you to get lost, shut the door in your face, or even physically assault you – turn the other cheek.

There is, of course, a clear danger with Flanders's Christian strategy. You can't go bottling all that anger up for years and years and expect there to be no repercussions. The chances are you'll be totally neurotic most of the time and then, one day, eventually explode. After years and years of having his garden tools borrowed and not given back, of having garbage dumped in his yard, of having his air conditioning stolen – in other words, after years and years of living next to Homer – Flanders eventually snaps when his house (and his house alone) is destroyed by a tornado. The result: he insults most of Springfield and then checks himself into a loony bin.

There's also another drawback. Flanders may be missing out on a golden opportunity for self-improvement. This type of criticism was developed by a guy called Friedrich Nietzsche. Nietzsche was, in effect, the mirror image of Flanders, which is presumably why Flanders's initials NF, are the mirror reverse of Nietzsche's FN.

Friedrich Nietzsche's critique of Ned, Barney and Homer

As we have seen, Homer's Epicureanism is a version of the first sort of approach to living the good life. Be happy with what you've got. So, too, in a slightly different way, is Marge's stoic approach. Someone who would have thrown up at the very thought of being happy with what you've got was the nineteenth-century German philosopher Friedrich Nietzsche (1844–1900), maybe because he didn't have very much at all, except for a nasty case of syphilis that he picked up during a youthful indiscretion at a brothel. That, and progressively worsening migraines – the two probably not being unconnected. You can understand Nietzsche not being happy with what he's got. And so you can understand Nietzsche developing an account of the good life based on the idea of not being happy with what you've got. You can see why Nietzsche's view chimed in so well with the guiding principle of modernity – the idea of self-fulfilment. For Nietzsche, life is all about overcoming – *transcending* – what you are and what you have in favour of what you might become. It's all about not being satisfied with what you are and what you have, and constantly improving yourself, becoming better than you are.

A good way of understanding Nietzsche is by contrasting his attitude to life with that of Ned Flanders. Towards the end of his life, he – Nietzsche, not Ned – decided to sum up his work and his teachings. This is never a good idea, particularly not when you're in the final throes of syphilitic confusion. But, anyway, Nietzsche's summation of his ten or so books was: *Dionysus against the Crucified*. The Crucified is, of course, Christ, and, by proxy, his Simpsonian earthly representative, Ned. Flanders is, in effect, the antithesis of everything Nietzsche stood for.

Nietzsche started off with the idea that human beings – because of the biological creatures they are – have various drives, desires and instincts. These are what we might call basic or *primitive* drives. We have already come across this idea when we looked at Freud earlier. It's not clear how many basic or primitive drives we have, but, obviously, the four Fs – feeding, fighting, fleeing and fucking – are going to be the classic examples. The characteristic that runs through all great human beings, Nietzsche thinks, is the ability to take these primitive drives and turn them into something else, something more worthwhile; something more *valuable*.

The key to greatness is to take your primitive desires, drives and instincts, and use them. Or, as Nietzsche puts it, the key is to *sublimate* them – transform them into something better. We've come across this idea of sublimation before, when we talked about Freud. Most people think Freud invented the idea of sublimation but, in fact, Nietzsche beat him to it by thirty years or so. The basic idea is that we can distinguish what we might call the *power* of a drive from the *expression* of that drive. A desire to drink beer, for example, has both a certain power and a certain expression. Its power is the strength of the grip it has over you, the motivation it provides you with to go and drink some beer. An extreme case would be Homer when he was on his 30 days abstention from alcohol. His resulting desire for beer is strong enough to get him to do all sorts of things – including, apparently, eating beer-soaked sand from underneath the sports ground's bleachers. The expression of the desire is, of course, drinking beer. Nietzsche's idea is that while the force or power that a desire provides is fairly constant, at least for short periods of time, the expression of a desire is variable. It can be altered, and sometimes it can be altered at will.

So, the key to sublimation is using the force of a drive or desire but changing its expression. The force of a desire whose expression is primitive – feeding, fighting, fleeing or fucking, for example – can be changed into something less primitive, say the desire to paint the house. This new desire will have both a certain force and a certain expression, and, once again, the force can be used and the expression transformed into something else, say the desire to paint not the house but the Sistine Chapel. In short, sublimation is the utilisation of the force of a desire coupled with the transformation of the expression of that desire. In sublimation, the force or power supplied by a desire is, as we might say, *channelled* into something else.

Throughout history, Nietzsche claimed, true greatness has only ever been achieved by those who were capable of constantly sublimating their desires – continually transforming them into higher and higher ones. A basic drive is transformed into one slightly less basic, and this in turn is transformed into something less basic, and so on. Eventually we arrive at the drives that, for Nietzsche, are the quintessence of human greatness. For Nietzsche, these were things like art and music. But what's distinctive about Nietzsche's philosophy is not so much his idea of the *product* of greatness – the sorts of things great people do – but his account of the *process* of greatness – the means by which great people become great.

It's easy to see why Nietzsche would have a problem with Flanders's approach to the good life. There are two basic problems. First, for Nietzsche, Flanders's approach is distinctly unhealthy. While we might be able to transform the expression of a desire, the force or power supplied by that desire cannot be changed. It's going to hang around one way or another. Flanders's strategy involves the repression of all recalcitrant desires. These wayward desires need to be sat on hard, given a good kicking, or whatever. We can try to do this, but we can never really quash their underlying force or power. Repressing our desires simply means that they are denied outward expression. So, where does their power go? It's turned inwards, turned back on Ned. The typical result of this will, Nietzsche claimed, be illness – psychological, physical or both. We came across this idea with our Freudian analysis of Tony Soprano in Chapter 2.

Secondly, and even more importantly, repressing your desires means that you lose out on a golden opportunity for self-improvement. All the power with which the drives in question provided you now has no useful outlet. It's just churning around inside you. If only you had sublimated, instead of repressed, you could have used this power for something really useful or valuable. You could have been better than you were. You could have been a Michelangelo or a Leonardo da Vinci. You could have been a contender; you could have been *someone*. Instead, you're just a bum.

Which gets us back to Barney, actually. Nietzsche would have had almost as much of a problem with Barney as he would with Flanders. Who knows the capacity for greatness that lies within Barney? We see clear glimpses of his potential when he wins first prize at the film festival for his portrayal of his life, or when he sails through the astronaut-training programme, despite stiff competition from Homer. Who knows what dark drives and passions burn inside Barney, drives and passions that might propel him to greatness? We will probably never know because, for the most part, what Barney feels, wants and desires is heavily numbed by his non-stop drinking of Duff beer. Karl Marx said that religion – and it was Christianity he had in mind – is the opium of the masses. Flanders represses his drives and desires with Christianity. Barney obliterates his with Duff. Why? Perhaps both Flanders and Barney find what is inside too painful, or too scary. If so, they are, according to Nietzsche, misguided. The pain and fear is something to be embraced, recognised as the friends they are.

Finally, Nietzsche wouldn't be particularly impressed with Homer's Epicurean approach to life either. For Nietzsche, as we have seen, greatness involves using your primitive desires. But this doesn't mean acting upon them, not in any straightforward way. Homer, with his 'be happy with what you've got' Epicurean approach, is a classic example of someone who believes in acting on his primitive drives and impulses, no matter how primitive they may be. Admittedly, he does believe it's best to restrict his desires to the easily satisfied ones. But if he has one of those, he's going to act on it. So, for example, if he desires to scratch his arse while drinking milk from the carton – as he did in the brilliant Sherry Bobbins ('no, not Mary Poppins!') episode – then that is what he is going to do. He wants beer, he drinks beer; he feels sleepy at work, he sleeps; he wants to eat a 12-foot-long sub, even though he's been working on it for a week and its definitely 'turned', then he eats it, or at least tries. If it itches, Homer's going to scratch. That's what Homer does.

Homer doesn't have the problems of repression associated with Flanders, nor does he have the sort of advanced liver damage associated with Barney.[25] However, on Nietzsche's view, Homer will always be a complete loser for the simple reason that he will never learn to sublimate his basic drives and desires. They're not around long enough for that. Homer's already acted on them before any sort of sublimation can take place. So there is no prospect of Homer getting any better than he already is. Which is great news for those of us for who like him just the way he is.

Lisa: the übergirl?

For Nietzsche, the person who is capable of sublimating their desires over and over again is what he called the *übermensch* – the *overman* or *superman*. For Nietzsche, it was always a *man* and not *overwoman* or even *overperson*. But Nietzsche, of course, had never come across Lisa Simpson. Of all the characters in *The Simpsons*, it is perhaps Lisa who most closely approximates what Nietzsche had in mind. So the question we are going to look at is this: can Lisa be regarded as a Nietzschean *übergirl*?

First of all, Lisa broadly agrees with Nietzsche on what makes life worth living: girly stuff like art, literature and, in particular, music. As she surveys her family – particularly her oafish father and loutish brother – she must indeed be tempted by Nietzsche's claim that 'Only as aesthetic phenomenon is the world, and the existence of man, eternally justified.' When she looks around her world, Lisa may well be struck with a peculiar sense of pointlessness. We

---

25. His heart, however, that's a different matter.

evolved slowly upwards from the primeval sludge, developing into, allegedly, higher and higher life forms. But why? What justification could there be for this, if all the process leads to is Homer and Bart Simpson? After millions and millions of years of birth, death, suffering and struggle, all we have to show for it are Homer and Bart – specimens that are, as Nietzsche puts it, *human, all too human*. But push this point further. Homer and Bart are no worse than anyone else. Everyone is, to a greater or lesser extent, blinkered, selfish and egotistical. We are progressively screwing the environment, thereby screwing ourselves in the process and exploiting other species on a monumental scale. All these things piss Lisa off no end, and so she would probably have to acknowledge, as do all of us, that in many ways the world would be a better place without us. So, it seems we have to ask the question: what justification could there by for humans?

Nietzsche's answer: only as an aesthetic phenomenon are human beings justified. We are justified because, and only because, Beethoven composed the Ninth Symphony, Goethe wrote *Faust* and Michelangelo painted the Sistine Chapel. These are the only sorts of things that could possibly make the existence of human beings worth it, at least according to Nietzsche. Lisa, I suspect, would agree with him – although she would probably insist on the inclusion of Bleeding Gums Murphy, her favourite saxophonist, on the list.

The second respect in which Lisa follows Nietzsche is in appreciating the value of sublimation. God knows, she has plenty of raw materials for it. The constant slights and irritations inflicted on her by her brother, and the regular disappointments visited on her by her father, provide her with the necessary impetus – the drive and desire – to transform herself into something better. And Lisa's life has been a constant transcending – overcoming – of her limitations. Despite the obvious limitation of having only three fingers, and rather short and stubby ones at that, she has driven herself on and forced herself to become a more than competent saxophonist. Despite her somewhat limited intelligence – she is intelligent but not as intelligent as at least one of her friends – she has pushed herself into becoming the best student in her class. Hell, she even managed to win the runner-up spot in the Miss Springfield beauty pageant.

Life for Lisa is a constant set of challenges, a constant set of invitations to become better than she is. It's the challenge, and the quest for self-overcoming, that is important, not anything else. And this brings us to the third sense in which Lisa is a Nietzschean. Happiness is way down on her list of priorities – it's one of the less important ingredients of the good life. Even her catchphrase is 'If anyone wants me I'll be in my room' – she's not exactly a ray of sunshine. It's very noticeable that pleasure and even happiness figure far less in Lisa's worldview than that of Bart or Homer. For the father and the brother, pleasure and happiness are the *raison d'être* of life, they're the whole point of everything. For Lisa, on the other hand, pleasure and happiness are, at most, a by-product of something far more important. This is the feeling that she is getting better – the feeling, as Nietzsche put it, that her power is increasing.

In many respects, then, Lisa is a most promising Nietzschean *übermensch*. Nietzsche might be forced to reappraise his rather negative view of woman if he had been fortunate enough to have a TV. And yet …

And yet …

And yet, there seems to be something missing – a tragic flaw in Lisa's personality. A clue to this is to be found in a rather important scene where, after Bart has been teasing her about her attitude to school, Lisa has a little fantasy – a waking dream – about him being impaled on her Nobel Peace Prize. This is a classic symptom of what Nietzsche called *ressentiment*. For some reason, Nietzsche always used the French form of the word when he discussed this concept. It is, pretty obviously, the French word for *resentment*, but Nietzsche used it in a slightly non-standard sense, a semi-technical sense, as it were.

Nietzsche's examples of *ressentiment* often involved the early Christian missionaries' descriptions of hell – the sort of description provided by a guy called Tertullian, for example. These were usually very graphic and typically involved, in gratuitous detail, accounts of red-hot pitchforks being stuck up people's bottoms, and stuff like that. What intrigued Nietzsche was that these early Christian missionary descriptions of hell also found a place for everyone who had gone upstairs – they had box seats, sort of heavenly corporate boxes, where they could observe the action and laugh at what was happening to those who had gone downstairs. Why would heaven have corporate boxes, particularly for the rather sick sort of entertainment on display? Or, to put the point another way, what sort of person would enjoy the spectacle of sinners having red-hot pitchforks stuck up their bums? Indeed, what kind of sick fuck would enjoy this spectacle so much that they would incorporate it into their conception of heaven? Nietzsche's answer is: the sort of person in whom *ressentiment* had built up to pathologically high levels. The sort of person who spends his life watching all the sinners going round having a great time on earth, going to all the good parties, having sex with all the attractive people, and who – quite literally – resents the hell out of them as a result.

Lisa's *ressentiment* pales in comparison to that of early Christians like Tertullian. Nonetheless, fondly imagining your brother impaled on your Nobel Peace Prize shows not only your fondness for irony but also a fairly significant level of resentment. And this is a problem if you ever want to be an *übermensch*. The reason is that *ressentiment* occurs because of a failure of sublimation. It is what happens when you fail to channel a drive, desire or emotion in an appropriate direction, when you fail to redirect its expression into something better or *higher*. The hostility Lisa undoubtedly – and sometimes quite reasonably – feels towards her brother could have been used by her. It could have been channelled, sublimated into something more useful. The fact that she feels *ressentiment* shows that her attempts to sublimate her feelings of hostility have failed. As a result, the feelings have been turned back into her; they're sloshing around inside her in the form of a useless and potentially unhealthy feeling of *ressentiment*. This, then, is one reason why Lisa might fall short of being a Nietzschean *übermensch*: she can sublimate a bit, but she can't, it seems, do it enough.

There's another reason. Nietzsche's recipe for greatness involves two separable elements. First, there is the existence of primitive desires of various sorts. Secondly, there is the ability to sublimate these desires continually and transform them into something better. So, Lisa can fall short of greatness for two reasons. One we have already looked at: she fails to sublimate continually her drives and desires. As her feelings of *ressentiment* seem to show, this is a bit of a problem for Lisa.

The other problem may be that her basic drives or desires are not strong enough. On Nietzsche's view, you shouldn't simply accept your desires; you should sublimate them. But you shouldn't try to moderate or reduce them either. That's the Flanders/Barney strategy, and Nietzsche would have none of it. On the contrary, you should try to intensify them, make them stronger than they already are. 'Man must become more evil; thus do I teach', as Nietzsche once put it. For it is these drives and desires that provide the raw materials you can use for sublimation. If your basic drives and desires are not strong enough, then you will always fall short of greatness.

Lisa, it seems, may have a problem with the strength of her primitive drives. One manifestation of this is her constant need to stick to the rules, to not do anything wrong; in marked contrast, it should be noted, to that of her brother. Another manifestation is her constant need for validation by society. For example, in the episode where school is cancelled because of a teachers' strike, she is constantly pestering Marge, and even Bart, to test her: *test me, grade me, evaluate me*! These are not the hallmarks of an *übergirl*. The overgirl, or overboy for that matter, is always characterised by a certain waywardness, a certain erraticness and unpredictability. The sense is always of an inner power that is barely contained. The *übergirl* would always appear, so to speak, as if she has a tiger by the tail. She can control her inner drives and desires just enough to sublimate them, but it's always touch and go; she's always on a knife edge. We get no real suggestion of this with Lisa.

The *übergirl* would also have a certain contempt for society's rules, recognising them to be a creation of other people and so, in essence, an impingement on his or her freedom, and hence his or her power. It is the creation of new values, rather than the acceptance of pre-existing values, that characterises the overgirl. In this respect, but probably only in this respect, Bart is more like *übermensch* than Lisa. 'Eat my shorts!' is one of Bart's classic rejections of the value systems imposed on him by others including, notably, Principal Seymour Skinner, who was on the receiving end of Bart's earliest use of this slogan. Bart, of course, could never be an *overboy*. He has got the flouting of convention and rejection of pre-existing values thing down very well. But there isn't the underpinning of sublimation and continual improvement to make this rebellion in any way significant. In fact, the whole idea of sublimation is completely alien to him. The sacrifice of short-term goals, and the sublimation of desires to meet long-term goals – this is something Bart never does.

Nevertheless, ironically enough for a girl who fondly imagined Bart being impaled on her Nobel Peace Prize, Lisa's failure to achieve *übergirl* status probably stems from her not being enough like Bart in this crucial respect. Whenever Lisa is creative, it is always within a framework of values and possibilities created by others. She is just too *safe*, and in her own rebellious way, too *conventional*. The genuine *übergirl* would look to transcend this framework, not work within it. And, at the end of the day, it is, I think, doubtful whether Lisa has the required strength or primitive drives or the required ability at sublimating these primitive drives to take this final step. Too bad.

And Bart? Why have I not said more about Bart? Bart exemplifies, as far as I can see, no philosophical system whatsoever – apart, possibly, from nihilism. And in this does his greatness lie. And the greatness of *The Simpsons* lies in providing just the sort of aesthetic phenomenon that, in Nietzsche's view, is required to justify eternally the existence of man.

eight
FRASIER

HOW CAN YOU KNOW YOURSELF?

Know thyself

For modernity, the self is, so to speak, our *inside*. Here is the philosopher Galen Strawson's exceptionally clear expression of the modern idea of the self:

> *The early realisation of the fact that one's thoughts are unobservable by others, the experience of the profound sense in which one is alone in one's head – these are among the deepest facts about the character of human life, and found the sense of the mental self. It is perhaps most often vivid when one is alone and thinking, but it can be equally vivid in a room full of people. It connects with a feeling that nearly everyone has intensely at some time – the feeling that one's body is just a vehicle or vessel for the mental thing that is what one really or most essentially is. I believe that the primary or fundamental way in which we conceive of ourselves is as a distinct mental thing – sex addicts, athletes, and supermodels included.*[26]

---

26. Galen Strawson, 'The self', *Journal of Consciousness Studies*, 4, 1997, 405–28, p. 407.

The real you is your inside, and your body is just something you use to carry this inside around. Consequently, if you want to know who and what you really are, you have to look inside. Introspection is the source of all self-knowledge. If you want to know thyself, then you know where to look.

We've already seen some of the things to which this idea of you as your inside can lead. The mistaken conception of happiness and pervasive sense of alienation that we discovered in Carrie Bradshaw's Manhattan was, perhaps, the most obvious one. Then, also, there was the difficulty we had, from our modern perspective, of understanding how life could be significant, important or ... *big*; a difficulty we encountered, in different ways, both in Sunnydale and in Jerry Seinfeld's version of New York. There were also the problems we had, again from our modern perspective, in understanding the significance of interpersonal relationships such as love and friendship that we encountered in yet another version of New York, oriented around Central Perk.

All these problems have a common root: the view of you and me around which modernity has been built. If all relations that the self enters into with things outside it are only identity-reflecting and not identity-constituting, then they cannot be as important as the relations the self enters into with *itself*. This, you might remember, is precisely how Carrie Bradshaw summed up what she had learned from seven years of *Sex and the City*. The most important relationship you have, she claimed, is the one you have with yourself. I must admit, I was very disappointed with Carrie in that final episode.[27] If the most important relationship is the one you have with yourself, then relations to things outside of you can have only a secondary status. No matter how important they are, or seem, they are not as

27. Marching into the sunset with her *fur coat* on, to boot!

important as the relationship you have with yourself. The modern conception of the self comes straight out of this. You – as a person – must be the sort of thing that can have a relationship with yourself irrespective of any relations you have to things outside of you. So, you love Big? Or you don't love Big you love Petrovski? Or Aidan. Or maybe you love no one at all? Who cares? You, the person you are, can persist through all these variations. Relations, like love, that you might have to people outside of you only reflect the person you are, but they don't make you the person you are. And we've seen the sort of problems to which this can lead.

In this chapter, I want to look at one final, characteristically modern, anxiety. The modern age tells us: fulfil yourself! Realise yourself! Be the best you can be! The anxiety I have in mind stems from a worrying suspicion that maybe all of us have from time to time: we have really have *no idea what this injunction means*! What is this *you* that must be realised or fulfilled? And how do you know whether it is being realised or fulfilled? In order to satisfy modernity's injunction, it seems you must first have some way of knowing who *you* are. But the modern view of the self, as we shall see, leads to all sorts of problems for the attempt to know who you are. If we adopt the modern view of the self, then it is, I think, highly likely that none of us ever really knows who we are. In fact, modernity gives us little reason for supposing that we are really anything at all. We are on the inside, so we are told. And if we want to know ourselves we must, accordingly, turn our attention inwards. But when we look inwards what we often find is *nothing at all*. And so modernity foists on us a deeply disturbing suspicion: that, at the end of the day, we may in fact *be* nothing at all.

These themes are complex and subtle. It is as well, then, that we are going to explore them using one of the most complex and subtle TV sitcoms: the incomparable *Frasier* (1993–2004).

I know what I like?

Frasier Crane is a psychiatrist, born in Seattle, but until recently living in Boston, where he used to hang out at a bar called Cheers, with his friends Norm, Cliff and Sam. He was also married to Lilith. She left him – which, as he admits, was painful. Then she came back to him, which, as he also admits, was excruciating. He finally decided to make a clean break and move back to Seattle, where he was to host a radio show. However, circumstances conspired to force him to allow his father Martin to move in with him. Martin is an ex-cop, who has been forced to retire early after taking a bullet in his hip. His injury meant that he was unable to live alone any more: he required the help of a physiotherapist/support worker. And so Daphne Moon – a Manchester girl with psychic abilities, or so she says – also moved in with them. The quartet is completed by Frasier's bother Niles. He doesn't live with them. At the time he is married to oft discussed but never seen Maris. But his growing infatuation with Daphne means that he is regularly to be found at Frasier's apartment.

What is this show all about? A superficial, but nonetheless correct, answer is: *snobbery*. Martin provides the baseline theme, one upon which Frasier and Niles are going to build. Martin is a no-nonsense, blue collar, regular guy who calls a spade a spade and … you can extend the stereotype as far as you like, but you probably get the picture. He is a man of few or no pretensions – utterly, and happily, oblivious to affectations regarding, for example, wine or coffee. And with food, he knows what he likes – typically a good steak, medium rare, down at The Sawmill – and what he doesn't like. He would rather be having a few beers with the boys down at Duke's rather than eating at a gourmet restaurant with his sons – or even without his sons, for that matter. And, on nights in, he is to be found on his faithful, if somewhat tatty, Lay-Z-Boy reclining armchair, drinking his Coors, and watching his beloved *Seahawks* (or, for that matter, *Sonics* or *Mariners*).

The thing about Martin is that he seems happy with what he is; he is a man entirely at ease with himself. And this drives Frasier and Niles mad! They are, of course, aficionados of the finer things life has to offer – or what they regard as the finer things anyway. Only the best, and most difficult to get into, restaurants will do. Only the finest wines, and only the most fashionable coffee are acceptable. So, they have different tastes, different values even. But this doesn't really get us to the heart of what bothers Frasier and Niles. No – what bothers them is that Martin is so at ease with himself; Martin is so *authentic*. And they can't believe he should be. In their classically trained minds, this sort of authenticity should be reserved for shepherds playing flutes or lyres in Arcadia. It should not be the province of the beer-drinking, Lay-Z-Boy-lying, Seahawk-supporting Martin Crane.

Martin is happy with what he is and therefore at ease with himself. The same can't be said of Frasier and Niles. There is a certain type of *anxiety* that Martin seldom, if ever, feels but which follows his two sons around like a bad smell. This stems from the greater role played by *should* or *ought* in the lives of Frasier and Niles. I'm not saying, of course, that Martin is not a moral man – quite the contrary. The sense of *should* or *ought* here is not a moral sense of the sort we looked at in the *Buffy* chapter. Nor is it what some people call a *petit-moral* sense – the sense of *should* involved in being polite, or having good manners. The sense of *should* or *ought* that dominates Frasier's and Niles's lives does not pertain to morality or etiquette. In fact, it is not entirely clear what it does pertain to. The sense of *should* involved is diaphanous, and difficult to pin down. That is, I think, part of the reason for their anxiety. Here's an example:

Frasier: That was around the time you thought the 1812 Overture was a great work of classical music.
Niles: Was I ever that young?

What's going on here? Niles (he was around nine years old at the time) liked the 1812 Overture. When his musical education had become more rounded – as he would now see it – he came to think that it was not a great work of classical music, and so stopped liking it. Why? Because what Niles likes is mediated through what he thinks he *should* like – what the canons of good musical taste tell him that he *ought* to like. With Niles, in this case at least, you can't separate what he *does* like from what he feels he *should* like: the two are bound tightly together. Niles, in this sort of case, is only going to permit himself to like what he feels he should like.

Frasier exhibits a similar profile. Once, he bought a painting because he believed, falsely, that it was the work of the famous (fictional) artist Martha Caxton. Mentioning this on his radio show, he gets a call from the artist, and decides to arrange a little impromptu unveiling soiree at his apartment. So, on Friday night we find him extolling – at *great* length – the virtues of this piece of work, to the supposed artist and a roomful of his guests, only for the artist to tell him, and everyone else, that she never painted the work. 'No, no' – he tries hopefully – 'you didn't paint it, you *created* it, you *gave birth* to it!' But, alas no. It's a forgery and Frasier is humiliated. The end result is that Frasier now decides he hates the painting and, being unable to get satisfaction from the gallery, ends up hanging it in one of the smaller toilets in his apartment. For Frasier, like Niles, you can't separate what he *does* like from what he feels he *should* like. The sense of *should* here corresponds to what some people – people like Frasier and Niles, actually – would call *taste* – and Frasier and Niles are dominated by it. For them, the *should* of good taste drives the *would* of what they would like. We all know people like this. Hell, some of us *are* people like this.

Martin isn't like this at all. Martin likes what he likes, and doesn't really dwell on why he likes it. And he certainly doesn't tend to dwell on whether he *should* like it. Not in the sense of *should* associated with good taste anyway. In the *moral* sense of should, of course, Martin is perfectly capable of questioning his desires and his behaviour. When Frasier buys him a telescope, he does worry about whether he should like peeking into the lives, and, more to the point, the apartments of other people. But this is a moral sense of should – Martin is not concerned with whether peeking into other people's apartments might contravene the canons of good taste, but whether it contravenes the rules of morality.

So Frasier and Niles have an extra *should* in their lives; a *should* of good taste. They find it difficult to establish any sense of what they like independently of what they think they should, in this sense, like. And this is a permanent source of anxiety for them. Of course, it's not like Frasier and Niles can always pull off this trick of only liking what they think they should like. They're only human, and their lapses are frequent. Niles's obsession with Daphne, for example, began around the second episode of series 1, and eventually culminated in his marrying her. But, for most of the series, his infatuation was unrequited. Daphne is portrayed as working-class Manchester. More than that, she's more than a little quirky – she claims to be psychic (of which, Frasier quips, 'we've decided to find it charming'). She is not at all the sort of well-heeled, well-educated and, in particular, *refined* person who, it seems, *should* appeal to the Harvard educated psychiatrist Niles Crane. Daphne is not going to go down well at the Seattle Arts Council bashes that Niles is disposed to attend, or the Seattle Fine Wine Tasting Society, of which he was once president. Nonetheless, Niles can't, it seems, help himself. That's the way it sometimes is with should and would. What you do like has a habit of getting away from you in the end, no matter how much of a slave you are to what you think you should like.

Exactly the same is true of Frasier. Recall, for example, the famous 'dirty girl' incident. The radio station has a new, female, boss – Mercedes Ruehl – who Frasier absolutely detests. Or, at least, that's his official line. She is loud, brassy, mercenary and attended an inferior university. Still, he is inexplicably drawn to her, and she to him, and their mutual attraction is increased by their habit of trading insults. Eventually, this culminates in them having sex in the control room. Frasier has been turned on by her calling him a 'bad boy', and she has been turned on by him calling her a 'dirty girl'. Unfortunately, the broadcasting equipment is – unbeknown to them – also turned on. And most of Seattle is treated to their verbal foreplay and its coital conclusion.

So, Frasier and Niles are snobs because, it seems, they allow considerations of what they *should* want to play a far greater role in their lives and determine, to a considerable extent, what they *would* or *do* want. Their domination by this *should* of good taste is, as we have seen, not total. But it is enough for them to count as snobs, at least relative to their father Martin. And this sort of snobbery, of course, goes hand in hand with a certain sort of anxiety. Frasier and Niles, of course, want to distance themselves from the masses – from the beer-swilling, Seahawks-supporting, tailgate-partying hoi polloi, with their risible knowledge of art, music, wine and food, and their bad taste in clothes. It is a matter of urgency for Frasier and Niles to distance themselves from such people because such people are, in effect, a *threat*. The threat is that Frasier and Niles are, in reality, not too different from those people at all. The danger is that underneath the suave exterior, beneath the thin veneer of civilisation, beats the heart of a savage – someone who actually likes the taste of beer, who wouldn't know a Martha Caxton from a David Hockney, someone who didn't even go to Harvard! The distance they need is given them by their pervasive use of *should* in their lives. The danger of becoming one of the masses is held at bay by their *taste*.

Martin, of course, is where the greatest danger lies. Not only is he of the same blood, and therefore, in one undeniable sense, one of them. More importantly, he often exhibits the sort of understanding of the boys, their problems and their foibles, that leaves them and their psychiatric training for dead. He has a ready and subtle wit, and often exhibits a level of mental agility that worries them profoundly. In one episode, for example, he regularly thrashes Frasier at chess. All this would be deeply unsettling for Frasier and Niles. Martin is a sort of *fifth column*, the one of them who is also one of us; the thin end of the wedge that threatens to undermine the distance Frasier and Niles have set up between themselves and the great unwashed.

So, at one level, *Frasier* is about snobbery and the anxieties that often accompany it. But this sort of snobbery is, I think, only a symptom of something deeper and far more interesting. It reveals a problem about the very idea, central to modernity, of *knowing yourself*.

I'm listening!

What does it mean to *know yourself*? According to modernity, you exist on the inside, and so knowing yourself involves turning your attention within – it involves introspection. So, the most straightforward explanation of the idea of knowing yourself would be that when you introspect, you become aware of yourself as the person you are. Knowing yourself amounts to knowing your *self*. Is this right? More importantly, what does it mean? When you turn you attention inwards, what exactly do you become aware of? Here is David Hume again, pointing out something that is, I think, quite important.

For my part, when I enter most intimately into something I call myself, I always stumble on some particular perception or other, of heat or cold, of light or shade, love or hatred, pain or pleasure. I can never catch myself at any time without a perception, and never can observe anything but the perception ... The mind is a kind of theatre, where several perceptions successively make their appearance, pass, re-pass, glide away, and mingle in an infinite variety of postures and situations ... The comparison of the theatre must not mislead us. They are the successive perceptions only that constitute the mind.

There is a lot going on here. First of all, when you introspect, when you turn your attention inwards, what do you find? Hume's answer, and I think he is right, is that you find what he refers to with the catch-all *perceptions*. By this he means to include:

thoughts and beliefs;
desires;
emotions;
feelings;
sensations;
hopes, fears, anticipations and expectations.

These are the sorts of things you find when you turn your attention inwards. But what you don't find, *in addition* to all these sorts of things, is the self of person that you are. What you find, in short, are states that a self or person might have – mental states or states of mind, as we now call them – but you don't find a self or person who has those states. At least, you don't find a self or person in any straightforward sense.

Some have inferred from Hume that you, therefore, really have no awareness of yourself. Maybe your sense of self – your sense of who you are – is just a hypothesis, one that you come up with to make sense of what you do experience when you turn your attention inwards. That is, you introspect, come across various states like thoughts, experiences and emotions, and hypothesise that there must be a self or person there that has all these things. But this, I think, is just way too simplistic.

Look at the page in front of you. You are presumably aware of the page. But what does that mean? Well, you may be aware of the whiteness of the paper, its rectangularity, the contrast of the black ink against that paper, and so on. In short, you are aware of various *properties* that the page has. Are you aware, *in addition to that*, of the page itself? Well, it is difficult to see how you could be. It is difficult, in fact, to see what that could possibly mean. What would it be to be aware of the page *in addition* to the various properties it has? But, if you are not aware of the page as something over and above its properties, does this mean that you are not really aware of the page at all, only its various properties? But that seems stupid. To say that you are only aware of various properties that the page has does not mean that you are not aware of the page. To be aware of the various properties of the page is, precisely, to be aware of the page. Some people say that the page is nothing more than the collection of properties that make it up. Others disagree; they claim there must be something there for the properties to attach to. But it doesn't matter for our purposes anyway. Properties such as whiteness and rectangularity are, at the very least, parts of the page. So when you are aware of these things, you are aware of part of the page. And no one is ever going to claim that in order to be aware of something, you have to be aware of *all* of it. Usually, we are aware of things by way of being aware of parts of them. So, being aware of the page simply is being aware of its various properties. Or, to put the same point another way: when you turn your attention to the page, you are aware of various properties and – *thereby* – aware of the page. You are aware of the page *by virtue of* being aware of its various properties. That's precisely what being aware of the page is.

We can take the same line with regard to Hume's comments on what we discover when we turn our attention inwards. To say that you become aware of thoughts, beliefs, desires, emotions, feelings, sensations and stuff like that does not mean that you do not become aware of your self. For becoming aware of such things may be precisely what becoming aware of your self is. You become aware of your self – of the person you are – *by virtue of* becoming aware of the various properties – thoughts, feelings, emotions, etc. – of this person.

Now, maybe, we are getting somewhere. We have worked out the sort of thing self-knowledge, if it exists, must be. To the extent we know ourselves, it must be through understanding our thoughts and beliefs, making sense of our feelings and emotions, correctly interpreting our desires, and hopes and fears. That's the sort of thing self-knowledge must be. Not some kind of acquaintance with a self that stands over and above these sorts of things (as if you could be acquainted with the page over and above its various properties!). So, the question then is, what is involved in knowing yourself in this sense?

Hume cautions us that the analogy of theatre is a limited one. What we find when we turn our attention inwards is just various states of mind – thoughts, feelings, emotions, and stuff like that. We do not find anyone or anything that corresponds to the spectator, the theatregoing observer. There is something very right about Hume's claim, but also something very wrong. To begin with what's right: when you're trying to explain what the self is, there's no point at all in bringing in the idea of a self whose function it is to watch the succession of conscious episodes – thoughts, experiences, and stuff like that – flash across the screen of the mind. This idea gets you nowhere. Your original problem was explaining what the self is. But if you bring in the imagery of the theatregoing observer, then you just replicate the problem. Your original problem was explaining what the self or person was. Now you have the problem of explaining what the theatregoing observer is – which, in fact, seems pretty much like the same problem.

One of the big mistakes in the history of philosophy – and it's still made today – was in thinking of consciousness as a sort of screen or stage on which conscious episodes – thoughts, experiences, feelings, emotions and so on – get displayed. Because this just forces you to bring in, explicitly or implicitly, someone or something that watches the screen – who *consciously* registers what is on the screen – and then you're back to your original problem: explaining what consciousness is. We can make much the same point about the self – which, after all, is a centre of consciousness. If we want to understand the self, then introducing another self isn't going to help us.

But there's also something very wrong about Hume's claim. Snobbery, as we have seen, is all about the ability to reflect on what you want or like, and then worry about whether you *should* want or like it. This sort of self-reflection is built into the nature of the self – or at least the snobbish self. So, it seems we are going to have to allow for a division *within* the self: a division between a *participatory* or *engaged* self and a *spectator* self. There is, it seems, a part of the self that does the wanting or the liking – this aspect of the self participates or is engaged in whatever it wants or likes – and a part of the self that observes the predilections of the engaged self and reflects on whether it should be wanting or liking what it wants or likes.

This is not just how it is for snobbish selves. Any time we think about things using the concept *should*, we get the same division between engaged and spectator self. Morality is an obvious example. As we saw in the *Buffy* chapter, genuine morality – of the sort involved in having a *soul* rather than merely a *chip* in your head – involves not only doing the right thing, but also doing the right thing because it is the right thing and because you want to do the right thing. So, morality involves the ability to reflect on your reasons for doing something, to evaluate them and to consider whether, all things considered, they are the best things – morally speaking – to do. And, as you no doubt recognise, this often takes the form of a sort of conversation – a conversation you have with yourself. How often do you find yourself praising yourself when you do something good, either morally good or prudentially good, or just damn clever: way to go, Mark! Or blaming yourself when you do something disappointing: Mark, you asshole!

So, often, the theatre analogy does, in fact, seem a good one. Just as the theatre is split into stage and audience, so too the self seems split into the self that acts, and the self that comments on and evaluates those actions. The possibility of any sort of self-evaluation seems to presuppose some sort of split in the self – a split between an engaged and a spectator self. There is the self that does things – thinks, experiences, feels, expects and hopes – and there is the self that provides the commentary – sometimes warm and encouraging, sometimes hostile and sarcastic – on those things.

Indeed, this is why TV provides such a good medium for moral matters. It provides a perfect medium for your spectator self to do what it does best: observe, comment and evaluate. And the great thing is that the characters on the TV do things so you don't have to. You are engaged with what they do – but in a vicarious way. Basically, they go proxy for you. You can try things out on TV – morally speaking, that is – that you wouldn't want to try out in real life.

But there's a big difference between the theatre, or TV for that matter, and the self. With TV, things are on screen right there in front of you. Nothing is, so to speak, hidden. Everything is, more or less, and allowing for a few plot twists or so, as it seems to be. In the self, on the other hand, nothing is what it seems. The relations between engaged self and spectator self are characterised by dissembling, illusion and sleight of hand. The self hides itself from itself. If *Frasier* has taught us anything, it has taught us this.

Just one more clarinet lesson

The engaged self is the self that acts – it thinks, experiences, emotes, feels, hopes and expects – all the stuff that makes life worth living. And thoughts, experiences, emotions, hopes and expectations, these are the sorts of things that can motivate you to do whatever it is you do. But, as Frasier Crane has taught us, your motivations can gradually transform themselves in order to make them more palatable both to you and other people. For example, Frasier has, somewhat inadvisedly, got himself into a slanging match with a Seattle newspaper columnist, Derek Mann. Mann started the whole thing off by saying that he hated Frasier Crane. Frasier responds on his radio show, and the whole thing escalates. The culmination: Mann challenges Frasier to a fight the following midday – high noon – outside Frasier's radio station. Being on the air when the challenge is made, Frasier, reluctantly, agrees. By the time he gets back to his apartment, however, he has changed his mind – much to the horror of his father, Martin. The real motivation for Frasier's change of mind is, of course, fear. However, realising that this is a motivation that is going to impress neither other people nor himself, Frasier dresses it up. What is really motivating him, he claims, is that decent, civilised people do not settle their disputes by way of brawls. He has a position to uphold in society, and can't be seen to stoop to that sort of behaviour, and so on.

This is an example of what the philosopher Jon Elster calls *alchemies of the self.* Alchemy was a discipline – a proto-science or pseudo-science, depending on who you ask – whose *raison d'être* was the transformation of 'base' metals such as lead into valuable metals such as gold. If Frasier's particular alchemy had been successful in this case, then the motivation of fear would gradually have become transformed into the desire to protect Seattle civilisation. His real – but unsavoury – motive would gradually have become transformed into his false – but far more praiseworthy – motive. He would actually – not just in his own mind, but truthfully – have become motivated by the desire to safeguard decent civility. The base metal of fear would have been transformed into the gold of civilised behaviour. However, the alchemical transformation is cut short by Martin, who points out, correctly, that this is just like the case of Eddie Kreely. When he was a schoolboy, Frasier was supposed to fight Eddie Kreely after school one day. He didn't show up – on the grounds that he had a *clarinet lesson*. Frasier's reluctance to fight Mann, Martin points out, is just one more clarinet lesson. Since Kreely was the son of one of Martin's colleagues, the whole thing has kind of pissed Martin off for the past thirty years or so.

Or consider another example. Recall Frasier's attempt to throw away his father's tattered, duct-taped old chair, and replace it with a shiny new model – one whose powerful vibrating action impressed Frasier, Niles and Daphne but not, unfortunately, Martin. Frasier's motives were not, perhaps, the best of ones. They were primarily aesthetic: the chair made his apartment look tatty, and Frasier wanted it gone. So, Frasier alchemically transforms this into a far more palatable motive. The story, and Niles helped him concoct this one, was that the old chair was a sort of transitional device for

Martin, a version of a comfort blanket, that helped him with the move into Frasier's apartment. But, now that the move was complete and reasonably successful, there was really no need for the chair any more. So, Frasier now comes to regard his motivation as one of helping his father move on from his old life and start properly living his new one. A noble motive indeed. Of course, it all goes pear-shaped, and Martin exposes Frasier's real motivations, forcing Frasier to star in a high school play to get it back.

Both of these are examples of not quite successful alchemies. And in both cases, it is Martin who undermines their success. Often, however, alchemies, whereby the self disguises its true motivation – not only from others but from itself – are successful. A false motivation, eventually, and after much work, becomes a real one. This can work both ways. A deplorable motivation can become a praiseworthy one. And a praiseworthy one can become a deplorable one. Cases of the latter sort are, however, much more rare – the self, apparently, likes to look good both to others and to itself. The principle at work is a familiar one. If you say something often enough people will believe it. Everyone knows that. What we tend to forget, however, is that we are one of those people. As Nietzsche put it: 'I did that says my memory. I cannot have done that says my pride. Eventually, my memory gives way.'

The games we play

The disguise of motivations – the tricks that the self plays on itself as well as others – is only part of a bigger game. The disguise is a necessary condition of role-playing. And this is what the self is really all about. Much of the humour of *Frasier*, in fact, lies in the suspicion that much of what the characters do is a form of role-playing. This is what allows us to laugh at Frasier and Niles: their ridiculous snobbery, their infatuation with 'good' restaurants, with fine wine, with exotic coffee. This is the first level of humour embodied in the series. Once, when they are talking about how good a restaurant is, and supporting this by explaining just how difficult it is to get into it – the telephone number is not listed, there's a huge waiting list and so on – Martin points out how ridiculous this is by quipping: 'If they only had a sniper on the roof, it would be a really good restaurant.' This level of humour is re-inforced when we see glimpses of Frasier and Niles being able to laugh at themselves because of their ridiculous snobbery.

> *Frasier*: This is just the sort of evening where two red-blooded, unattached guys on the tear should go down to a sports bar and grab a few bruskies.
> *Niles*: Yes, but where should *we* go …

This is the second level of humour: ironic detachment from the role – cultured snob – that they are playing. When this happens, we see that it is a role, and nothing more. We all suspect what the story behind it is. Frasier and Niles were effeminate children, bullied and ridiculed by their peers at school, always picked last for sports, and so on. The only way they could carve out their own niche – make a place for themselves in the world – was by way of their intelligence, and the level of culture that this intelligence allowed them to appreciate. And so they became cultured snobs as a way of separating themselves off from everyone else and making out a case for their own importance in a schoolboy world that regarded them with contempt. So, playing the role of cultured snob – or cultured *ingénue*, as they would no doubt prefer – was a response to a clear need. It wasn't the sort of thing that comes naturally or, indeed, frivolously – few roles ever are – but something that was necessary and had to be carefully cultivated and constructed. Their occasional ironic detachment from this role allows us to see it for the role that it is.

Roles like this are often responses to needs, either real or merely perceived. Developing this sort of role is part of what Nietzsche calls *giving style to one's character*. It is ultimately, according to Nietzsche, an expression of the *will to power*. It is the desire to make oneself more important in the world by giving oneself a clear place in it and by clearly differentiating oneself from everyone else. In so doing, you present yourself as someone who has *something to offer*.

However, it would be a mistake to think this is just restricted to the Crane sons. Martin is also role-playing. His role as the blue-collar, no-nonsense, what you see is what you get father is, despite its obvious difference from that of his sons, no less a role. Indeed, we strongly suspect that living with Frasier, and his constant proximity to both sons, has sharpened or accentuated the role he is playing. Roles, remember, are often responses to needs, real or perceived. In many ways, Martin cannot compete with his Harvard-educated sons: he cannot compete with their encyclopaedic knowledge of fine wines, fine art and fine apparel – even though their knowledge might be significantly less encyclopaedic than he takes it to be. So, what does he do? He accentuates his own role. In doing so, he cuts out a niche for himself in the Crane household – the no-nonsense purveyor of good, honest advice that can only come from a long life crammed full of varied experiences. In doing this, he is not only able to carve out a niche – hence a level of importance – for himself, but is also, by way of some well-timed barbs, able to accomplish some subtle undermining of the roles played by his sons. It's the sort of undermining that the well-educated are frequently likely to meet at the hand of the less well-educated. It has the form: 'Sure, he's book smart but ...' Martin is, however, more subtle in his role-playing. It's far less clear that he is playing a role at all – though he is. This gives him something extra, something that his sons can't offer: *subtlety*.

Daphne seems to have adopted a similar strategy to Martin – the no-nonsense, Mancunian working-class girl, abundant in homespun down-to-earth wisdom, who tells it like it is. The experience Martin has gained from a long life – the long life she has not yet lived – is, instead, passed down to her by Grammy Moone. Of course, she adds a psychic twist to her speciality – a twist that would not appeal to the pragmatic Martin. But the type of role she plays is, broadly speaking, similar to Martin's. And this is really no surprise. Both her role and Martin's are, to a considerable extent, reactions to those of Frasier and Niles. Frasier and Niles have done well in cultivating and constructing their roles – they are, by now, far and away the most powerful roles in the Crane household. Other roles, therefore, become *reactive* ones – ones whose rationale, to some extent, is to react against the roles of Frasier and Martin.

There is nothing, as far as I can see, wrong with any of this. It's not like we have a choice anyway. All of us have to carve out a place for ourselves in this world. All of us have to find ways of making ourselves appear special. All of us have to make a case for ourselves as people with something to offer. Role-playing is something we do all the time, and we do it because, basically, we have to. However, what this does do is undermine the possibility of the sort of self-knowledge that modernity seems to require. Be true to yourself? Be true to what? Develop yourself to the best of your abilities? Develop what?

Remind me, what is it you do again?

The title of this section is Frasier's reply to a question once raised by an exasperated Niles: 'Who really knows why anyone does anything?' Niles, you remember, is also a psychiatrist. The question nicely sums up the predicament of self-knowledge in the modern world. So far we have been looking at two ideas. The first is that the possibility of self-evaluation and self-knowledge seems to rest on a bifurcation of the self into two parts: the *engaged* self, the self that thinks and acts, and the *spectator* self, the self that observes and comments on this thinking and acting. The second is the idea that a large part of how we think and what we do is bound up with some or other role that we are playing. When we put these two ideas together, what we get is a real problem about the possibility of self-knowledge: of knowing who and what you are.

Which is the real self – the real *you*? The engaged thinking and acting you? Or the spectator you, the you that observes, evaluates and comments on this thinking and acting you? There is little reason for thinking that either engaged or spectator self is any more free of role-playing than the other. Take the engaged self. The way you think, feel and act is often bound up with the roles you take yourself to be playing. Frasier's reaction to a good meal, the enjoyment he feels from the meal, is thoroughly bound up with the role of cultured gourmand that he frequently plays. His differing reactions to the 'Martha Caxton' painting – both when he thought it was a genuine Caxton and after he discovered it wasn't – these reactions are thoroughly bound up with his frequently adopted role of connoisseur of fine art. The roles Frasier plays determine what he feels he *should* like, and these, as we have seen, play a huge role in determining what he, in fact, does like. Frasier's engaged self is one that is thoroughly entwined with the roles he plays.

But so too is his spectator self. The spectator self is the one that monitors his engaged self – that observes, reflects on and often comments on what is happening in the engaged self. If Frasier's engaged self consists of his cognitive and emotional reactions to what is going on in the world, then his spectator self consists of his cognitive and emotional reactions to what is going on in his engaged self. But these latter reactions are also bound up with the roles he is playing, and for precisely the same reasons as the case of the engaged self. Frasier is the kind of person who is going to feel what he thinks he *should* feel – whether these feelings are about what is going on in the world or what is going on in Frasier's head.

The result is that you, at least if you are anything like Frasier, are split into two halves – engaged self and spectator self – both of which are thoroughly bound up, perhaps inextricably entwined, with the roles they are playing. Think of the consequences of this. The spectator self is supposed to be your route to self-knowledge. What you know of yourself, you know because this spectator self is supposed to be able to observe, evaluate and comment on what it is you are thinking and what it is you are doing. But the (engaged) self that it is observing, evaluating and commenting upon is not a patent one: it is not transparent to the spectator self. Instead, it is observing, evaluating and commenting upon a succession of roles that the engaged self has constructed in order to carve out a niche for itself in the world; in order to make the world believe that it has something to offer.

But neither is the spectator self separate from these sorts of roles. Not only is the *object* of self-knowledge a collection of roles, so too is the *route* to this knowledge. Your observation, evaluation and commentary on your engaged self is itself shot through with various roles that you play. It is difficult to see how it could be any other way – not if we buy into the significance of role-playing. Playing a role not only involves doing things a certain way, and thinking thoughts of a certain sort. Being really convincing in a role depends on – indeed demands – reacting to what you do and what you think in the right sort of way. What sort of way? The way someone in your role would react to those actions and those thoughts. Without this, the phoniness of the role player soon becomes evident. Without this sort of self-monitoring, the self is not sufficiently immersed in its roles to be able to carry them off. So, in the good role player, both engaged self and spectator self are thoroughly immersed in the roles they play. We can't separate the spectator self from the roles it plays any more than we can separate the engaged self from those roles.

The situation is something like that of a story. A story has been written about someone and by someone. You have to understand the story. But the subject of the story is mysterious and reclusive. They reveal themselves only occasionally, and only in veiled hints of their real nature. They appear only in various roles that they play – various, if you like, ceremonies at which they are present. And you have to try and understand them from this. But that's only the beginning of the complications. For the author of the story is not exactly a balanced or accomplished storyteller. Whether their story provides an accurate, balanced and fair representation of their subject is of no importance to them. They have their own vested interests, and are going to tell the story in the way it suits them – irrespective of whether things really happened in the way they tell it. So, they accentuate some of the veiled appearances of the story's subject, and they neglect others. Some appearances are assigned an importance that, someone else might think, is out of all proportion to their real significance. And other appearances are played down or even ignored when, at least arguably, they are of central impor-tance to the whole story.

If you like biographies, then the chances are you've read one like this. You'll probably admit that it wasn't exactly helpful. The chances are, however, that they reveal about as much about their subjects as your knowledge of yourself reveals about you. In the case of self-knowledge – the knowledge of who and what you are – you are both the subject and the author of the story. But, still, this doesn't look particularly good for the possibility of self-knowledge. What you are trying to get to know is a contrary and obstructive persona, and you are trying to get to know it by way of a dogmatic and opinionated persona. What is self-knowledge in this modern age? Nothing more, it seems, than a bigoted attempt to understand an unaccommodating subject.

Self, fulfilment

Sometimes it's difficult to avoid the suspicion that modernity, when you look at it closely, just vanishes before your eyes. The twin pillars of modernity are *self* and *fulfilment*. But, I suppose the principal thing that has emerged on our voyage through the philosophy of the modern age is that it is difficult, truly difficult, to find these anywhere we've been.

Each one of us is a self, modernity tells us, that has no identity-constituting relations to things outside it. Any such relations – be they relations of obligation, friendship, love, morality, or whatever – may be identity-reflecting but they are not identity-constituting. As such, each one of us, from the modern perspective, is an *inside*. The real you lies within, and the way you know who – and what – you are is by turning your attention inwards. This explains the mood of introspectionism that has permeated, even dominated, modernity. And this explains why modernity has converted all of the most important things in life – happiness, love, affection, obligation – into the sorts of things that might be found on the inside: feelings of some sort.

The real you lies on the inside, modernity tells us. The problem is: when we look inside we find no such thing.

Fulfilment – or development, or realisation, or whatever you want to call it – is the name of the modern game. But modernity has degraded the concept of value to such an extent that the idea of fulfilment no longer has any genuine content. Value always, ultimately, comes from *you*. Things, including other people, are instrumentally valuable because of the role they can make to your own project of self-realisation. Value stems from the choices you make. Above all, value is not out there in the world – it comes from you: it is a matter of how you *feel* about things.

But this degrading of value threatens to undermine the very idea of self-fulfilment. It does this by flattening down the notion of a choice – by making all choices equally valuable. In order for some choices to be valuable, other choices have to be less valuable. And if all choices are equally valuable, then no choice is valuable. The result is that all forms of self-fulfilment are equally legitimate and valuable. No way of fulfilling yourself is any *worse* than any other. Therefore, no way of fulfilling yourself is any *better* than any other. And this robs the idea of self-fulfilment of any genuine content. If no matter what you do you fulfil yourself just as much as if you had done the exact opposite, then the idea of fulfilment means nothing.

We've seen this strand of modernity at work in the tendency to chip away at the *bigness* of life, the tendency of us moderns to be fascinated by the facile, to busy ourselves with little things, to base our lives around the search for, as Nietzsche would put it, a *pitiable comfort*. There is a lack of *bigness* to modern life that ultimately undermines modernity's second pillar: the idea of self-fulfilment.

Therefore, it seems that modernity stands condemned *by its own principles*. The things it needs, the conceptual pillars that hold it up – the inner self and fulfilment of that self – are things that, by its own principles, it cannot have. Some people – the sort of people who would use the term *modernity* – refer to this undermining of a view by its own principles as a *deconstruction* of that view. That's all a deconstruction is. You deconstruct a view by giving it enough rope to hang itself. You show that, when push comes to shove, the view condemns itself out of, so to speak, its own mouth.

It does, however, seem a little harsh to go around deconstructing modernity before we've had time even to get the hang of it properly. There we all are, trying to drag ourselves out of pre-modernity, trying to put ourselves into a properly modern way of thinking, and some bastard comes along and says: too late, mate! Time's up! You feel like one of those people who finally worked out how to set the time on their VHS recorder just as the DVD revolution was getting going. And, besides, no one has a clue what a decent post-modernity would look like. If you stray into the wrong part of town, you'll find various academics (mostly from English departments) crapping on about free play of values, and stuff like that – like (a) that's anything new, and (b) they have any idea what they are talking about. Trust me: here, no one really has a clue.

Whatever a post-modern condition is going to look like, the undermining of the idea of the self as something inner is going to be the key. For that is really the central idea on which modernity was built. Most of the other things follow from that – with a bit of coaxing. And what is the self if not an inner object, an ego of some sort? Well that, as they say, is a different book.

A wish

Thanks for buying this book. If I could repay you with a wish it would be that you find something in your life so important that without it you would not be the same person. If you're lucky you'll have it already. Modernity can make no sense of this wish. And that, in a nutshell, is the problem of modernity.